Options

Options

The Investor's Complete Toolkit

Robert W. Kolb

NEW YORK INSTITUTE OF FINANCE

NEW YORK • TORONTO • SYDNEY • TOKYO • SINGAPORE

Library of Congress Cataloging-in-Publication Data

Kolb, Robert W.
    Options : the investor's complete toolkit / Robert W. Kolb.
      p. cm.
    Includes index.
    ISBN 0-13-638933-3
    1. Options (Finance)—United States. 2. Options (Finance)
  I. Title.
  HG6024.U6K65 1991   91-21430
  332.63'228—dc20   CIP

Printed in the United States of America

10 9 8 7 6

This publication is designed to provide accurate and authoritative information in regard to the subject matter covered. It is sold with the understanding that the publisher is not engaged in rendering legal, accounting, or other professional service. If legal advice or other expert assistance is required, the services of a competent professional person should be sought.
—*From the Declaration of Principles jointly adopted by a Committee of the American Bar Association and a Committee of Publishers and Associations*

ISBN 0-13-638933-3

ATTENTION: CORPORATIONS AND SCHOOLS

NYIF books are available at quantity discounts with bulk purchase for educational, business, or sales promotional use. For information, please write to: Prentice Hall Special Sales, 240 Frisch Court, Paramus, New Jersey 07652. Please supply: title of book, ISBN number, quantity, how the book will be used, date needed.

 NEW YORK INSTITUTE OF FINANCE
Paramus, NJ 07652

A Simon & Schuster Company

On the World Wide Web at http://www.phdirect.com

Prentice-Hall International (UK) Limited, *London*
Prentice-Hall of Australia Pty. Limited, *Sydney*
Prentice-Hall Canada Inc., *Toronto*
Prentice-Hall Hispanoamericana, S.A., *Mexico*
Prentice-Hall of India Private Limited, *New Delhi*
Prentice-Hall of Japan, Inc., *Tokyo*
Simon & Schuster Asia Pte. Ltd., *Singapore*
Editora Prentice-Hall do Brasil, Ltda., *Rio de Janeiro*

To Lori

Preface

In *Options: The Investor's Complete Toolkit,* a strategy of building knowledge from the simple to the more complex is followed. Chapter 1 introduces the essential institutional features of the U.S. options market. Chapter 2 begins the analytical portion of the book. When an option is at expiration, there is no difference between an American and European option. Also, it is easy to specify what the price of an option must be when it is about to expire. Chapter 2 explains the value of option positions when options are about to expire. Understanding the payoffs on options at expiration provides the basic building block for understanding the value of options before expiration.

Chapter 3 considers option values before expiration. We assume that traders in option markets are money hungry and not foolish. Such traders will exploit any trading opportunity that offers a sure profit with no risk and no investment. By assuming that no such profit opportunities exist, we learn much about what option prices can rationally prevail. Thus, in Chapter 3, we place rational bounds on option prices. We are able to place these limitations on option prices based solely on our assumptions of greed and the absence of stupidity. These boundaries are not exact, because we do not specify the exact price of an option. Nonetheless, they give considerable guidance as to what the price of an option should be.

To specify the exact price that an option should have requires a model of how stock prices can move. Chapter 4 begins by considering a very simple model of stock price movements. First, we assume that an option will expire soon and that the stock price can change only once before the option expires. Also, we assume the stock price can only go up by a certain percentage or down by a certain percentage before the option expires. Next, we allow slightly more realism by allowing the stock price to change more frequently before the option expires. Finally, we allow the stock price to change continuously. Under each circumstance, we can say precisely what the option price should be. By following this building block approach, we can gain a great deal of understanding of the factors that affect option prices. In addition, we can understand the principles of option pricing without suffering mathematical fatigue. At the end of Chapter 4, we are able to specify prices for options that conform very closely to the prices we observe in the marketplace.

In Chapter 5 we consider the impact of dividends on option prices. Option pricing is much simpler if the stocks that underlie options have no dividends. Unfortunately, real world options are typically written on stocks with dividends. Chapter 5 shows how to adjust our thinking about options to accommodate dividends. Chapter 5 also extends our option pricing principles to options written on goods other than stock. For instance, we explain options on foreign exchange, options on futures, and options on stock indexes.

Chapter 6 explains how to use **OPTION!**, the software that accompanies this book. **OPTION!** works on almost any IBM PC or compatible. For computers equipped with a graphics board, **OPTION!** can graph option values and the profits and losses from a wide variety of option strategies. **OPTION!** is very easy to use. Chapter 6 begins with a Quick Start section. Most people familiar with the computer can be running **OPTION!** within three minutes of touching the disk. (This is not an exaggeration.) This book explains all of the principles used in **OPTION!**, but it is possible to use the software without reading the book.

Acknowledgments

The preparation of this book has benefitted from the assistance of a number of people. Andrea Coens provided timely editing and many useful suggestions about the design of the book. James Debevec of the University of Miami helped to test the software. T. Harikumar of the University of Miami also tested the software and made a number of useful suggestions to enhance the presentation of material. In addition, Harikumar used the pre-publication version of the book in his class, as I did. Ray Chiang of the University of Miami, Gerry Gay of Georgia State University, Tom Schneeweis of the University of Massachusetts, Shantaram Hegde of the University of Connecticut, Dick Rendleman of the University of North Carolina, and Joanne Hill of Paine Webber all read the manuscript and offered numerous helpful suggestions. Ron Best and Marcus Ingram of Georgia State University read the entire manuscript and checked every calculation. Val Rubler helped prepare the references. Sandi Schroeder prepared the index. Linde Barrett managed the production of the book and oversaw all of the business details involved in bringing it to life. The students in my futures and option class in Spring 1990 studied from the page proofs of the book, giving me a chance to test the book in the classroom before publication. To all of you, my sincere thanks. Of course, I alone remain responsible for any remaining deficiencies.

Contents

3 Bounds on Option Prices   64

4 Option Pricing Models   103

5 Applications of Option Pricing Models   151

6 OPTION! Software   192

Index   212

1

The Options Market

Introduction

Everyone has options. When buying a car we can add more equipment to the automobile that is "optional at extra cost." In this sense, an option is a choice. This book examines options in financial markets. These are a very specific type of option—an option created through a financial contract. This chapter defines the options created by these financial contracts, and we show how participants in financial markets can use these special option contracts.

Options have played a role in security markets for many years, although no one can be certain how long. Initially, options were created by individualized contracts between two parties. However, until recently, there was no organized exchange for trading options. The development of option exchanges stimulated greater interest and more active trading of options. In many respects, the recent history of option trading can be regarded as an option revolution. This chapter considers the options exchanges and the well-defined options contracts that trade on these exchanges.

In modern options trading, an individual can contact a broker and trade an option on an exchange in a matter of moments. This chapter explains how orders flow from an individual to the exchange, and it shows how the order is executed and confirmed for the trader. At first, the options exchanges only traded options on stocks. Now exchanges trade options on a wide variety of underlying goods, such as bonds, futures contracts, and foreign currencies. The chapter concludes with a brief consideration of these diverse types of options.

The importance of options goes well beyond the profit motivated trading that is most visible to the public. Today, sophisticated institutional traders use options to execute extremely complex strategies. For instance, large pension funds and investment banking firms trade options in conjunction with stock and bond portfolios to control risk and capture additional profits. Corporations use options to execute their financing strategies and to hedge unwanted risks that they could not avoid in any other way. Option research has advanced in step with the exploding option market. Scholars have found that there is an option way of thinking that allows many financial decisions to be analyzed using an option framework. Together, these developments constitute an options revolution.

What Is an Option?

Every exchange traded option is either a **call option** or a **put option.**[1] The owner of a call option has the right to purchase the underlying good at a specific price, and this right lasts until a specific date. The owner of a put option has the right to sell the underlying good at a specific price, and this right lasts until a specific date. In short, the owner of a call option can call the underlying good away from someone else. Likewise, the owner of a put option can put the good to someone else by making the opposite party buy the good. To acquire these rights, owners of options buy them from other traders by paying the price, or premium, to a seller.

CALL OPTION

The right to purchase the underlying good at a specific price, with this right lasting for a specific time.

PUT OPTION

The right to sell the underlying good at a specific price, with this right lasting for a specific time.

Options are created only by buying and selling. Therefore, for every owner of an option, there is a seller. The seller of an option is also known as an **option writer.** The seller receives payment for an option from the purchaser. In exchange for the payment received, the seller confers rights to the option owner. The seller of a call option receives payment and, in exchange, gives the owner of a call option the right to purchase the underlying good at a specific price with this right lasting for a specific time. The seller of a put option receives payment from the purchaser and promises to buy the underlying good at a specific price for a specific time, if the owner of the put option chooses.

In these agreements, all rights lie with the owner of the option. In purchasing an option, the buyer makes payments and receives rights to buy or sell the underlying good on specific terms. In selling an option, the seller receives payment and promises to sell or purchase the underlying good on specific term—at the discretion of the option owner. With put and call options and buyers and sellers, four basic positions are possible. Notice that the owner of an option has all the rights. After all, that is what the owner purchases. The seller of an option has all the obligations, because the seller undertakes obligations in exchange for payment.

Every option has an underlying good. Through most of this book, we will speak of a share of stock as the underlying good. However, all the principles that we will develop apply to options on different underlying goods. The call writer gives the purchaser the right to demand the underlying good from the writer. However, the writer of a call need not own the underlying good when he or she writes the option. If a seller writes a call and does not own the underlying good, the call is a **naked call**. If the writer owns the underlying good, he has sold a **covered call**. When a trader writes a naked call, he undertakes the obligation of immediately securing the underlying good and delivering it if the purchaser of the call chooses to exercise the call.

CALL BUYER

Purchases the right to buy the underlying good at a specific price, with this right lasting a specific time.

CALL SELLER OR CALL WRITER

Receives payment and promises to deliver the underlying good at a specific price, if the call owner so chooses, within a specific time.

PUT BUYER

Purchases the right to sell the underlying good at a specific price, with this right lasting a specific time.

PUT SELLER OR PUT WRITER

Receives payment and promises to buy the underlying good at a specific price, if the put owner so chooses, within a specific time.

An Option Example

Consider an option with a share of IBM stock as the underlying good. Assume that today is March 1 and that IBM shares trade at $110. The market, we assume, trades a call option to buy a share of IBM at $100 with this right lasting until August 15 and the price of this option being $15. In this example, the owner of a call must pay $100 to acquire the stock. This $100 price is called the **exercise price** or the **striking price**. The price of the option, or the **option premium**, is $15. The option expires in 5.5 months, which gives 168 days until expiration.

If a trader buys the call option, he pays $15 and receives the right to purchase a share of IBM stock by paying an additional $100, if he so chooses, by August 15. The seller of the option receives $15, and she promises to sell a share of IBM for $100 if the owner of the call chooses to buy before August 15. Notice that the price of the option, the option premium, is paid when the option trades. The premium the seller receives is hers to keep whether or not the owner of the call decides to exercise the option. If the owner of the call exercises his option, he will pay $100 no matter what the current price of IBM stock may be. If the owner of the option exercises his option, the seller of the option will receive the $100 exercise price when she delivers the stock as she promised.

At the same time, puts will trade on IBM. Consider a put with a striking price of $100 trading on March 1 that also expires on August 15. Assume that the price of the put is $5. If a trader purchases a put, he pays $5. In exchange, he receives the right to sell a share of IBM for $100 at any time until August 15. The seller of the put receives $5, and she promises to buy the share of IBM for $100 if the owner of the put option chooses to sell before August 15.

In both the put and call example, the payment by the purchaser is gone forever at the time the option trades. The seller of the option receives the payment and keeps it, whatever the owner of the option decides to do. If the owner of the call exercises his option, then he pays the exercise price as an additional amount and receives a share. Likewise, if the owner of the put exercises his option, then he surrenders the share and receives the exercise price as an additional amount. The owner of the option may choose never to exercise. In that case, the option will expire on August 15. The payment the seller receives is hers to keep whether or not the owner exercises. If the owner chooses not to exercise, the seller has a profit equal to the premium received and does not have to perform under the terms of the option contract.

Why Trade Options?

Options trading today is more popular than ever before. For the investor, options serve a number of important roles. First, many investors trade options to speculate on the price movements of the underlying stock. However, investors could merely trade the stock itself. As we will see, trading the option instead of the underlying stock can offer a number of advantages. Call options are always cheaper than the underlying stock, so it takes less money to trade calls. Generally, but not universally, put options are also cheaper than the underlying goods. In relative terms, the option price is more volatile than the price of the underlying stock, so investors can get more price action per dollar of investment by investing in options instead of investing in the stock itself.

Options are extremely popular among sophisticated investors who hold large stock portfolios. Accordingly, institutional investors, such as mutual funds and pension funds, are prime users of the options market. By trading options in conjunction with their stock portfolios, investors can carefully adjust the risk and return characteristics of their entire investment. As we will see, a sophisticated trader can use options to increase or decrease the risk of an existing stock portfolio. For example, it is possible to combine a risky stock and a risky option to form a riskless combined position that performs like a risk-free bond.[2]

Many investors prefer to trade options rather than stocks in order to save transaction costs, to avoid tax exposure, and to avoid stock market restrictions.[3] We already mentioned that some investors trade options to achieve the same risk exposure with less capital. In many instances, traders can use options to take a particular risk position and pay lower transaction costs than stocks would require. Likewise, specific provisions of the tax code may favor option trading over trading the underlying stock. If different traders face different tax schedules, one may find advantage in buying options and another may find advantage in selling options, relative to trading stocks. Finally, the stock and option markets have their own institutional rules. Differences in these rules may stimulate option trading. For example, selling stock short is highly restricted.[4] By trading in the option market, it is possible to replicate a short sale of stock and to avoid some stock market restrictions.[5]

Options Exchanges

Trading options undoubtedly grew up with the development of financial markets. In the 19th century, investors traded options in an informal market; however, the market was subject to considerable corruption. For example, some sellers of options would refuse to perform as obligated. In the 20th century, the United States developed a more orderly market called the Put and Call Broker and Dealers Association. Member firms acted to bring buyers and sellers of options together. However, this was an over-the-counter market. The market had no central exchange floor, and standardization of option contract terms was not complete. The lack of an exchange and imperfect standardization of the contracts kept this option market from flourishing.

In 1973, the Chicago Board of Trade, a large futures exchange, created the Chicago Board Options Exchange (CBOE). The CBOE is an organized options exchange that trades highly standardized option contracts. It opened on April 26, 1973 to trade calls; put trading began in 1977. Since 1973, other exchanges have begun to trade options, with annual trading of about 300,000,000 options. The U.S. option exchanges and the main items they trade are:

American Stock Exchange	Stocks, options on individual stocks, and options on stock indexes
Chicago Board of Trade	Futures, options on futures for agricultural goods, precious metals, stock indexes, and debt instruments
Chicago Board Options Exchange	Options on individual stocks, options on stock indexes, and options on Treasury securities
Chicago Mercantile Exchange	Futures, options on futures for agricultural goods, stock indexes, debt instruments, and currencies
Coffee, Sugar and Cocoa Exchange	Futures and options on agricultural futures
Commodity Exchange (COMEX)	Futures and options on futures for metals
Kansas City Board of Trade	Futures and options on agricultural futures
MidAmerica Commodity Exchange	Futures and options on futures for agricultural goods and precious metals
Minneapolis Grain Exchange	Futures and options on agricultural futures
New York Cotton Exchange	Futures and options on agricultural, currency, and debt instrument futures

New York Futures Exchange	Futures and options on stock indexes
New York Mercantile Exchange	Futures and options on energy futures
New York Stock Exchange	Stocks and options on individual stocks and a stock index
Pacific Stock Exchange	Options on individual stocks and a stock index
Philadelphia Stock Exchange	Stocks, futures, and options on individual stocks, currencies, and stock indexes

For these exchanges, stock options dominate options on other goods. However, index options have been gaining in importance. For example, in 1988, the CBOE traded more options on indexes than it traded on individual stocks.

The Option Contract

One of the major reasons for the success of options exchanges is that they offer standardized contracts. In a financial market, traders want to be able to trade a good quickly and at a fair price. They can do this if the market is **liquid**. A liquid market provides an efficient and cost effective trading mechanism with a high volume of trading. Standardizing the options contract has helped promote liquidity. The standardized contract has a specific size and expiration date. Trading on the exchange occurs at certain well-publicized times, so traders know when they will be able to find other traders in the marketplace. The exchange standardizes the exercise prices at which options will trade. With fewer exercise prices, there will be more trading available at a given exercise price. This too promotes liquidity.

Each option contract is for 100 shares of the underlying stock. Exercise prices are specified at intervals of $10, $5, or $2.50, depending on the share price. For example, IBM trades in the $100 range and IBM options have exercise prices spaced at $5 intervals. Every option has a specified expiration month. The option expires on the Saturday after the third Friday in the exercise month. Trading in the option ceases on the third Friday, but the owner may exercise the option on the final Saturday.

Reading Option Prices

Table 1.1 shows typical price quotations from a U.S. newspaper. Prices are for January 26 for trading IBM options. On that day, IBM closed at 96 7/8 per share. The table shows listings for IBM options with striking prices of $90, 95, 100, and 105. It would not be unusual for other striking prices to be represented as well. Options expire in February, March, and April of the same year, and the table shows option prices for both puts and calls. An "r" indicates that the option was not traded on the day for which prices are reported, while an "s" shows that the specific option is not listed for trading.[6]

Table 1.1

Option Price Quotations

IBM		CALLS			PUTS		
96 7/8		FEB	MAR	APR	FEB	MAR	APR
	90	6 5/8	s	9 1/8	5/8	s	1 3/8
	95	2 7/8	4 3/8	5 1/2	1 5/8	2 5/8	3 1/8
	100	7/8	1 7/8	3 1/8	4 5/8	r	6 1/4
	105	1/4	13/16	1 5/8	9 1/2	r	11

As an example, consider the call option with a striking price of $100 that expires in March. This option has a price of $1 7/8 or $1.875. This is the price of the call for a single share. However, each option contract is written for 100 shares. Therefore, to purchase this option, the buyer would pay $187.50 for one contract. Owning this call option would give the buyer the right to purchase 100 shares of IBM at $100 per share until the option expires in March.

We can learn much from a careful consideration of the price relationships revealed in the table. First, notice that option prices are generally higher the longer the time until the option expires. This is true for both calls and puts. Other things being equal, the longer one has the option to buy or sell, the better. Thus, we expect options with longer terms to expiration to be worth more. Second, for a call, the lower the striking price, the more the call option is worth. For a call, the striking price is the amount the call holder must pay to secure the stock. The lower the amount one must pay, the better; therefore, the lower the exercise price, the more the call is worth. Third, for a put option, the higher the striking price, the more the put is worth. For a put, the striking price is the value the put holder receives when he exercises his option to sell the put. Therefore, the more the put entitles its owner to receive, the greater the value of the put. A moment's reflection shows that these simple relationships make sense. Following chapters explore these and similar relationships in detail.

Option Trading Procedures

Every options trader needs to be familiar with the basic features of the market. This section explores the action that takes place on the market floor and the ways in which traders away from the exchange can have their orders executed on the exchange. From its image in the popular press and television, one gets the impression that the exchange floor is the scene of wild and chaotic action. While the action may become wild, it is never chaotic. Understanding the role of the different participants on the floor helps dispel the illusion of chaos. Essentially, there are three types of people on the exchange floor: traders, clerical personnel associated with the traders, and exchange officials. First we describe the system that the CBOE uses. Later, we note some differences among exchanges.

Types of Traders

There are three different kinds of traders on the floor of the exchange: market makers, floor brokers, and order book officials. A trader who trades for his own account is a market maker. A trader who executes orders for another is a floor broker. The order book official is an employee of the exchange who makes certain kinds of option trades and keeps the book of orders awaiting execution at specified prices.

The Market Maker—The typical market maker owns or leases a seat on the options exchange and trades for his or her own account to make a profit. However, as the name implies, the market maker has an obligation to make a market for the public by standing ready to buy or sell options. Typically, a market maker will concentrate on the options of just a few stocks. Focusing on a few issues allows the market maker to become quite knowledgeable about the other traders who deal in options on those stocks.

Market makers follow different trading strategies, and they switch freely from one strategy to another. Some market makers are scalpers. The scalper follows the psychology of the trading crowd and tries to anticipate the direction of the market in the next few minutes. The scalper tries to buy if the price is about to rise and tries to sell just before it falls. Generally, the scalper holds a position for just a few minutes, trying to make a profit on moment to moment fluctuations in the option's price. By contrast, a position trader buys or sells options and holds a position for a longer period. This commitment typically rests on views about the underlying worth of the stock or movements in the economy. Both scalpers and position traders often trade option combinations. For example, they might buy a call at a striking price of 90 and sell a call with a striking price of 95. Such a combination is called a **spread**. A spread is any option position in two or more related options. In all such combination trades, the trader seeks to profit from a change in the price of one option relative to another.

The Floor Broker—Many option traders are located away from the trading floor. When an off-the-floor trader enters an order to buy or sell an option, the floor broker has the job of executing the order. Floor brokers typically represent brokerage firms, such as Merrill Lynch or Prudential Bache. They work for a salary or receive commissions, and their job is to obtain the best price on an order while executing it rapidly. Almost all brokers have support personnel that assist in completing trades. For example, major brokerage firms will have clerical staff that receive orders from beyond the trading floor. These individuals deal with all of the record keeping necessary to execute an order and assist in transmitting information to and from the floor brokers. In addition, many brokerage firms engage in proprietary trading—trading for their own account. Therefore, they have a number of trained people on the floor of the exchange to seek trading opportunities and to execute transactions through a floor broker.

The Order Book Official—The order book official is an employee of the exchange who can also trade. However, the official cannot trade for his or her own account. Instead, the order book official primarily helps to facilitate the flow of orders. The order book is the listing of orders that are awaiting execution at a specific price. The order book official discloses the best limit orders (highest bid and lowest ask) awaiting execution. In essence, the order book official performs many of the functions of a specialist on a stock exchange. However, the order book official cannot trade for his own account. The order book official also has support personnel to help keep track of the order book and to log new orders into the book as they come in.

Exchange Officials—Exchange officials comprise the third group of floor participants. We have already noted that the order book official and assistants are exchange employees. They serve the special function we described above. However, there are other exchange employees on the floor, such as price reporting officials and surveillance officials. After every trade, price reporting officials enter the order into the exchange's price reporting system. The details of the trade immediately go out over a financial reporting system so that traders all over the world can obtain the information reflected in the trade. This process takes just a few seconds. Then traders and other interested parties around the world will know the price and quantity of a particular option that just traded. In addition to personnel involved with price reporting, the exchange has personnel on the floor to monitor floor activity. The exchange has the responsibility of providing an honest marketplace, so it strives to maintain an orderly market and to ensure that brokers and market makers follow exchange rules.

Other Trading Systems

The alignment of personnel described here follows the practice at the CBOE and the Pacific Stock Exchange. Other exchanges, such as the American and Philadelphia Stock Exchanges, use a specialist instead of an order book official. In this system, the specialist keeps the limit order book but does not disclose the outstanding orders. Also, the specialist alone bears the responsibility of making a market, rather than relying on a group of market makers. In place of market makers, these exchanges have registered option traders who buy and sell for their own account or act as brokers for others.

One of the most important differences between the two systems is the role of the market makers and registered option traders. At the CBOE and the Pacific Stock Exchange, a market maker cannot act as a broker and trade for his account on the same day. The same individual can play different roles on different days, however. Restricting individuals from simultaneously acting as market makers and brokers helps avoid a conflict of interest between the role of market maker and broker. The system of allowing an individual simultaneously to trade for himself (as a market maker) and to execute orders for the public (a broker) is called dual trading. Many observers believe that dual trading involves inherent conflicts of interest between the role of broker and market maker. For example, consider a dual trader who holds an order to execute as a broker. If this dual trader suddenly confronts a very attractive trading opportunity, he may well decide to take it for his own profit, rather than executing the order for his customer.

Types of Orders

Every option trade falls into one of four categories. It can be an order to:

1. open a position with a purchase;
2. open a position with a sale;
3. close a position with a purchase; or
4. close a position with a sale.

For example, a trader could open a position by buying a call and later close that position by selling the call. Alternatively, one could open a position by selling a put and close the position by buying a put. An order that closes an existing position is an **offsetting order**.

As in the stock market, there are numerous types of orders in the options market. The simplest order is a market order. A market order instructs the floor broker to transact at whatever price is currently available in the marketplace. For example, one might place an order to buy 1 call contract for a stock at the market. The floor broker will fill this order immediately at the best price currently available. As in the stock market, the alternative to a market order is a limit order. In a limit order, the trader instructs the broker to fill the order only if certain conditions are met. For example, assume an option trades for $5 1/8. In this situation, one might place a limit order to buy an option only if the price is $5 or less. In a limit order, the trader tells the broker how long to try to fill the order. If the limit order is a day order, the broker is to fill the order that day if it can be filled within the specified limit. If the order cannot be filled that day, the order expires. Alternatively, a trader can specify a limit order as being good–until–canceled. In this case, the order stays on the limit order book indefinitely.

Order Routing and Execution

To get a better idea of how an order is executed, let's trace an order from an individual trader. A college professor in Miami decides that today is the day to buy an option on IBM. He calls his local broker and places a market order to buy a call. The broker takes the order and makes sure she has recorded the order correctly. The broker then transmits the order to the brokerage firm's representatives at the exchange. Usually this is done over a computerized system operated by the brokerage firm.

The brokerage firm's clerical staff on the floor of the exchange receives the order and gives it to a runner. The runner quickly moves to the trading area and finds the firm's floor broker who deals in IBM options. The floor broker executes the order by trading with another floor broker, a market maker, or an order book official. Then the floor broker records the price obtained and information about the opposite trader. The runner takes this information from the floor broker back to the clerical staff on the exchange floor. The brokerage firm clerks confirm the order to the Miami broker, who tells the professor the result of the transaction. In the normal event, the entire process takes about two minutes and the professor can reasonably expect to receive confirmation of his order in the same phone call used to place the order.

The Clearinghouse

In executing the trade just described, the buyer of a call has the right to purchase 100 shares of IBM at the exercise price. However, it might seem that the buyer of the call is in a somewhat dangerous position, because the seller of the call may not want to fulfill his part of the bargain if the price of IBM rises. For example, if IBM sells for $120, the seller of the call may be unwilling to part with the share for $100. The purchaser of the call needs a mechanism to secure his position without having to force the seller to perform.

The clearinghouse, the Options Clearing Corporation (OCC), performs this role. After the day's trading, the OCC first attempts to match all trades. For the college professor's transaction, there is an opposite trading party. When the broker recorded the purchase for the professor, she traded with someone else who also recorded the trade. The clearinghouse must match the paperwork from both sides of the transaction. If the two records agree, the trade is a matched trade. This process of matching trades and tracking payments is called **clearing**. Every options trade must be cleared. If records by the two sides of the trade disagree, the trade is an **outtrade** and the exchange works to resolve the disagreement.

Assuming the trade matches, the OCC guarantees both sides of the transaction. The OCC becomes the seller to every buyer and the buyer to every seller. In essence, the OCC interposes its own credibility for that of the individual traders. This has great advantages. The college professor did not even know the name of the seller of the option. Instead of being worried about the credibility of the seller, the professor needs only to be satisfied with the credibility of the OCC. But the OCC is well capitalized and anxious to keep a smoothly functioning market. Therefore, the college professor can be assured that the other side of his option transaction will be honored. If an option trader fails to perform as promised, the OCC absorbs the loss and proceeds against the defaulting trader. Because the OCC is a buyer to every seller and a seller to every buyer, it has a zero net position in the market. It holds the same number of short and long positions. Therefore, the OCC has very little risk exposure from fluctuating prices.

Margins

Besides having a net zero position, the clearinghouse further limits its risk by requiring margin payments from its clearing members. A clearing member is a securities firm having an account with the clearinghouse. All option trades must be channeled through a clearing member to the clearinghouse. Most major brokerage firms are clearing members. However, individual market makers are not clearing members, and they must clear their trades through a clearing member. In effect, the clearing member represents all of the parties that it clears to the clearinghouse. By demanding margin payments from its clearing members, the clearinghouse further ensures its own financial integrity. Each clearing member in turn demands margin payments from the traders it clears. The margin payments are immediate cash payments that show the financial integrity of the traders and help to limit the risk of the clearing member and the clearinghouse.

To understand margins, we recall that there are four basic positions: long a call or long a put and short a call or short a put. The margin rules differ with the type of position. First, options cannot be bought on credit. The buyer of an option pays the full price of the option by the morning of the next business day. For example, the college professor in Miami who buys a call this afternoon must pay his broker in full for the purchase by the next morning. For short traders, margin rules are very important.

The Federal Reserve Board sets minimum margin requirements for option traders. However, each exchange may impose additional margin requirements. Also, each broker may require margin payments beyond those required by the Federal Reserve Board and the exchanges. A single broker may also impose different margin requirements on different customers. Because these option requirements may differ so radically and because they are subject to frequent adjustment, this section illustrates the underlying principles of margin rules.[7]

The seller of a call option may be required to deliver the stock if the owner of a call exercises his option. Therefore, the maximum amount the seller can lose is the value of the share. If the seller keeps money on deposit with the broker equal to the share price, then the broker, clearing member, and clearinghouse are completely protected. This sets an upper bound on the reasonable amount of margin that could be required. Sometimes the seller of a call has the share itself on deposit with the broker. In this case, the seller has sold a **covered call**—the call is covered by the deposit of the shares with the broker. If the call is exercised against the seller of a covered call, the stock is immediately available to deliver. Therefore, there is no risk to the system in a covered call. Accordingly, the margin on a covered call is zero.

If the seller of a call does not have the underlying share on deposit with the broker, the seller has sold an uncovered or naked call. We have just seen that the maximum possible loss is the value of the share. For this type of transaction, the margin is 30 percent of the stock price plus the difference between the stock price and the exercise price. Consider the following example. Assume that IBM trades for $100 and a trader sells a call option on IBM with an exercise price of $90. The margin will be $30 per share plus the $10 difference between the exercise price and the stock price. For one contract of 100 shares, the margin will be $4,000. Now assume the same prices, except that the trader sells an option with an exercise price of $110. In this case, the margin will be $30 per share, minus the $10 difference between the stock price and the exercise price We can express this relationship as follows:

Naked Call Margin per Share = .3 × S + (S − E)

S = Stock Price
E = Exercise Price

For the writer of a put, the worst result is being forced to buy a worthless stock at the exercise price. This worst case gives a loss equal to the exercise price. Therefore, if the margin equaled the exercise price, the broker, clearing member, and clearinghouse would be fully protected. Instead of demanding such complete protection, the minimum margin for selling a put is the same as for selling a call:

Naked Put Margin per Share = .3 × S + (E − S)

If the computations of margin for naked puts and calls do not exceed $2.50 per share, the minimum margin per share is $2.50 or $250 per contract.

The margins we have been discussing are initial margin requirements. The trader must make these margin deposits when he or she first trades. If prices move against the trader, he or she will be required to make additional margin payments. To see why such a system is necessary, consider the seller of a naked IBM call with an exercise price of $90 when IBM stock sells for $100. Above, we computed the initial margin for this transaction as $40 per share. Assume now that IBM stock rises to $140 per share. Now the trader may be required to surrender a share of stock worth $140 in exchange for a payment of only $90. This would represent a loss of $50 per share, which exceeds the initial margin of $40 per share. Now if the trader defaults, the broker, clearing member, and clearinghouse will be at risk, unless they require additional margin. As the stock price starts to rise and cause losses for the short trader, the broker requires additional margin payments, called maintenance margin. By requiring maintenance margin payments, the margin system protects the broker, clearing member, and clearinghouse from default by traders. This system also benefits traders, because they can be confident that payments due to them will be protected from default as well.

Many option traders trade option combinations. Margin rules apply to these transactions as well, but the margin requirements reflect the special risk characteristics of these positions. For many option combinations, the risk may be less than the risk of a single long or short position in a put or call.[8]

Commissions

As we have seen, the same brokerage system that trades stocks can execute option transactions. In stocks, commission charges depend on the number of shares and the dollar value of the transaction. A similar system applies for call option contracts. The following schedule shows a representative commission schedule from a discount broker. Full-service brokerage fees can be substantially higher.[9] In addition to these fees, each transaction can be subject to certain minimum and maximum fees. For instance a broker might have a maximum fee per contract of $40.

Representative Discount Brokerage Commissions

Dollar Value of Transaction	Commission
$0-2,500	$29 + 1.6% of principal amount
$2,500-10,000	$49 + 0.8% of principal amount
$10,000 +	$99 + 0.3% of principal amount

As an example of commissions with this fee schedule, assume that you buy 5 contracts with a quoted price of $6.50. The cost of the option would be $650 per contract, for a total cost of $3,250. The commission would be: $29 + .016 × $3,250 = $81. For the same dollar value of a transaction in stocks, the commission tends to be lower. However, once the dollar amount of the transaction approaches $10,000, commissions on stocks and options tend to be similar.

Even though the commission per dollar of options traded may be higher than for stocks, there can be significant commission savings in trading options. In our example, the option price is $6.50 per share of stock. The share price might well be $100 or more. If it were $100, trading 500 shares would involve a transaction value of $50,000. Commissions on a stock transaction of $50,000 would be much higher than commissions on our option transaction. Trading the option on a stock and trading the stock itself can give positions with very similar price actions. Therefore, option trading can provide commission savings over stock trading. This principle holds, even though option commissions tend to be higher than stock commissions for a given dollar transaction.

Another way to see this principle is to realize that options inherently have more leverage than a share of stock. As an example, assume the stock price is $100 and the option on the stock trades for $6.50. If the stock price rises 3 percent to $103, the option price could easily rise 30 percent to $8.45. On a percentage basis, the option price moves more than the stock price. Unfortunately for option traders, this happens for price increases and decreases. With this greater leverage, the same dollar investment in an option will give a greater dollar price movement than investment in the stock.

Taxation

Taxation of option transactions is no simple matter. We cannot hope to cover all of the nuances of the tax laws in this brief section. However, we can illustrate the basic principles. Profits and losses on options trading are treated as capital gains and losses. Therefore, option profits and losses are subject to all the regular rules that pertain to all capital gains and losses. In brief, capital gains are taxed as regular income, just like wages from employment. Capital losses offset capital gains and thereby reduce taxable income. However, capital losses are deductible only up to the amount of capital gains plus $3,000. Any excess capital loss cannot be deducted, but must be carried forward to offset capital gains in subsequent years. For example, assume that a trader has capital gains of $17,500 from securities trading. Unfortunately for the trader, he also has $25,000 in capital losses. Therefore, $17,500 of the losses completely offset the capital gains, freeing the trader from any taxes on those gains. This leaves $7,500 of capital losses to consider. The trader can then use $3,000 of this excess loss to offset other income, such as wages. In effect, this protects $3,000 of wages from taxation. The remaining $4,500 of losses must be carried forward to the next tax year, where it can be used to offset capital gains realized in that tax year.

Option transactions give rise to capital gains and losses, and the tax treatment differs for buyers and sellers of options. If you buy an option and sell it later, the capital gain or loss equals the difference in the purchase and sale price. If you buy an option and it expires worthless, the capital loss equals the full purchase price of the option. If you buy a call option and exercise the option to acquire the stock, there is no immediate tax consequence. Instead, the original price of the option is added to the exercise price paid to acquire the stock. The taxable capital gain or loss will then occur when the stock is sold. If you buy a put option and exercise it, you deliver a share of stock. The purchase price of the put is treated as part of the cost of the stock. The capital gain or loss is figured on the sale price of the stock measured against the original cost of the stock plus the price of the put.

If you sell an option and the option expires worthless, the capital gain equals the full proceeds from the sale. The capital gain is realized in the year the option expires. If you close your option position by offsetting, the difference in the sales price and offsetting price determines the amount of the capital gain or loss. If the option is exercised against you, you adjust the price of the stock by the proceeds from the option. For example, if a call option is exercised against you, you must deliver the stock. Delivering the stock closes the stock transaction, so there will be a capital gain or loss on the stock transaction. The proceeds received for selling the call that was exercised against you increase the sale price of the stock for computing the capital gain or loss on the stock. Similarly, if a put option is exercised against you, you receive stock. The price of the stock for tax purposes equals the exercise price you had to pay, plus the price you received when you sold the put.

There are other special and more complicated rules for taxing option transactions, so the account here is not definitive. Additional complications arise for some options on stock indexes, for example. Also, there are special tax rules designed to prevent option trading merely to manipulate taxes.

American and European Options

There are two fundamental kinds of options: the American option and the European option. An **American option** permits the owner to exercise at any time before or at expiration. The owner of a **European option** can exercise only at expiration. Thus, the two kinds of options differ because the American option permits early exercise. To this point, we have considered option values only at expiration. If the option is at expiration, American and European options will have the same value. Both can be exercised immediately or be allowed to expire worthless. Prior to expiration, we will see that the two options are conceptually distinct. Further, they may have different values under certain circumstances. In this chapter, and through the remainder of the book, we will need to distinguish the principles that apply to each kind of option.

Consider any two options that are just alike, except one is an American option and the other is a European option. By saying that the two options are just alike, we mean that they have the same underlying stock, the same exercise price, and the same time remaining until expiration. The American option gives its owner all the rights and privileges that the owner of the European option possesses. However, the owner of the American option also has the right to exercise the option before expiration if he desires. From these considerations, we can see that the American option must be worth at least as much as the European option.

The owner of an American option can treat the option as a European option just by deciding not to exercise until expiration. Therefore, the American option cannot be worth less than the European option. However, the American option can be worth more. The American option will be worth more if it is desirable to exercise earlier. Under certain circumstances, which we explore later, the right to exercise before expiration can be valuable. In this case, the American option will be worth more than the otherwise identical European option.

In some cases, the right to exercise before expiration will be worthless. For these situations, the American option will have the same value as the European option. In general, the European option is simpler and easier to analyze. However, in actual markets, most options are American options. This is true both in the United States and throughout the world. We should not associate the names "American" and "European" with geographic locations. In the present context, the names simply refer to the time at which holders can exercise these options.

Information Sources

A wide variety of sources are available to provide more information about option markets and option trading. These include materials provided by various option exchanges and the Option Clearing Corporation. In addition, there are numerous periodicals and books about options. Most exchanges offer a variety of free booklets about option trading risk and option strategies. Two monthly periodicals provide continuing coverage of the futures and options industry:

Futures and Options World
Metal Bulletin, Inc.
220 Fifth Avenue
New York, New York   10001

Futures
219 Parkade
Cedar Falls, Iowa   50613

Futures and Options World is published in Great Britain and covers the international scene more extensively. *Futures* also features international coverage, but it focuses more specifically on futures and the Chicago exchanges in particular.

There are many books written on trading strategies. Many of these are of dubious value because they pretend that their readers can become rich by following their advice. The following books emphasize trading strategies but do not propound get rich quick schemes:

Lawrence G. McMillan, *Options as a Strategic Investment*, (New York: New York Institute of Finance, 1986).
Gary L. Gastineau, *The Options Manual*, 3rd Edition, (New York: McGraw-Hill Book Company, 1988).

The mathematics of option pricing are formidable. While this text tries to explain option pricing principles, it does so with relatively little mathematics. The following books are mathematically much more demanding than this one:

John C. Cox and Mark Rubinstein, *Options Markets*, (Englewood Cliffs, New Jersey: Prentice-Hall, Inc., 1985).

Peter Ritchken, *Options: Theory, Strategy, and Applications*, (Glenview, IL: Scott, Foresman and Company, 1987).

John Hull, *Options, Futures, and other Derivative Securities*, (Englewood Cliffs, New Jersey: Prentice-Hall, Inc., 1989).

Robert A. Jarrow and Andrew Rudd, *Option Pricing*, (Homewood, IL: Richard D. Irwin, Inc., 1983).

Summary

This chapter has introduced the options market. In the short time since options started trading on the Chicago Board Options Exchange, options have helped to revolutionize finance. They permeate the world of speculative investing and portfolio management. Corporations use them in their financing decisions to control risk. Beyond their uses as trading vehicles, options provide a new way to analyze many financial transactions.

The chapters that follow build an understanding of the option revolution on several levels. Foremost, we seek to build an understanding of option trading and speculating as a topic that is interesting in its own right. However, by following the argument of this book, the reader will develop skills in financial thinking that will apply to many problem areas. After completing the book, the careful reader should even be able to analyze many financial problems using an option framework. At that point, the reader has become part of the option revolution.

Questions and Problems

1. State the difference between a call and a put option.

2. How does a trader initiate a long call position, and what rights and obligations does such a position involve?

3. Can buying an option, whether a put or a call, result in any obligations for the option owner? Explain.

4. Describe all of the benefits that are associated with taking a short position in an option.

5. What is the difference between a short call and a long put position. Which has rights associated with it, and which involves obligations? Explain.

6. Consider the following information. A trader buys a call option for $5 that gives the right to purchase a share of stock for $100. In this situation, identify: the exercise price, the premium, and the striking price.

7. Explain what happens to a short trader when the option he or she has sold expires worthless. What benefits and costs has the trader incurred?

8. Explain why an organized options exchange needs a clearinghouse.

9. What is the difference between an American and a European option?

10. Assume a trader does not want to continue holding an option position. Explain how this trader can fulfill his or her obligations, yet close out the option position.

Notes

1. There are also some other more complicated types of options that are not traded on exchanges. For example, an **exchange option** is an option to exchange one asset for another. As we will see when we discuss options on futures, there is a **delivery option** that gives a trader the right to choose which of several assets to surrender. There are still other types of options, but the most important market for options is the option exchange, where just put and call options trade.

2. Christopher K. Ma and Ramesh P. Rao, "Information Asymmetry and Options Trading," *The Financial Review*, 23:1, February 1988, 39–51, discuss the different roles that options can play for informed and uninformed traders. The informed trader is one with special knowledge about the underlying stock; the uninformed trader has no special knowledge. In their analysis, the informed trader tends to take an outright position in the option, while the uninformed trader is likely to use options to reduce the risk of an existing stock position. While these factors may benefit market participants, the same authors analyze the effect of new listing of options on stock prices in "The Effect of Call-Option-Listing Announcement on Shareholder Wealth," *Journal of Business Research*, 15:5, October 1987, 449–465. Ma and Rao show that the listing of an option on a stock that never had options before leads to stock price declines and thus to a loss of shareholder wealth. Apparently, this drop in stock prices reflects the market's view that new option trading is likely to make the stock more

volatile. However, Ma and Rao also find that stock prices rebound when the option actually begins to trade.

3.   Consider an option position and a stock position designed to give the same profits and losses for a given movement in the stock price. If we consider a short-term investment horizon, the option strategy will almost always be cheaper and incur lower transaction costs. This is not necessarily true for a long-term investment horizon. All exchange-traded options are dated; that is, they expire within the next few months. Therefore, maintaining an option position in the long-term involves trading to replace expiring options. By contrast, taking the stock position requires only one transaction, and the stock can be held indefinitely. Therefore, the repeated transaction costs incurred with the option strategy can involve greater transaction costs in the long-term than the stock strategy.

4.   Selling stock short involves borrowing a share, selling it, repurchasing the share later, and returning it to its owner. The short seller hopes to profit from a price decline by selling before the decline and repurchasing after the price falls. Rules on the stock exchange restrict the timing of short selling and the use of short sale proceeds.

5.   Stephen A. Ross, "Options and Efficiency," *Quarterly Journal of Economics*, 90 February 1976, 75–89, shows that options serve a useful economic role by completing markets. In a complete market, a trader can trade for any pattern of payoffs that he or she desires. The more nearly complete a market is, the greater is its likely efficiency. Thus, because options help to complete markets, they contribute to economic efficiency and thereby raise the welfare level of society as a whole.

6.   The "r" and "s" have no specific meaning. However, this is the convention used by *The Wall Street Journal* for its option price reports.

7.   George Sofianos, "Margin Requirements on Equity Instruments," *Federal Reserve Bank of New York Quarterly Review*," 13:2, Summer 1988, 47–60, explains margin rules in more detail. Stephen Figlewski, "Margins and Market Integrity: Margin Setting for Stock Index Futures and Options," *Journal of Futures Markets*, 4:3, Fall 1984, 385–416, argues that margins on stocks are set too high relative to margins on options and futures. According to his analysis, the margin requirements give different levels of protection for different instruments.

8.   Margins can be devilishly complicated. Andrew Rudd and Mark Schroeder, "The Calculation of Minimum Margin," *Management Science*, 28 (December 1982), 1368–1379 present a linear program to compute minimum margin under a variety of scenarios.

9.   A discount broker executes unsolicited orders for its customers. It provides little or no research information but seeks to offer fully competitive order execution at reduced prices. Charles Schwab and Quick and Reilly are two leading discount brokerage firms. By contrast, full discount brokers typically have account executives that actively solicit orders from their customer base. The full discount broker also maintains a research department.

2

Option Payoffs at Expiration

Introduction

This chapter considers the factors that determine the value of an option. When an option is about to expire, it is relatively easy to determine its value. Thus, we begin our analysis by considering option values at expiration. When we say that an option is at expiration, we mean that the owner has a simple choice: exercise immediately or allow the option to expire as worthless. We specify precisely the value of an option at expiration as a function of the stock price and the exercise price. We also give rules for whether an owner should exercise an option or allow it to expire.

With all assets, we consider either the value of the asset or the profit or loss incurred from trading the asset. The value of an asset equals its market price. As such, the value of an asset does not depend on the purchase price. However, the profit or loss on the purchase and sale of an asset depends critically on the purchase price. In considering options, we keep these two related ideas strictly distinct. We present graphs for both the value of options and the profits from trading options, but we want to be sure not to confuse the two. By graphing the value of options and the profits or losses from options at expiration, we start to develop our grasp of option pricing principles. To focus on the principles of pricing, we ignore commissions and other transaction costs in this chapter.

Option traders often trade options with other options and with other assets, particularly stocks and bonds. This chapter also considers the payoffs from combinations of options. Many of these combinations have colorful names such as spreads, straddles, and strangles. Beyond the terminology, these combinations interest us because they offer special profit and loss characteristics. We also explore the particular payoff patterns that traders can create by trading options in conjunction with stocks and bonds.

We can use **OPTION!**, the software that accompanies this book, to explore the concepts we develop in this chapter. The first module of **OPTION!** analyzes values, profits, and losses at expiration. **OPTION!** can prepare reports of outcomes, and it can graph profit and losses of all the combinations we explore in this chapter.

Stocks

We begin our analysis with the two most familiar securities—common stock and a default-free bond. Figure 2.1 presents the graph of the value of a share of stock and a bond at a certain date. The graph expresses the value of a share of stock and the value of a bond as functions of stock price. In other words, we graph the stock price, or stock value, against the stock price. In the graph, a line runs from the bottom left to the upper right corner. Also, the graph has a horizontal line that intersects the Y-axis at $100.

The diagonal line depicts the value of a single share of the stock. When the stock price on the X-axis is $100, the value of the stock is $100. The horizontal line reflects the value of a $100 face value default-free bond at maturity. The value of the bond does not depend on the price of the stock. Because it is default-free, the bond pays $100 when it matures, no matter what happens to the stock price. For convenience, we assume that the bond matures in one year, and we graph the value of the stock and bond on that future date. Notice that the value of these instruments does not depend in any way on the purchase price of the instruments.

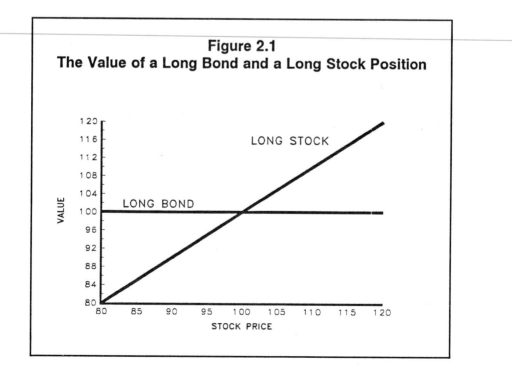

Figure 2.1
The Value of a Long Bond and a Long Stock Position

We now consider possible profits and losses from the share of stock and the risk-free bond. Let us assume that the stock was purchased for $100 and that the pure discount (zero-coupon) risk-free bond was purchased one year before maturity at $90.91. This implies an interest rate of 10 percent on the bond. Figure 2.2 graphs the profit and losses from a long and short position in the stock. The solid line running from the bottom left to the top right of Figure 2.2 shows the profits and losses for a long position of one share in the stock, assuming a purchase price of $100. When the stock price is $100, our graph shows a zero profit. If the stock price is $105, then there is a $5 profit, equal to the stock price of $105 minus the purchase price of $100.

The dotted line in Figure 2.2 runs from the upper left corner to the bottom right corner. The dotted line shows the profits or losses from a short position of one share, assuming that the stock was sold at $100. Throughout this book, we used dotted lines to indicate short positions in value and profit and loss graphs. If the stock is worth $105, the short position shows a loss of $5. The short trader loses $5 because he sold the stock for $100. Now with the higher stock price, the short trader must pay $105 to buy the stock and close the short trade. This will

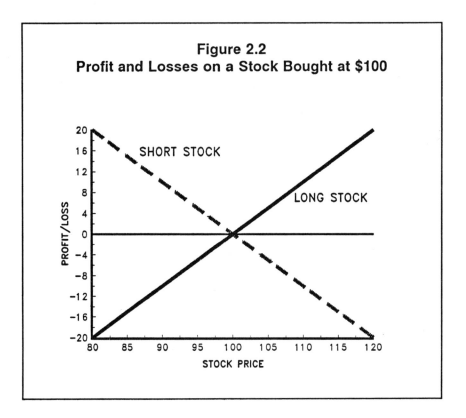

Figure 2.2
Profit and Losses on a Stock Bought at $100

give a loss of $5. As Figure 2.2 shows, the short trader bets that the stock price will fall. For example, if the stock price falls to $93, the short trader can buy the stock at that price and repay the person from whom he borrowed the share. Assuming the short trader sold the share at $100, these transactions provide a $7 profit.

Before leaving the stock, consider the profit and loss profile for a combination of a position that is long one share and short one share. If the stock trades at $105, the long position has a profit of $5 and the short position has a loss of $5. Similarly, if the stock trades at $95, the long position has a loss of $5 and the short position has a profit of $5. No matter what stock price we consider, the profits and losses from the long and short positions cancel each other. The profit or loss is always zero. Thus, taking a long and short position in exactly the same good is a foolish exercise.

Figure 2.3 graphs the profits from the bond that we considered. The purchase price of the bond is $90.91 and it matures in one year, paying $100 with certainty. The profit equals the payoff of $100 minus the cost of $90.91. Thus, the owner of the bond has a sure profit of $9.09 at expiration. Figure 2.3 shows this profit with the solid line in the upper portion of the graph. Similarly, the issuer of the bond will lose $9.09. The issuer receives $90.91, but pays $100. Presumably, the issuer has some productive use for the bond proceeds during the year that will yield more than $9.09.

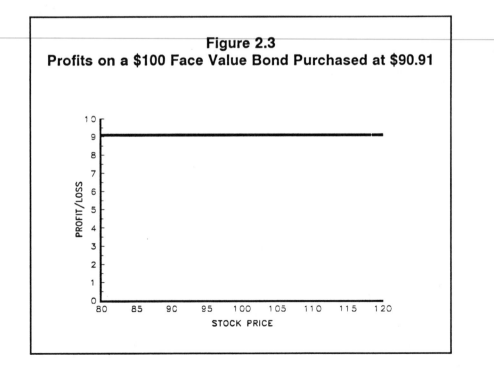

Figure 2.3
Profits on a $100 Face Value Bond Purchased at $90.91

Arbitrage

To explain the value of options, we rely throughout the book on the concept of **arbitrage**—trading to make a riskless profit with no investment. Consider the following example of arbitrage, in which we ignore transaction costs. Some stocks trade on both the New York and Pacific Stock Exchanges at the same time. Suppose that IBM sells for $100 on the New York Stock Exchange and for $102 on the Pacific Stock Exchange. With these prices a trader can simultaneously buy a share in New York and sell the same share on the Pacific Exchange for a $2 profit.

This transaction provides an arbitrage profit. First, there is no investment, because the trader buys and sells the same good at the same time. Second, the profit is certain once the trader enters the two positions. Notice that we ignore transaction costs in this example. We also ignore other real–world problems, such as execution risk, the risk that we cannot execute both transactions simultaneously at the quoted prices. Nonetheless, the example shows a classic case of arbitrage and the trader who engages in such transactions is called an **arbitrageur**.

Properly functioning financial markets allow no such arbitrage opportunities. If the two prices of our example prevailed, arbitrageurs would trade exactly as we described. They would buy the cheap share, and sell the expensive share. Of course, they would do this for as many shares as possible, not just the single share of our example. These transactions would generate a tremendous demand for IBM shares in New York and a tremendous supply of IBM shares on the Pacific Exchange. This high demand would raise the price of shares in New York, and the great supply would cause prices on the Pacific Exchange to fall. The prices on the two exchanges would continue to adjust until they were equal, which would remove the arbitrage opportunity. If a financial market functions properly, there should be no such arbitrage opportunities in the market. In other words, in a smoothly functioning market, traders are alert and immediately compete away such opportunities as they arise. These reflections give rise to a **no–arbitrage principle**.

While we have assumed that there are no transaction costs, we can see their effect within the framework of our example. Assume that the transaction cost of monitoring the market and trading one share is $.10. In our example, a trader must trade two shares, buying a share in New York and selling it on the Pacific Exchange. Thus, the trader faces transaction costs of $.20 to exploit the strategy we have considered. Now assume that the price of a share is $100 in New York and $100.15 on the Pacific Exchange. The trader cannot trade profitably on such a small discrepancy. If he tries, he will pay $100 for the New York share and incur $.20 in transaction costs to get a share worth $100.15. Thus, the arbitrage attempt loses $.05. This example shows that small differences in prices can persist if the difference is less than the cost of trading to exploit the difference.

We know that such small discrepancies in prices can persist in actual markets; however, we ignore these differences for the sake of simplicity in our examples, and we continue to assume that transaction costs are zero.

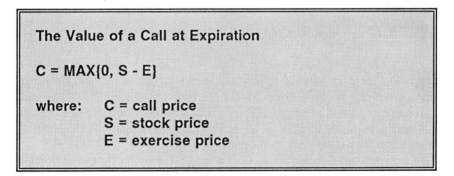

No-Arbitrage Principle

In a properly functioning financial market, prices adjust to prevent arbitrage—trading to make a risk–free profit with no investment. We can analyze prices assuming that they provide no arbitrage opportunities.

Call Options

We now consider the value of call options at expiration, along with the profits or losses that come from trading call options. We noted that the owner of an option has an immediate choice when the option is at expiration: exercise the option or allow it to expire worthless. Therefore, the value of the option will either be zero or it will be the exercise value or the **intrinsic value**—the value of the option if it is exercised immediately. As we will see, the value of an option at expiration depends only on the stock price and the exercise price of the option. The value of a call at expiration equals zero, or the stock price minus the exercise price, whichever is greater.

The Value of a Call at Expiration

$$C = MAX\{0, S - E\}$$

where: C = call price
        S = stock price
        E = exercise price

To understand this principle, let us consider a call option with an exercise price of $100 and assume that the underlying stock trades at $95. At expiration, the call owner may either exercise the option or allow it to expire worthless. With the prices we just specified, the call owner must allow the option to expire.

If the owner of the call exercises the option, he pays $100 and receives a stock that is worth $95. This gives a loss of $5 on the exercise, so it is foolish to exercise. Instead of exercising, the owner of the call can merely allow the option to expire. If the option expires, there is no additional loss involved with the exercise, because the owner of the call avoids exercising. In our example:

$$S - E = \$95 - \$100 = -\$5$$

The call owner need not exercise. By allowing the option to expire, the call owner acknowledges the zero value of the option. With our example numbers at expiration:

$$C = MAX\{0, S - E\} = MAX\{0, \$95 - \$100\} = MAX\{0, -\$5\} = 0$$

We can extend this example to any ending stock price we wish to consider. For any stock price less than the exercise price, the value of S - E will be negative. Therefore, for any stock price less than the exercise price, the call will be worthless. If the stock price equals the exercise price, the value of S - E equals zero, so the call will still be worthless. Therefore, for any stock price equal to or less than the exercise price at expiration, the call is worth zero.

If the stock price exceeds the exercise price, the call is worth the difference between the stock price and the exercise price. Assume that the stock price is $103. The call option with an exercise price of $100 now allows the holder to exercise the option by paying the exercise price. Therefore, the owner of the call can acquire the stock worth $103 by paying $100. This gives an immediate payoff of $3 from exercising. Notice that this example conforms to our principle. Using these numbers we find:

$$C = MAX\{0, S - E\} = MAX\{0, \$103 - \$100\} = MAX\{0, \$3\} = \$3$$

For the call of our example, Figure 2.4 graphs the value of the call at expiration. Here the value of the call equals the maximum of zero or the stock price minus the exercise price. As the graph shows, the value of the call is unlimited, at least in principle. If the stock price were $1000 at expiration, the call would be worth $MAX\{0, S-E\} = \$900$. This graph has the characteristic shape for a long position in a call option.

Figure 2.4 also shows the value of a short position in the same call option. The dotted line graphs the short position. (For stock prices between 0 and $100, both graphs lie on the same line.) Notice that the short position has a zero value for all stock prices equal to or less than the exercise price. If the stock price exceeds the exercise price, the short position is costly. Assume that the stock price is $107 at expiration. In this case, the call owner will exercise the option. The seller of the call must then deliver a stock worth $107 and receive the

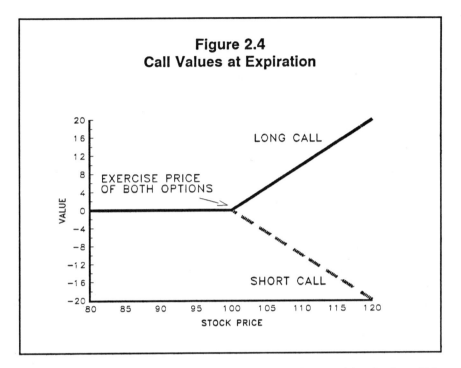

Figure 2.4
Call Values at Expiration

exercise price of $100. This means that holding a short position in the call is worth -$7. The short position never has a value greater than zero, and when the stock price exceeds the exercise price, the short position is worse than worthless. From this consideration, it appears that no one would ever willingly take a short position in a call option. However, this leaves out the payments made from the buyer to the seller when the option first trades.

Continuing with our same example of a call option at expiration with a striking price of $100, we consider profit and loss results. We assume that the call option was purchased for $5. To profit, the holder of a long position in the call needs a stock price that will cover the exercise price and the cost of acquiring the option. The seller of a call receives payment when the option first trades. The seller continues to hope for a stock price at expiration that does not exceed the exercise price. However, even if the stock price exceeds the exercise price, there may still be some profit left for the seller. Figure 2.5 graphs the profit and losses for the call option positions under the assumptions we have been considering. Graphically, bringing profits and losses into consideration shifts the long call graph down by the $5 purchase price and shifts the short call graph up by the $5 purchase price.

We can understand Figure 2.5 for both the long and short positions by considering a few key stock values. We begin with the long position. To acquire a long position in the call option, the trader paid $5. If the stock price is $100 or less, the value of the option is zero at expiration and the owner of the call lets it expire. Therefore, for any stock price less than the $100 exercise price, the call owner simply loses the entire purchase price of the option. If the stock price at expiration is above $100 but less than $105, the graph shows that the holder of the long call still has a loss, but the loss is not a total loss of the $5 purchase price. For example, if the stock price at expiration is $103, the long call holder loses $2 in total. The call owner exercises, buying the $103 stock for $100 and makes $3 on the exercise. This $3 exercise value, coupled with the $5 paid for the option, gives a net loss of $2. If the stock price is $105, the holder of the call makes an exercise value of $5. This exactly offsets the purchase price of the option, and there is no profit or loss. From this example, we see that the holder of a call makes a zero profit if the stock price equals the exercise price plus the price paid for the call. To profit, the call holder needs a stock price that exceeds the exercise price plus the price paid for the call.

Figure 2.5 shows several important points. First, for the call buyer, the worst that can happen is losing the entire purchase price of the option. Comparing Figure 2.5 with Figure 2.2, we can see that the potential dollar loss is much greater if we hold the stock rather than the call. However, a small drop in the stock price can cause a complete loss of the option price. Second, potential profits from a long position in a call option are theoretically unlimited. The

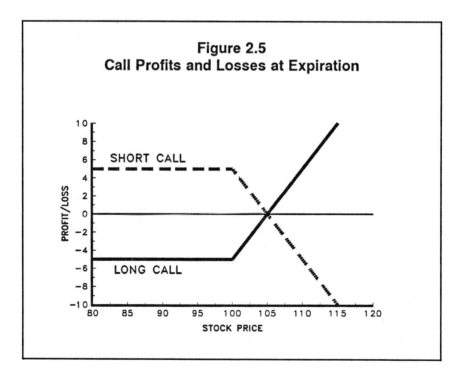

Figure 2.5
Call Profits and Losses at Expiration

profits depend only on the price of the stock at expiration. Third, our discussion and graph show that the holder of a call option will exercise any time the stock price at expiration exceeds the exercise price. The call holder will exercise to reduce a loss or to capture a profit.

We now consider profit and losses on a short position in a call option. When the long trader bought a call, he paid $5 to the seller. As we noted in Chapter 1, the premium paid by the purchaser at the time of the initial trade belongs to the seller no matter what happens from that point forward. As Figure 2.5 shows, the greatest profit the seller of the call can achieve is $5. The seller attains this maximum profit when the holder of the call cannot exercise. In our example, the seller's profit is $5 for any stock price of $100 or less. This makes sense because the call owner will allow the option to expire worthless for any stock price at expiration at or below the exercise price.

If the call owner can exercise, the seller's profits will be lower and the seller may incur a loss. For example, if the stock price is $105, the owner of the call will exercise. In this event, the seller will be forced to surrender a share worth $105 in exchange for the $100 exercise price. This represents a loss for the seller in the exercise of $5, which exactly offsets the price the seller received for the option. So with a stock price of $105, the seller makes a zero profit, as does the call owner. If the stock price exceeds $105, the seller will incur a loss. For example, with a stock price of $115, the call owner will exercise. At the exercise, the seller of the call delivers a share worth $115 and receives the $100 exercise price. The seller thereby loses $15 on the exercise. Coupled with the $5 the seller received when the option traded, the seller now has a net loss of $10.

In summary, we can note two key points about the profits and losses from selling a call. First, the best thing that can happen to the seller of a call is never to hear any more about the transaction after collecting the initial premium. As Figure 2.5 shows, the best profit for the seller of the call is to keep the initial purchase price. Second, potential losses from selling a call are theoretically unlimited. As the stock price rises, the losses for the seller of a call continue to mount. For example, if the stock price went to $1,000 at expiration, the seller of the call would lose $895.

Figure 2.5 also provides a dramatic illustration of one of the most important and sobering points about options trading. The profits from the buyer and seller of the call together are always zero. The buyer's gains are the seller's losses and vice versa. Therefore, the options market is a **zero–sum game**; there are no net profits or losses in the market.[1] The trader who hopes to speculate successfully must be planning for someone else's losses to provide his profits. In other words, the options market is a very competitive arena, with profits being possible only at the expense of another trader.

Call Options at Expiration and Arbitrage

What happens if option values stray from the relationships we analyzed in the preceding section? In this section, we use the concept of arbitrage to show that call option prices must obey the rules we just developed.[2] If prices stray from these relationships, arbitrage opportunities arise. In the preceding section, we considered an example of a call option with an exercise price of $100. At expiration, with the stock trading at $103, the price of a call option must be $3. In this section, we show that any other price for the call option will create an arbitrage opportunity. If the price is too high, say $4, there is one arbitrage opportunity. If the call is too cheap, say $2, there is another arbitrage opportunity. To see why the call must trade for at least $3, consider the arbitrage opportunity that arises if the call is only $2. In this case, the money hungry arbitrageur would transact as follows.

Transaction	Cash Flow
Buy 1 call	-2
Exercise the call	-100
Sell the share	+103
Net Cash Flow	+$1

These transactions give an arbitrage profit. First, there is no investment because all the transactions occur simultaneously. The only cash flow is a $1 cash inflow. Second, the profit is certain once the trader enters the transaction. Therefore, these transactions meet our conditions for arbitrage: they offer a riskless profit without investment. If the call were priced at $2, traders would follow our strategy mercilessly. They would madly buy options, exercise, and sell the share. These transactions would cause tremendous demand for the call and a tremendous supply of the share. These supply and demand forces would subside only after the call and share price adjust to prevent the arbitrage.

We now consider why the call cannot trade for more than $3 at expiration. If the call price exceeds $3, a different arbitrage opportunity arises. If the call is priced at $4, for example, arbitrageurs would simply sell the over-priced call. Then they would wait to see whether the purchaser of the call exercises. Transactions for both possibilities—the purchaser exercises or does not exercise—appear on the next page.

If the purchaser exercises, the arbitrageur has already sold the call and received $4. Now to fulfill his exercise commitment, the seller acquires a share for $103 in the market and delivers the share. Upon delivery, the seller of the call receives the exercise price of $100. These three transactions yield a profit of $1. If the purchaser foolishly neglects to exercise, the situation is even better for the arbitrageur. The arbitrageur already sold the call and received $4. If the purchaser fails to exercise, the option expires and the arbitrageur makes a full $4 profit. The worst case scenario still provides the arbitrageur with a profit of $1. Therefore, these transactions represent an arbitrage transaction. First, there is no investment. Second, the transactions ensure a profit.

If such option prices prevailed, traders would madly sell call options. The excess supply of options at the $4 price would drive down the price of the option. The process would stop only when the price relationships offer no more arbitrage opportunities. This happens when the price of the call and stock conform to the relationships we developed in the preceding section. In other words, prices in financial markets must conform to our no-arbitrage principle by adjusting to eliminate any arbitrage opportunity.

The Purchaser Exercises

Transaction		Cash Flow
Sell 1 call		+4
Buy 1 share		–103
Deliver share and collect exercise price		+100
	Net Cash Flow	+$1

The Purchaser Does Not Exercise

Transaction		Cash Flow
Sell 1 call		+4
	Net Cash Flow	+$4

Put Options

This section deals with the value of put options and the profits and losses from buying and selling puts when the put is at expiration. In most respects, we can analyze put options in the same way we analyzed call options. At expiration, the holder of a put has two choices—exercise or allow the option to expire worthless. If the holder exercises, he surrenders the stock and receives the exercise price. Therefore, the holder of a put will exercise only if the exercise price exceeds the stock price. The value of a put option at expiration equals zero, or the exercise price minus the stock price, whichever is higher.

We can illustrate this principle with an example. Consider a put option with an exercise price of $100 and assume that the underlying stock trades at $102.

At expiration, the holder of the put can either exercise or allow the put to expire worthless. With an exercise price of $100 and a stock price of $102, the holder cannot exercise profitably. To exercise the put, the trader would surrender the stock worth $102 and receive the exercise price of $100, thereby losing $2. Consequently, if the stock price is above the exercise price at expiration, the put is worthless. With our example numbers we have:

$$P = MAX\{0, E - S\} = MAX\{0, \$100 - \$102\} = MAX\{0, -\$2\} = 0$$

Now consider the same put option with the stock trading at $100. Exercising the put requires surrendering the stock worth $100 and receiving the exercise price of $100. There is no profit in exercising and the put is at expiration, so the put is still worthless. In general, if the stock price equals or exceeds the exercise price at expiration, the put is worthless.

The Value of a Put Option at Expiration

$P = MAX\{0, E - S\}$

where: P = put price
          S = stock price
          E = exercise price

When the stock price at expiration falls below the exercise price, the put has value. In this situation, the value of the put equals the exercise price minus the stock price. For example, assume the stock trades at $94 and consider the same put with an exercise price of $100. Now the put is worth $6 because it gives its owner the right to receive the $100 exercise price by surrendering a stock worth only $94. Using these numbers we find:

$$P = MAX\{0, E - S\} = MAX\{0, \$100 - \$94\} = MAX\{0, \$6\} = \$6$$

Figure 2.6 graphs the value of our example put option at expiration. The graph shows the value of a long position as the solid line and the value of a short position as the dotted line. For stock values equaling or exceeding the $100 exercise price, the put has a zero value. If the stock price is below the exercise price, however, the put is worth the exercise price minus the stock price. As our example showed, if the stock trades for $94, the put is worth $6. The graph reflects this valuation.

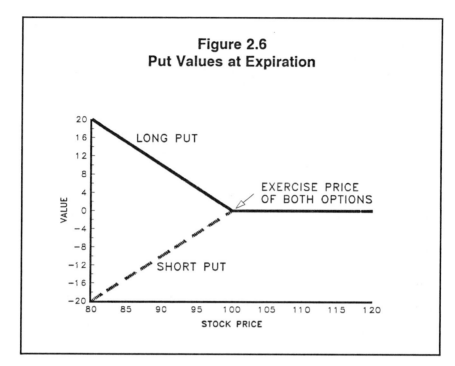

Figure 2.6
Put Values at Expiration

Figure 2.6 also shows the value of a short position in the put. For stock prices equaling or exceeding the exercise price, the put has a zero value. This zero value results from the fact that the holder of the long put will not exercise. However, when the stock price at expiration is less than the exercise price, a short position in the put has a negative value, which results from the opportunity that the long put holder has to exercise. For example, if the stock price is $94, the holder of a short position in the put must pay $100 for a stock worth only $94 when the long put holder exercises. In this situation, the short position in the put will be worth -$6.

Our analysis of put values parallels our results for call options in several ways. First, as we saw with the values of call options at expiration, the value of long and short positions in puts always sum to zero for any stock price. We noted in our discussion of call options that the option market is a zero-sum game. The same principle extends to put options with equal force. Second, we see for put options, as we noted for call options, that a short position can never have a positive value at expiration. The seller of a call or put hopes that nothing happens after the initial transaction when he collects the option price. The best outcome for the seller of either a put or a call is that there will be no exercise and that the option will expire worthless. Third, noting that a short put position has a zero value at best, we might wonder why anyone would accept a short position. As we saw with a call option, the rationality of selling a put requires us to consider the sale price. This leads to a consideration of put option profits and losses.

We continue with our example of a put option with an exercise price of $100. Now we assume that this option was purchased for a price of $4. We consider how profits and losses on long and short put positions depend on the stock price at expiration. As we did for calls, we consider a few key stock prices.

First, we analyze the profits and losses for a long position in the put, where the purchase price is $4 and the exercise price is $100. If the stock price at expiration exceeds $100, the holder of the put cannot exercise profitably and the option expires worthless. In this case, the put holder loses $4, the purchase price of the option. Likewise, if the stock price at expiration equals $100, there is no profitable exercise. Exercising in this situation would only involve surrendering a stock worth $100 and receiving the $100 exercise price. Again, the buyer of the put option loses the purchase price of $4. Therefore, if the stock price at expiration equals or exceeds the exercise price, the buyer of a put loses the full purchase price. Figure 2.7 shows the profits and losses for long and short positions in the put.

If the stock price at expiration is less than the exercise price, there will be a benefit to exercising. For example, assume the stock price is $99 at expiration. Then, the owner of the put will exercise, surrendering the $99 stock and

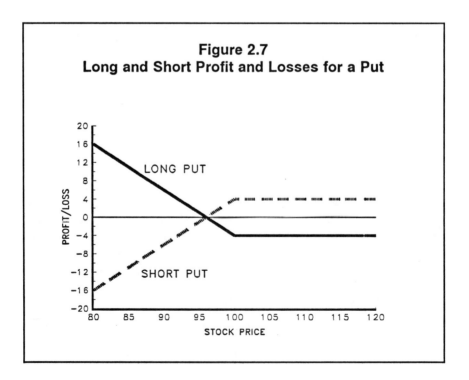

**Figure 2.7
Long and Short Profit and Losses for a Put**

receiving the $100 exercise price. In this case, the exercise value of the put is $1. With the $99 stock price, the holder of the put makes $1 on the exercise but has already paid $4 to acquire the put. Therefore, the total loss is $3. If the stock price is $96 at expiration, the buyer of the put makes a zero profit. The $4 exercise value exactly offsets the price of the put. When the stock price is less than $96, the put buyer makes a profit. For example, if the stock price is $90 at expiration, the owner of a put exercises. In exercising, he surrenders a stock worth $90 and receives the $100 exercise price. This gives a $6 profit after considering the $4 purchase price of the option.

Option Combinations

This section discusses some of the most important ways that traders can combine options. By trading option combinations, traders can shape the risk and return characteristics of their option positions, which allow more precise speculative strategies. For example, we will see how to use option combinations to profit when stock prices move a great deal, or when they stagnate.

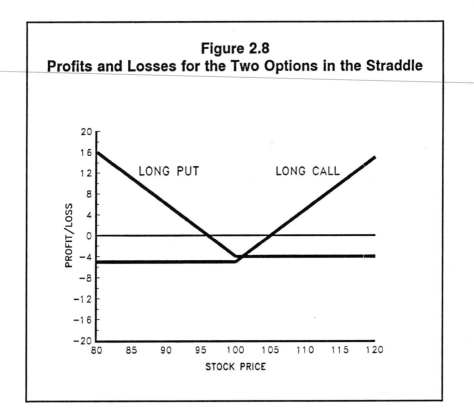

Figure 2.8
Profits and Losses for the Two Options in the Straddle

The Straddle

A **straddle** consists of a call and a put with the same exercise price and the same expiration. The buyer of a straddle buys the call and put, while the seller of a straddle sells the same two options.[3] Consider a call and put, both with $100 exercise prices. We assume the call costs $5 and the put trades for $4. Figure 2.8 shows the profits and losses from purchasing each of these options. The profit and losses for buying the straddle are just the combined profits and losses from buying both options. Figure 2.9 shows the profits and losses from buying and selling the straddle. As the graph shows, the maximum loss for the straddle buyer is the cost of the two options. Potential profits are almost unlimited for the buyer if the stock price rises or falls enough.

Because the options market is always a zero-sum game, the short trader's profits and losses mirror those of the long position. As Figure 2.9 shows, the maximum profit for the short straddle trader occurs when the stock price at expiration equals the exercise price. If the stock price equals the exercise price, the straddle owner cannot exercise either the call or the put profitably. Therefore,

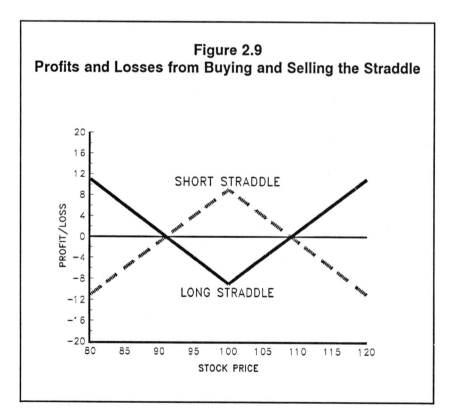

Figure 2.9
Profits and Losses from Buying and Selling the Straddle

both options expire worthless and the short straddle trader keeps both option premiums for a total profit of $9. However, if the stock price diverges from the exercise price, the long straddle holder will exercise either the call or the put. Any exercise decreases the short trader's profits and may even genei: te a loss. If the stock price exceeds the exercise price, the call owner will exercise against the short trader. If the stock price is less than the exercise price, the long trader exercises his or her put and the short trader will lose the exercise value of the put.

As Figure 2.9 shows, the short trader essentially bets that the stock price will not diverge too far from the exercise price, so the seller is betting that the stock price will not be too volatile. In making this bet, the straddle seller risks theoretically unlimited losses if the stock price goes too high. Likewise, the short traders losses are almost unlimited if the stock price goes too low. The short trader's cash inflows equal the sum of the two option prices. At expiration, the short trader's cash outflow equals the exercise result for the call and for the put. If the call is exercised against him at expiration, the short trader loses the difference between the stock price and the exercise price. If the put is exercised against him, the short trader loses the difference between the exercise price and the stock price.

The Strangle

Like a straddle, a **strangle** consists of a put and a call on the same underlying good. In a strangle both options have the same expiration date, but the call has an exercise price above the stock price and the put has an exercise price below the stock price. Therefore, a strangle is just like a straddle, but the put and call have different exercise prices. The long strangle trader buys the put and call, while the short trader sells the two options. To illustrate the strangle, we use a call with an exercise price of $85 and a put with an exercise price of $80. The call price is $3 and the put price is $4.

Figure 2.10 graphs the profits and losses for long positions in these two options. The call has a profit for any stock price above $88, and the put has a profit for any stock price below $76. However, for the strangle to profit, prices must drop further than $76 or rise higher than $88. Figure 2.11 shows the profits and losses from buying and selling the strangle based on these two options. The total outlay for the two options is $7. To break even, either the call or the put must give an exercise profit of $7. The call makes an exercise profit of $7 when the stock price is $7 above the exercise price of the call. This price is $92. Similarly, the put has an exercise profit of $7 when the stock price is $73. Any stock price between $73 and $92 results in a loss on the strangle. Any stock price outside the $73-$92 range gives a profit on the strangle.

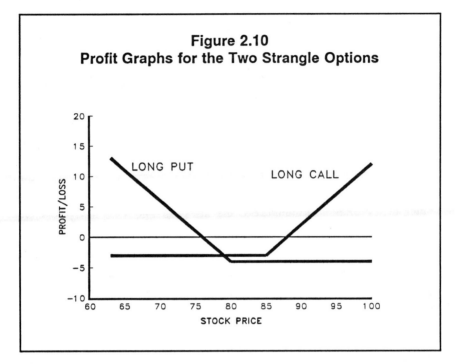

Figure 2.10
Profit Graphs for the Two Strangle Options

Figure 2.11 shows that buying a strangle is betting that the stock price will move significantly below the exercise price on the put or above the exercise price on the call. The buyer of the strangle has the chance for very large profits if the stock price moves dramatically away from the exercise prices. Theoretically, the profit on a strangle is boundless. A stock price at expiration of $200, for example, gives a profit on the strangle of $108.

For the short position, the profits are just the negative values of the profits for the long position. Figure 2.11 shows the profits and losses for the short strangle position as dotted lines. At any stock price from $80–$85, the short strangle has a $7 profit. Between these two prices, the long trader cannot profit by exercising either the put or the call, so the short trader keeps the full price of both options. For stock prices below $80, the straddle buyer exercises the put, and for stock prices above $85, the straddle buyer exercises the call. Any exercise costs the short trader, who has a profit if the stock price stays within the $73–$92 range. However, for very low stock prices, the short strangle position gives large losses, as it does for very high stock prices. Therefore, the short strangle trader is betting that stock prices stay within a fairly wide band. In essence, the short strangle trader has a high probability of a small profit, but accepts the risk of a very large loss.

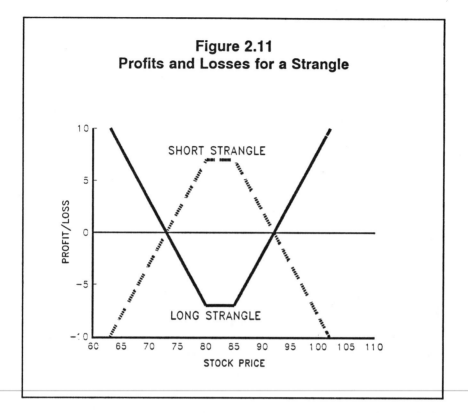

Figure 2.11
Profits and Losses for a Strangle

The Bull Spread with Call Options

A **bull spread** in the options market is a combination of call options designed to profit if the price of the underlying good rises.[4] Both calls in a bull spread have the same expiration, but they have different exercise prices. The buyer of a bull spread buys a call with an exercise price below the stock price and sells a call option with an exercise price above the stock price. The spread is a "bull" spread, because the trader hopes to profit from a price rise in the stock. The trade is a "spread," because it involves buying one option and selling a related option. Compared to buying the stock itself, the bull spread with call options limits the trader's risk. However, it also limits the profit potential compared to the stock itself.

To illustrate this spread, assume that the stock trades at $100. One call option has an exercise price of $95 and costs $7. The other call has an exercise price of $105 and costs $3. To buy the bull spread, the trader buys the call with the $95 exercise price, and sells the other. The total outlay for the bull spread is $4. Figure 2.12 graphs the profits and losses for the two call positions individual-

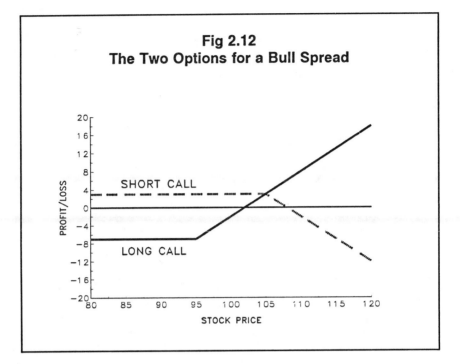

Fig 2.12
The Two Options for a Bull Spread

ly. The long position profits if the stock price moves above $102. The short position profits if the stock price does not exceed $108. As the graph shows, low stock prices result in an overall loss on the position, because the cost of the long position outweighs the amount received from the short position. It is also interesting to consider prices at $105 and above. For every dollar by which the stock price exceeds $105, the long position has an extra dollar of profit. However, at prices above $105, the short position starts to lose money. Thus, for stock prices above $105, the additional gains on the long position match the losses on the short position. Therefore, no matter how high the stock price goes, the bull spread can never give a greater profit than it does for a stock price of $105.

Figure 2.13 graphs the bull spread as the solid line. For any stock price at expiration of $95 or below, the bull spread loses $4. This $4 is the difference between the cash inflow for selling one call and buying the other. The bull spread breaks even for a stock price of $99. The highest possible profit on the bull spread comes when the stock sells for $105. Then the bull spread gives a $6 profit. For any stock price above $105, the profit on the bull spread remains at $6. Therefore, the trader of a bull spread bets that the stock price goes up, but he hedges his bet. We can see that the bull spread protects the trader from losing any more than $4. However, the trader cannot make more than a $6 profit. We can compare the bull spread with a position in the stock itself in Figure 2.2.

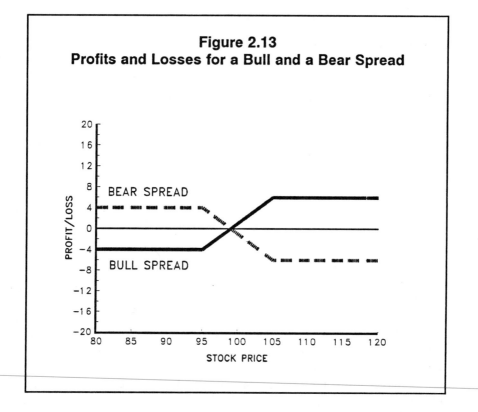

Figure 2.13
Profits and Losses for a Bull and a Bear Spread

Comparing the bull spread and the stock, we find that the stock offers the chance for bigger profits, but it also has greater risk of a serious loss.

Figure 2.13 also shows the profit and loss profile for a bear spread with the same options. A **bear spread** is a combination of options designed to profit from a drop in the stock price. In our example, the bear spread is just the short positions that match the bull spread. In other words, the short position in the bull spread is a bear spread. The dotted line shows how profit and losses vary if a trader sells the call with the $95 strike price and buys the call with the $105 strike price. This position exactly mirrors the bull spread we have considered. In a bear spread, the trader bets that the stock price will fall. However, the bear spread also limits the profit opportunity and the risk of loss compared to a short position in the stock itself. We can compare the profit and loss profiles of the bear spread in Figure 2.13 with the short position in the stock shown as the dotted line in Figure 2.2.[5]

The Butterfly Spread

In a **butterfly spread**, a trader buys one call with a low exercise price and buys one call with a high exercise price, while selling two calls with a medium exercise price. The spread profits most when the stock price is near the medium exercise price at expiration. In essence, the butterfly spread gives a payoff pattern similar to a straddle. Compared to a straddle, however, a butterfly spread offers lower risk at the expense of reduced profit potential.

As an example of a butterfly spread, assume that a stock trades at $100 and a trader buys a spread by trading options with the following prices. As the table shows, the buyer of a butterfly spread sells two calls with a striking price near the stock price and buys one each of the calls above and below the stock price.

	Exercise Price	Option Premium
Long 1 Call	$105	$3
Short 2 Calls	$100	$4
Long 1 Call	$95	$7

Figure 2.14 graphs the profits and losses from each of these three option positions. (This is the most complicated option position we consider.) To understand the profits and losses from the butterfly spread, we need to combine these profits and losses, remembering that the spread involves selling two options and buying two.

Let us consider a few critical stock prices to see how the butterfly spread profits respond. The critical stock prices always include the exercise prices for the options. First, if the stock price is $95, the call with an exercise price of $95 is worth zero and a long position in this call loses $7. The long call with the $105 exercise price also cannot be exercised, so it is worthless, giving a loss of the $3 purchase price. The short call position gives a profit of $4 per option and the spread sold two of these options, for a $8 profit. Adding these values gives a net loss on the spread of $2, if the stock price is $95. Second, if the stock price is $100, the long call with a striking price of $95 loses $2 (the $5 stock profit minus the $7 purchase price). The long call with an exercise price of $105 loses its full purchase price of $3. Together, the long calls lose $5. The short call still shows a profit of $4 per option, for a profit of $8 on the two options. This gives a net profit of $3 if the stock price is $100. Third, if the stock price is $105 at expiration, the long call with an exercise price of $95 has a profit of $3. The long call with an exercise price of $105 loses $3. Also, the short call position loses $1 per option for a loss on two positions of $2. This gives a net loss on the butterfly spread of $2. In summary we have: a $2 loss for a $95 stock price, a $3 profit for a $100 stock price, and a $2 loss for a $105 stock price.

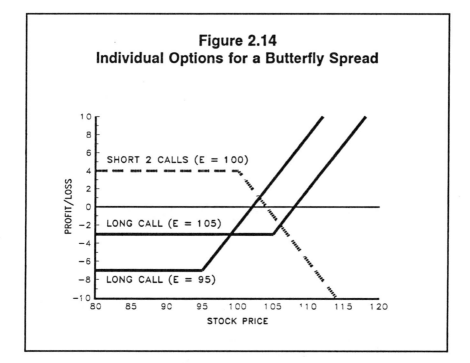

Figure 2.14
Individual Options for a Butterfly Spread

Figure 2.15 shows the entire profit and loss graph for the butterfly spread. At a stock price of $100, we noted a profit of $3. This is the highest profit available from the spread. At stock prices of $95 and $105, the spread loses $2. For stock prices below $95 or above $105, the loss is still $2. As the graph shows, the butterfly spread has a zero profit for stock prices of $97 and $103. The buyer of the butterfly spread essentially bets that stock prices will hover near $100. Any large move away from $100 gives a loss on the butterfly spread. However, the loss can never exceed $2. Comparing the butterfly spread with the straddle in Figure 2.9, we see that the butterfly spread resembles a short position in the straddle. Compared to the straddle, the butterfly spread reduces the risk of a very large loss. However, the reduction in risk necessarily comes at the expense of a chance for a big profit.

Combining Options with Bonds and Stocks

Thus far we have considered some of the most important combinations of options. We now show how to combine options with stocks and bonds to adjust payoff patterns to fit virtually any taste for risk and return combinations. These combinations will show us the relationships among the different classes of securities. By combining two types of securities, we can generally imitate the

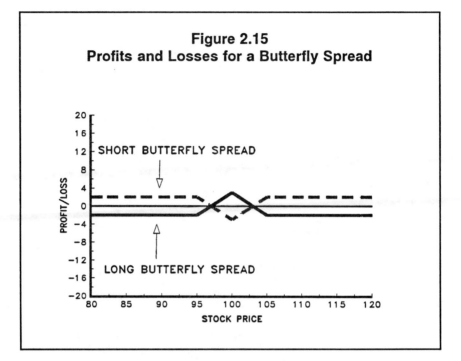

Figure 2.15
Profits and Losses for a Butterfly Spread

payoff patterns of a third. In addition, this section extends the concepts we have developed earlier in this chapter. Specifically, we learn more about shaping the risk and return characteristics of portfolios by using options.

In this section we consider four combinations of options with bonds or stocks. First, we explore portfolio insurance. During the 1980s, portfolio insurance became one of the most discussed techniques for managing the risk of a stock portfolio. We illustrate some of the basic ideas of portfolio insurance by showing how to insure a stock portfolio. Second, we show how to use options to mimic the profit and loss patterns of the stock itself. For investors who do not want to invest the full purchase price of the stock, it is possible to create an option position that gives a profit and loss pattern much like the stock itself. Third, by combining options with the risk-free bond, we can duplicate the underlying stock. In this situation, the option and bond position gives the same profit and loss pattern as the stock and it has the same value as the stock as well. Finally, we show how to combine a call, a bond, and a share of stock to duplicate a put option.

Portfolio Insurance: Stock plus a Long Put

Along with program trading, portfolio insurance was a dominant investing technique developed in the 1980s. **Portfolio insurance** is an investment management technique designed to protect a stock portfolio from severe drops in value. Investment managers can implement portfolio strategies in various ways. Some use options, while others use futures, and still others use combinations of other instruments. We analyze a simple strategy for implementing portfolio insurance with options. Portfolio insurance applies only to portfolios, not individual stocks. Therefore, for our discussion we assume that the underlying good is a well-diversified portfolio of common stocks. We may think of the portfolio as consisting of the Standard & Poors 100. This is convenient because a popular stock index option is based on the S&P 100. Therefore, the portfolio insurance problem we consider is protecting the value of this stock portfolio from large drops in value.[6]

In essence, portfolio insurance with options involves holding a stock portfolio and buying a put option on the portfolio.[7] If we have a long position in the stock portfolio, the profits and losses from holding the portfolio consist of the profits and losses from the individual stocks. Therefore, the profits and losses for the portfolio resemble the typical stock's profits and losses. As an example,

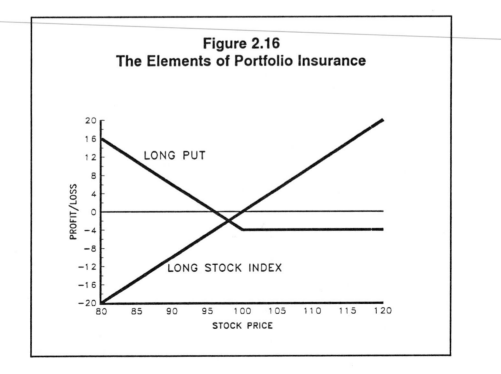

Figure 2.16
The Elements of Portfolio Insurance

consider an investment in the stock index at a value of 100.00. Figure 2.16 shows the profit and loss profiles for an investment in the index at 100 and for a put option on the index. The figure assumes that the put has a striking price of 100.00 and costs 4.00 (we are expressing all values in terms of the index). Figure 2.17 shows the effects of combining an investment in the index stocks and buying a put on the index. For comparison, Figure 2.17 also shows the profits and losses from a long position in the index itself.

The insured portfolio, the index plus a long put, offers protection against large drops in value. If the stock index suddenly falls to 90.00, the insured portfolio loses only 4.00. No matter how low the index goes, the insured portfolio can lose only 4.00 points. However, this insurance has a cost. Investment in the index itself shows a profit for any index value over 100.00. By contrast, the insured portfolio has a profit only if the index climbs above 104.00. In the insured portfolio, the index must climb high enough to offset the price of buying the insuring put option. Because the put option will expire, keeping the portfolio insured requires that the investor buy a series of put options to keep the insurance in force. In Figure 2.17, notice that the combined position of a long index and a long put gives a payoff shape that matches a long position in a call. Like a call, the insured portfolio protects against extremely unfavorable outcomes as the stock price falls. This similarity between the insured portfolio and a call

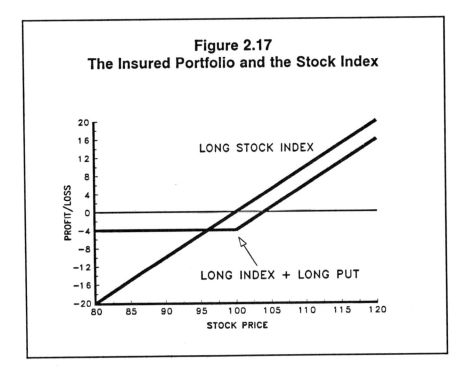

Figure 2.17
The Insured Portfolio and the Stock Index

position suggests that a trader might buy a call and invest the extra proceeds in a bond in order to replicate a position in an insured portfolio.

As a further comparison, we consider the likely profits from holding the stock portfolio and the insured portfolio. Let us assume that the option expires in one year. The stock portfolio is expected to appreciate about 10 percent and have a standard deviation of 15 percent. We also assume that the returns on the stock portfolio are normally distributed. Thus, a $100 investment in the stock portfolio would have an expected terminal value of $110 in one year. Under these assumptions, Figure 2.18 shows the probability distribution of the stock portfolio's terminal value. With a standard deviation of 15 percent there is approximately a two-thirds chance that the terminal value of the portfolio will lie between $95 and $125 dollars. This conclusion results from a feature of the normal distribution. About 67 percent of all observations from a normal distribution lie within one standard deviation of the mean.

With the insured portfolio, we have already seen that the maximum loss is $4. Therefore, the terminal value of the insured portfolio must be at least $96. However, Figures 2.17 and 2.18 imply that there is a good chance that the insured portfolio's terminal value will be $96. For the stock portfolio, any terminal value of $100 or less gives a $96 terminal value for the insured portfolio. While the insured portfolio protects against large losses, it has a lower

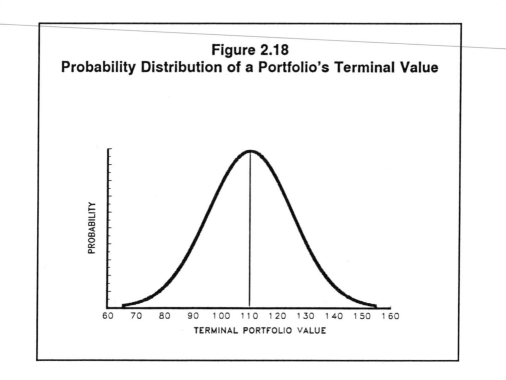

Figure 2.18
Probability Distribution of a Portfolio's Terminal Value

chance of a really large payoff. For the insured portfolio to have a terminal value of $136, for example, the stock portfolio must be worth $140. This is two standard deviation's above the expected return on the stock portfolio, however, and there is little chance of such a favorable outcome.

Figure 2.19 compares the distribution of returns for the stock and for the insured portfolios. The figure presents the cumulative probability distribution for each portfolio. For the stock portfolio, the line in Figure 2.19 merely presents the cumulative probability consistent with Figure 2.18. The kinked line in Figure 2.19 corresponds to the insured portfolio. The probability of a terminal value below $96 for the insured portfolio is zero, because that is exactly what the insurance guarantees. However, there is a very good chance that the terminal value for the insured portfolio will be $96. The probability of a $96 terminal value for the insured portfolio equals the probability that the stock portfolio will be worth $100 or less. As the graph shows, this probability is 25 percent. Notice also that the probability of a $96 or lower terminal value for the stock portfolio is 18 percent. This means that there is an 82 percent chance that the stock portfolio will outperform the insured portfolio, because there is an 82 percent chance that the stock portfolio will be worth more than $96.

As we consider terminal stock portfolio values above $96, we see that the line for the insured portfolio lies above the line for the stock portfolio in Figure

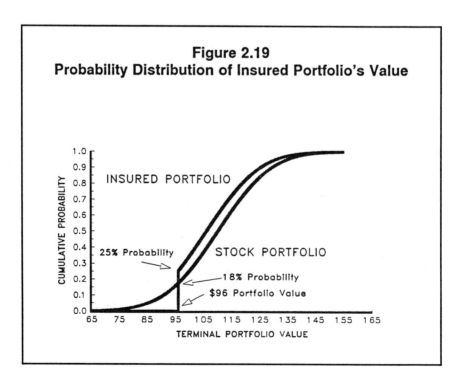

Figure 2.19
Probability Distribution of Insured Portfolio's Value

2.19. Consider a $110 terminal value for the stock portfolio. Because the distribution is normal and the expected return is 10 percent, there is a 50 percent chance that the terminal value of the stock portfolio will be $110 or less. Because the line for the insured portfolio lies above the line for the stock portfolio, there is a higher probability that the insured portfolio's value will be $110 or less. The probability of a terminal value for the insured portfolio of $110 or less is 61 percent. Correlatively, there is a 50 percent chance of a terminal stock portfolio value above $110 and only a 39 percent chance of a terminal value above $110 for the insured portfolio. Thus, because the insured portfolio's cumulative probability line lies above that for the stock portfolio at higher terminal prices, the stock portfolio has a better chance of higher returns. Figure 2.19 shows that the insured portfolio sacrifices chances of a large gain to avoid the chance of a large loss. Which investment is better depends on the risk preferences of the investor. The important point to recognize is the role of options in adjusting the returns distribution for the underlying investment. With options, we can adjust the distribution to fit our tastes—subject to the risk and return trade-off governing the entire market.[8]

Finally, we also observe that the insured portfolio has the same profits and losses as a call option. In fact, the profit and loss graph for the insured portfolio matches that of a call option with a striking price of 100.00 and a price of 4.00. This does not mean, however, that the insured portfolio and such a call option would have the same value. At expiration, the call will have no residual value beyond its profit and loss at that moment. By contrast, the insured portfolio will still include the underlying value of the investment in the stock index. Therefore, for a particular time horizon, two different investments can have the same profit and loss patterns without having the same value.

Mimicking Stock: Long Call plus a Short Put

By combining a long position in a call and a short position in a put, we can create an option position that has the same basic profit and loss pattern as investing in a stock. For a stock priced at $100, consider call and put options with exercise prices of $100. Assume that the call costs $7 and the put costs $3. We want to compare two investments. The first investment is buying one share of stock for $100. The second investment is buying one call for $7 and selling one put for $3.

When the options expire, the two investments have parallel profits and losses. However, the profit on the stock will always be $4 greater than the profit on the option position. For example, assume the stock price is $110 at expiration. The stock has a profit of $10 and the option investment has a profit of $6. For the option position, the put expires worthless and the call has an exercise value of $10. From this exercise value we subtract the $4 net investment required to purchase the option position. Figure 2.20 graphs the profits and losses for both options, the stock, and the combined option position.

Investing in the stock costs $100, while the option position costs only $4. Yet the option position profits mimic those of the stock fairly closely. In a sense, the options give very high leverage by simulating the stock's profits and losses with a low investment. Many option traders view this high leverage of options as one of their prime advantages. Thus, a very small investment in the option position gives a position that mimics the profits and losses of a much more costly investment in the stock. In other words, the option position is much more elastic than the similar stock position.

The profit on the stock is always $4 greater than the profit on the option position. However, the stock investment costs $100, while the option position costs only $4. Therefore, the stock costs $96 more than the option position to guarantee a certain $4 extra profit over the option position. While the long call plus short put option position mimics the profits and losses on the stock, it does not duplicate the stock. As we will see, we can duplicate the stock by adding investment in the risk-free bond to the option position.

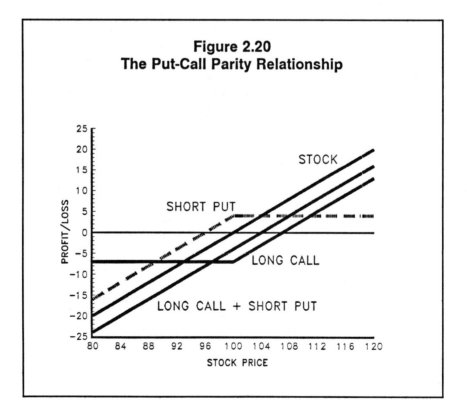

Figure 2.20
The Put-Call Parity Relationship

Duplicating Stock: Long Call, plus a Short Put, plus Bonds

As we have just seen, a long call combined with a short put can mimic the profit and loss pattern on the underlying stock. By adding an investment in the risk-free bond, we can create an investment that will duplicate the stock's profits and losses and its value as well. Therefore, this section shows that a long call, plus a short put, plus the right investment in the risk-free bond, can duplicate a stock investment.

To duplicate a stock, let us consider the same stock selling for $100 and the same options we considered in the previous section. Comparing just the value of the stock position versus the value of the option position at expiration, the stock position will always be worth $100 more than the option position. For example, assume the stock price is $120 at expiration. Then, the stock investment is worth $120. The option position will be worth $20, because the call can be exercised for $20 and the put will be worthless. To duplicate the stock value by using options, we need to buy a risk-free bond that pays $100 at expiration. We can think of this investment as buying a one-year Treasury-bill with a face value of $100. Notice that the payoff on the Treasury-bill equals the exercise price for the options. We now have two equivalent portfolios:

Investment	Cash Flow
Portfolio A	
Long position in the stock	$100
Portfolio B	
Long position in the call	-$7
Short position in the put	+3
A bond paying the exercise price of $100 at expiration	?

Thus far, we have not said how much the bond should cost. However, we can employ our no-arbitrage condition for guidance. We know that both portfolios will have the same value in one year when the option expires. To avoid arbitrage, the two portfolios must have the same value now as well. This condition implies that the bond must cost $96 and that the interest rate must be 4.17 percent.

To see why the bond must cost $96, we consider the arbitrage opportunity that results with any other bond price. For example, assume that the bond costs $93. With this low bond price, Portfolio A is too expensive relative to Portfolio B. To exploit the arbitrage opportunity, we sell the overpriced Portfolio A and buy the underpriced Portfolio B, transacting as follows:

Transaction	Cash Flow
Sell the stock	$100
Buy the call	-7
Sell the put	+3
Buy the bond	-93
Net Cash Flow	+$3

When the options expire in one year, we can close out all the positions without any additional investment. To close the position, we buy back the stock and honor any obligation we have from selling the put. Fortunately, we will have $100 in cash from the maturing bond we bought. For example, if the stock price at expiration is $90, our call is worthless and the put is exercised against us. Therefore, we use the proceeds from the maturing T-bill to pay the $100 exercise price for the put that is exercised against us. We now have the stock and in return use it to close our short position in the stock. The total result at expiration is that we can honor all obligations with zero cash flow. This is true no matter what the stock price is. Therefore, the cheap price on the bond gave us an arbitrage profit of $3 when we made the initial transaction. The transactions are an arbitrage because they require no investment and offer a riskless profit. With an initial cash inflow of $3, there is clearly no investment. Also, we make a riskless profit immediately when we transact. The only price for the bond that rules out arbitrage is $96.

If the bond is priced higher than $96, then Portfolio B is overpriced relative to Portfolio A. We then sell Portfolio B and buy Portfolio A. Again, we have an arbitrage profit. To see how to make an arbitrage profit from a bond price that is too high, assume the bond price is $98. We then transact as follows:

Transaction	Cash Flow
Buy the stock	-$100
Sell the call	7
Buy the put	-3
Sell the bond	+98
Net Cash Flow	+$2

In one year, the options will expire and the bond will mature. Selling the bond means that we borrow $98 and promise to repay $100, so we will owe $100 on the bond at expiration. However, no matter what the stock price is at expiration, we can dispose of the stock and close the option positions for a cash inflow of $100. This gives exactly what we need to pay our debt on the bond. For example, assume the stock price is $93. The call we sold expires worthless but we can exercise the put. When we exercise the put, we deliver the stock and receive the $100 exercise price. This amount repays the bond debt.

Duplicating a Stock

$$S = C - P + Ee^{-rt}$$

where: Ee^{-rt} = the present value of the exercise price, or the price of a bond that pays the exercise price when the options expire

Note: The call and put have the same exercise price E and the same expiration.

Duplicating a Put Option: The Put–Call Parity Relationship

We have just seen that we can buy a call, short a put, and invest in a risk-free bond to duplicate investment in a stock. In fact, with any three of these four instruments, we can duplicate the fourth. This section illustrates **put–call parity**—the relationship between put, call, stock, and bond prices. Specifically, put-call parity shows how to duplicate a put option by selling the stock, buying a call, and investing in a risk-free bond. Put-call parity asserts that a put is worth the same as a long call, short stock, and a risk-free investment that pays the exercise price on the common expiration date of the put and call.

Put-Call Parity

$$P = C - S + Ee^{-rt}$$

Note: The call and put must have the same exercise price and expiration.

To create a put from the other instruments, we use our previous example of a stock selling at $104, a call option worth $7 with a strike price of $100, and a bond costing $96 that will pay $100 in one year. From these securities, we can duplicate the put option costing $3 with an exercise price of $100. To duplicate the put, we transact as follows:

Investment	Cash Flow
Portfolio C	
Buy the call	-$7
Sell the stock	+104
Buy a bond that pays the exercise price at maturity	-$96
	-$3

In buying Portfolio C, we have the same cash outflow of $3 that buying the put requires. To show that Portfolio C is equivalent to a put with a $3 price and a $100 exercise price, we consider the value of Portfolio C when the stock price equals, exceeds, or is less than $100.

If the stock price is $100 at expiration, Portfolio C is worthless. We cannot exercise the call. However, we receive $100 from the bond, with which we buy the stock. This disposes of the entire portfolio. Also, for any stock price above $100, Portfolio C is worthless. We can then exercise the call and use the proceeds from the bond to pay the exercise price on the call. This gives us the stock, which we owe to cover our earlier sale of the stock. Finally, for a stock price less than $100, Portfolio C is worth the difference between the exercise price and the stock price. If the stock price is $95, the call option expires worthless. We receive $100 on the bond investment and use $95 of this to repurchase the stock that we owe. Thus Portfolio C is worth $5.

Considering our profits on Portfolio C, we lose $3 for any stock price of $100 or more, because Portfolio C is then worthless at expiration and it costs $3. For any stock price at expiration less than $100, Portfolio C is worth the exercise price of $100 minus the stock price. Notice that this is an exact description of the profit and losses on the put. Therefore, Portfolio C duplicates the put option with an exercise price of $100 that costs $3.

Put-call parity has another important implication. Assume that S = E. In this situation, the call will be worth more than the put. To prove this principle, consider the following re-arrangement of the put-call parity formula:

$$C - P = S - Ee^{-rt}$$

If S = E, the right hand side of this equation must be positive, because the exercise price E is being discounted. Therefore, the quantity C - P must also be positive, and this implies that the call price must exceed the put price in this special circumstance.

Summary

This chapter has explored the value and profits from option positions at expiration. The concept of arbitrage provided a general framework for understanding option values and profits. We began by studying the characteristic payoffs for positions in single options, noting that there are four basic possibilities of being long or short a call or a put.

We then considered how to combine options to create special positions with unique risk and return characteristics. These combinations included options to create a straddle, a strangle, a bull spread, and a butterfly spread. A trader can either buy or sell each of these option combinations. Each gives its own risk and return profile, which differs from the position in a single option.

We also considered combinations among options, stocks, and bonds. We saw how to insure a portfolio by using a put option. We also showed that a combination of options could mimic the profit and loss profile of a stock. To duplicate the investment and payoffs of a stock, we used a call, a put, and investment in a risk-free bond. The mimicking portfolio has the same profits and losses at a future date. A duplicating portfolio has the same initial and terminal values. We also showed how to create a put by trading a call, a stock, and the risk-free bond. This illustrated the put-call parity relationship. In general, we conclude that put, call, bond, and stock prices are all related.

Questions and Problems

1. Consider a call option with an exercise price of $80 and a cost of $5. Graph the profits and losses at expiration for various stock prices.

2. Consider a put option with an exercise price of $80 and a cost of $4. Graph the profits and losses at expiration for various stock prices.

3. For the call and put in questions 1 and 2, graph the profits and losses at expiration for a straddle comprised of these two options. If the stock price is $80 at expiration, what will be the profit or loss? At what stock price (or prices) will the straddle have a zero profit?

4. A call option has an exercise price of $70 and is at expiration. The option cost $4 and the underlying stock trades for $75. Assuming a perfect market, how would you respond if the call is an American option? State exactly how you might transact. How does your answer differ if the option is European?

5. A stock trades for $120. A put on this stock has an exercise price of $140 and is about to expire. The put trades for $22. How would you respond to this set of prices? Explain.

6. If the stock trades for $120 and the expiring put with an exercise price of $140 trades for $18, how would you trade?

7. Consider a call and a put on the same underlying stock. The call has an exercise price of $100 and costs $20. The put has an exercise price of $90 and costs $12. Graph a short position in a strangle based on these two options. What is the worst outcome from selling the strangle? At what stock price or prices does the strangle have a zero profit?

8. Assume that you buy a call with an exercise price of $100 and a cost of $9. At the same time, you sell a call with an exercise price of $110 and a cost of $5. The two calls have the same underlying stock and the same expiration. What is this position called? Graph the profits and losses at expiration from this position. At what stock price or prices will the position show a zero profit? What is the worst loss that the position can incur? For what range of stock prices does this worst outcome occur? What is the best outcome and for what range of stock prices does it occur?

9. Consider three call options with the same underlying stock and the same expiration. Assume that you take a long position in a call with an exercise price of $40 and a long position in a call with an exercise price of $30. At the same time, you sell two calls with an exercise price of $35. What position have you created? Graph the value of this position at expiration. What is the value of this position at expiration if the stock price is $90? What is the position's value for a stock price of $15? What is the lowest value the position can have at expiration? For what range of stock prices does this worst value occur?

10. Assume that you buy a portfolio of stocks with a portfolio price of $100. A put option on this portfolio has a striking price of $95 and costs $3. Graph the combined portfolio of the stock plus a long position in the put. What is the worst outcome that can occur at expiration? For what range of portfolio prices will this worst outcome occur? What is this position called?

11. Consider a stock that sells for $95. A call on this stock has an exercise price of $95 and costs $5. A put on this stock also has an exercise price of $95 and costs $4. The call and the put have the same expiration. Graph the profit and losses at expiration from holding the long call and short put. How do these profits and losses compare with the value of the stock at

expiration? If the stock price is $80 at expiration, what is the portfolio of options worth? If the stock price is $105, what is the portfolio of options worth? Explain why the stock and option portfolio differ as they do.

12. Assume a stock trades for $120. A call on this stock has a striking price of $120 and costs $11. A put also has a striking price of $120 and costs $8. A risk-free bond promises to pay $120 at the expiration of the options in one year. What should the price of this bond be? Explain.

13. In the preceding question, if we combine the two options and the bond, what will the value of this portfolio be relative to the stock price at expiration? Explain. What principle does this illustrate?

14. Consider a stock that is worth $50. A put and call on this stock have an exercise price of $50 and expire in one year. The call costs $5 and the put costs $4. A risk-free bond will pay $50 in one year and costs $45. How will you respond to these prices? State your transactions exactly. What principle do these prices violate?

Notes

1. Recall that we are ignoring transaction costs. In the options market, both buyers and sellers incur transaction costs. Therefore, the options market is a negative sum game if we include transaction costs in our analysis.

2. The arbitrage arguments used in this chapter stem from a famous paper by Robert C. Merton, "Theory of Rational Option Pricing," *Bell Journal of Economics and Management Science*, 4, Spring 1973, 141-183.

3. The buyer of a straddle need not be matched with a trader who specifically sells a straddle. Opposite the buyer of a straddle could be two individuals, one of whom sells a call and the other of whom sells a put.

4. It is also possible to execute similar strategies with combinations of put options.

5. The reader should note that the use of terms such as bear spread and bull spread is not standardized. While this book uses these terms in familiar ways, other traders may use them differently.

6.   Three introductory studies of portfolio insurance are: Peter A. Abken, "An Introduction to Portfolio Insurance," *Federal Reserve Bank of Atlanta Economic Review*, 72:6, Nov/Dec 1987, 2-25; and Thomas J. O'Brien, "The Mechanics of Portfolio Insurance," *Journal of Portfolio Management*, 14:3, Spring 1988, 40-47. In his paper, "Simplifying Portfolio Insurance," *Journal of Portfolio Management*, 14:1, Fall 1987, 48-51, Fischer Black shows how to insure a portfolio without using option pricing theory, and he shows how to establish an insured portfolio without a definite horizon date.

7.   It is possible to create an insured portfolio without using options. These alternative strategies employ stock index futures with continuous rebalancing of the futures position. Because of this continuous rebalancing, these strategies are called "dynamic hedging" strategies. Hayne E. Leland, "Option Pricing and Replication with Transaction Costs," *Journal of Finance*, 40, December 1985, 1283-1301 discusses these dynamic strategies. With a dynamic strategy, the insurer must re-balance the portfolio very frequently, leading to a trade-off between having an exactly insured portfolio and high transaction costs. J. Clay Singleton and Robin Grieves discuss this trade-off in their paper, "Synthetic Puts and Portfolio Insurance Strategies," *Journal of Portfolio Management*, 10:3, Spring 1984, 63-69. Richard Bookstaber, "Portfolio Insurance Trading Rules," *Journal of Futures Markets*, 8:1, February 1988, 15-31, discusses some recent technological innovations in portfolio insurance strategies and foresees increasing complexity and sophistication in the implementation of insurance techniques.

8.   Several studies have explored the cost of portfolio insurance. Richard J. Rendleman, Jr. and Richard W. McEnally, "Assessing the Cost of Portfolio Insurance," *Financial Analysts Journal*, 43, May/June 1987, 27-37, compare the desirability of an insured portfolio relative to a utility-maximizing strategy. They conclude that only extremely risk-averse investors will be willing to incur the costs of insuring a portfolio. Richard Bookstaber found similar results in his paper, "The Use of Options in Performance Structuring: Modeling Returns to Meet Investment Objectives," in *Controlling Interest Rate Risk: New Techniques and Applications for Money Management*, edited by Robert B. Platt (New York: John Wiley), 1986. According to Bookstaber, completely insuring a portfolio costs about 25 percent of the portfolio's total return. C. B. Garcia and F. J. Gould, "An Empirical Study of Portfolio Insurance," *Financial Analysts Journal*, July/August 1987, 44-54, find that fully insuring a portfolio causes a loss of returns of about 100 basis points. They conclude that an insured portfolio is not likely to out-perform a static portfolio of stocks and T-bills. Roger

G. Clarke and Robert D. Arnott study the costs of portfolio insurance directly in their paper, "The Cost of Portfolio Insurance: Tradeoffs and Choices," *Financial Analysts Journal*, 43:6, November/December 1987, 35–47. Clarke and Arnott explore the desirability of only insuring part of the portfolio, increasing the risk of the portfolio, and attempting to insure a portfolio for a longer horizon. As they conclude, transaction costs are an important factor in choosing the optimal strategy.

3

Bounds on Option Prices

Introduction

This chapter continues to use no–arbitrage conditions to explore option pricing principles. In the last chapter we considered the prices options could have at expiration, consistent with no–arbitrage conditions. In this chapter we consider option prices before expiration. Extending our analysis to options with time remaining until expiration brings new factors into consideration.

The value of an option before expiration depends on five factors: the price of the underlying stock, the exercise price of the option, the time remaining until expiration, the risk-free rate of interest, and the possible price movements on the underlying stock.[1] In this chapter, we focus on the intuition underlying the relationship between put and call prices and these factors. The next chapter builds on these intuitions to specify these relationships more formally.

We first consider how option prices respond to changes in the stock price, the time remaining until expiration, and the exercise price of the option. These factors set general boundaries for possible option prices. Later in the chapter, we discuss the influence of interest rates on option prices and we consider how the riskiness of the stock affects the price of the option.

The Boundary Space for Call and Put Options

In Chapter 2, we saw that the value of a call option at expiration must be:

$$C = MAX\{0, S - E\} \qquad \qquad 3.1$$

Similarly, the value of a put at expiration is:

$$P = MAX\{0, E - S\} \qquad \qquad 3.2$$

where: C = *the call price*
P = *the put price*
S = *the stock price*
E = *the exercise price*

Corresponding to equations 3.1 and 3.2, we saw that call and put options had distinctive graphs that specified their values at expiration. Figure 2.4 for a call and Figure 2.6 for a put gave the value of the options at expiration. These two figures simply graph equations 3.1 and 3.2, respectively. Now we want to consider the range of possible values for call and put options more generally. Specifically, we want to analyze the values that options can have before expiration.[2]

Said another way, we want to explore the values of options as a function of the stock price, S, the exercise price, E, and the time remaining until expiration, t. In chapter 2, we only considered options that were at expiration, with t = 0. Thus, we were considering option values for various ranges of stock price and exercise prices, but with zero time to expiration. Now, we want to consider option prices when the stock price, the exercise price, and the time to expiration all vary.

Before expiration, call and put values need not conform to equations 3.1 and 3.2. Therefore, our first task is to determine the entire possible range of prices that calls and puts may have before expiration. We call this range of possibilities the **boundary space** for an option. Once we specify the largest range of possible prices, we consider no–arbitrage principles that will help us specify the price of an option more precisely.

The Boundary Space for a Call Option

To define the boundary space for a call option, we consider extreme values for the variables that affect call prices. Because we first focus on the stock price, exercise price, and the time remaining until expiration, we consider extremely high and low values for each of these variables. First, the value of a call option will depend on the stock price. We have already seen that a call option at expiration is worth more the greater the price of the stock. Second, the value of a call option depends on the exercise price of the option. Third, the value of a call can depend on the time remaining until the option expires.

The owner of a call option receives the stock upon exercise. The stock price represents the potential benefit that will come to the holder of a call, so the higher the stock price, the greater the value of a call option. We have already observed this to be true at expiration, as equation 3.1 shows. Also, the exercise price is a cash outflow if the call owner exercises. As such, the exercise price represents a potential liability to the call owner. The lower the liability associated with a call, the better for the call owner. Therefore, the lower the exercise price, the greater the value of a call. Finally, consider the time remaining until expiration. For clarity we focus on two American options that differ only because one has a longer time remaining until expiration. Comparing these two options, we see that the one with the longer time until expiration gives every benefit that the one with the shorter time until expiration does. At a given moment, if the shorter-term option permits expiration, so does the option with a longer term until expiration. In addition, the longer-term option allows the privilege of waiting longer to decide whether to exercise. Generally, this privilege of waiting is quite valuable, so the option with the longer life will tend to have a higher value. However, no matter what happens, the option with the longer life must have a price at least as great as the option with the shorter life. We will see that the same holds true for European options. The longer the time until expiration, the greater the value of the option, holding other factors constant.

We have seen that lower exercise prices and longer lives generally contribute to the value of an option. Therefore, the value of an option will be highest for an option with a zero exercise price and an infinite time until expiration. Similarly, the value will be lowest for an option with a higher exercise price and the shortest time until expiration. A call that is about to expire, with $t = 0$, will be the call with the lowest price for a given stock price and a given exercise price. We already know the possible values that such an expiring option can have. This value is simply the call option's price at expiration, which is given by equation 3.1. At the other extreme, the call with the highest possible value for a given stock price will be the call with a zero exercise price and an infinite time until expiration.

This call option with a zero exercise price and an infinite time until it expires allows us to exercise the option with zero cost and acquire the stock. In short, we can transform this option into the stock anytime we wish without paying anything. Therefore, the value of this call must equal the price of the underlying stock. If we can get the stock for zero any time we wish, the price of the call cannot be more than the stock price. Also, the price of the call cannot exceed the stock price, because the call can only be used to acquire the stock. Therefore, we know that a call on a given stock, with a zero exercise price, and an infinite time to expiration must have a value equal to the stock price. In this special limiting case $C = S$.

> **The price of a call option with a zero exercise price and an infinite time until expiration must equal the price of the underlying stock.**

From this analysis, we have now determined the upper and lower bounds for the price of a call option before expiration. Figure 3.1 depicts the boundaries for the price of a call option as the interior area between the upper and lower bounds. The upper bound for any call option is the stock price. The figure shows this boundary as the 45 degree line from the origin. Along this line, the call

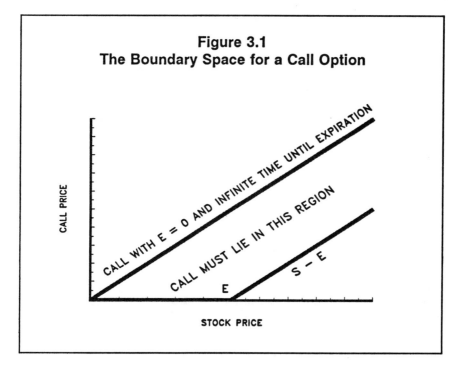

Figure 3.1
The Boundary Space for a Call Option

option is worth the same as the stock. The lower bound is the value of the call option at expiration. At expiration, if the stock price is at or below the exercise price, the call is worth zero. For any stock price above the exercise price, the expiring call is worth the stock price minus the exercise price. Therefore, the value of a call option must always fall somewhere on or within the bounds given by these lines. Later in this chapter, we develop principles that help us to specify much more precisely where within these bounds the actual option price must lie.

The Boundary Space for a Put Option

We now consider the range of possible put prices. We have already considered prices for puts at expiration, and we found the value of a put at expiration to conform to equation 3.2. Equation 3.2 gives the lower bound for the value of a put option. To find the upper bounds for a put option, we need to consider the best possible circumstances for the owner of a put option.

Upon exercise, the owner of a put surrenders the stock and receives the exercise price. The most the put holder can receive is the exercise price, and he can obtain this only by surrendering the stock. Therefore, the lower the stock price, the more valuable the put must be. This is true before expiration and at expiration, as we have already seen. For an American put, this exercise can occur

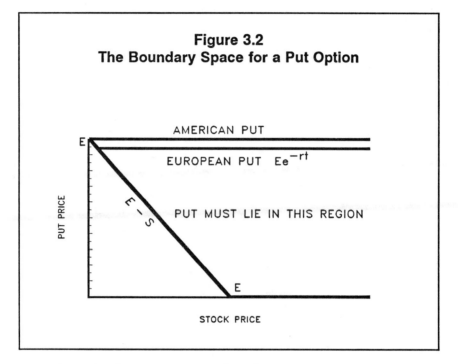

Figure 3.2
The Boundary Space for a Put Option

at any time. Therefore, the maximum value for an American put is the exercise price. The price of an American put equals the exercise price if the stock is worthless and sure to remain worthless until the option expires. If the put is a European put, it cannot be exercised immediately, but only at expiration. For a European put before expiration, the maximum possible price equals the present value of the exercise price. The European put price cannot exceed the present value of the exercise price, because the owner of a European put must wait until expiration to exercise.

Figure 3.2 shows the bounds for American and European puts. The price of a put can never fall below the maximum of zero or E - S. This is the put's value at expiration, which equation 3.2 specifies. For an American put, the price can never exceed E. For a European put, the price can never exceed the present value of the exercise price, Ee^{-rt}. Therefore, the interior of Figure 3.2 defines the range of possible put prices. By developing more exact no-arbitrage conditions, we can say where in this interior area the price of a put can be found.[3]

Relationships Between Call Prices

In this section we focus on price relationships between call options. These price differences arise from differences in exercise price and time until expiration. We have already seen in an informal way that the exercise price is a potential liability associated with call ownership. The greater the value of this potential liability, the worse for the value of the call option. In this section, we illustrate this principle more formally by appealing to our familiar no-arbitrage arguments. We use similar no-arbitrage arguments to explicate other pricing relationships.

The Lower the Exercise Price, the More Valuable the Call—Let us consider a single underlying stock on which there are two call options. The two call options have the same expiration date, but one option has a lower exercise price than the other. In this section, we want to show why the option with the lower exercise price must be worth as much or more than the option with the higher exercise price. For example, assume that two calls exist that violate this principle:

	Time Until Expiration	Exercise Price	Call Price
Call A	6 months	$100	$20
Call B	6 months	$95	$15

These two calls violate our principle because Call A has a higher exercise price and a higher price. These prices give rise to an arbitrage opportunity, as we now show. Faced with these prices, the trader can transact as follows:

Transaction	Cash Flow
Sell Call A	+$20
Buy Call B	-$15
Net Cash Flow	+$5

Once we sell Call A and buy Call B, we have a sure profit of at least $5. To see this, we consider profits and losses for various stock prices, such as $95 and below and $100 and above. If the stock price is $95, neither option can be exercised. If the stock price stays at $95 or below, both options expire worthless, and we keep our $5 from the initial transactions. If the stock price is greater than $100, say $105, Call A will be exercised against us. When that happens, we surrender the stock worth $105 and receive $100, losing $5 on the exercise against us. However, we ourselves exercise Call B, receiving the stock worth $105 and paying the exercise price of $95. So, we can summarize our profits and losses from the exercises that occur when the stock trades at $105.

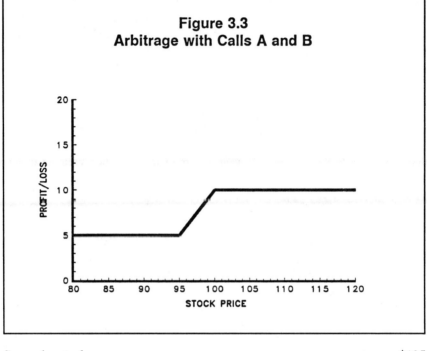

Figure 3.3
Arbitrage with Calls A and B

Surrender stock	–$105
Receive $100 exercise price	+100
Pay $95 exercise price	–95
Receive stock	+105
Net Cash Flow	+$5

As the calculation shows, if Call A is exercised against us, we exercise Call B and make $5 on the double exercise. Therefore, we make a total of $10, $5 from the initial transaction and $5 on the exercises.

Next, we consider what happens if the stock price lies between $95 and $100, say at $97. This outcome is also beneficial for us, because the option we sold with a $100 strike price cannot be exercised against us. However, we can exercise our option. When we exercise, we pay the $95 exercise price and receive a stock worth $97. We add the $2 profit on this exercise to the $5 we made initially, for a total profit of $7. Figure 3.3 graphs the total profit on the position for all stock prices. With a stock price at or below $95, we make $5 because neither option can be exercised. With a stock price of $100 or above, we make $10—$5 from our initial transaction and $5 from the difference between the two exercise prices. If the stock price is between $95 and $100, we make $5 from our initial transaction plus the difference between the stock price and the $95 exercise price we face.

These transactions guarantee an arbitrage profit of at least $5, and perhaps as much as $10. Figure 3.3 reflects the arbitrage profit because it shows there is at least a $5 profit for any stock price. If the profit and loss graph shows profits for all possible stock prices with no investment, then there is an arbitrage opportunity. In the real world, an investment strategy that requires no initial investment may show profits for some stock price outcomes, but it must also show losses for other stock prices. Otherwise, there is an arbitrage opportunity.

In stating our principle, we said that the call with the lower exercise price must cost at least as much as the call with the higher exercise price. Why doesn't the call with the lower exercise price have to cost more than the call with the higher exercise price? In most real market situations, the call with the lower exercise price will, in fact, cost more. However, we cannot be sure that will happen as a general rule. To see why, assume the stock underlying calls A and B trades for $5 and there is virtually no chance that the stock price could reach $90 before the two options expire. When the underlying stock is extremely far out-of-the-money, the calls might have the same, or nearly the same, price. In such a situation, both calls would have a very low price. If it is certain that the stock price can never rise to the lower exercise price, both calls would be worthless.

The Difference in Call Prices Cannot Exceed the Difference in Exercise Prices—Consider two call options that are similar in all respects except that they have exercise prices that differ by $5. We have already seen that the price of the call with the lower exercise price must equal or exceed the price of the call with the higher exercise price. Now we show that the difference in call prices cannot exceed the difference in exercise prices. We illustrate this principle by considering two call options with the same underlying stock:

	Time Until Expiration	Exercise Price	Call Price
Call C	6 months	$ 95	$10
Call D	6 months	$100	$ 4

The prices of Calls C and D do not meet our condition, and we want to show that these prices give rise to an arbitrage opportunity. To profit from this mispricing, we trade as follows:

Transaction		Cash Flow
Sell Call C		+$10
Buy Call D		−4
	Net Cash Flow	+$6

Selling Call C and buying Call D gives a net cash inflow of $6. Because we sold a call, however, we also have the risk that the call will be exercised against us. We now show that no matter what stock price occurs, we still make a profit.

If the stock price is $95 or below, both options expire worthless, and we keep our initial cash inflow of $6. If the stock price exceeds $100, Call C is exercised against us and we exercise Call D. For example, assume the stock price is $102. We exercise, pay the $100 exercise price, and receive the stock. Call C is exercised against us, so we surrender the stock and receive the $95 exercise price. Therefore, we lose $5 on the exercise. This loss partially offsets our initial cash inflow of $6. Thus, for any stock price of $100 or more, we make $1. We now consider stock prices between $95 and $100. If the stock price is $98, Call C will be exercised against us. We surrender the stock worth $98 and receive $95, for a $3 loss. The option we own cannot be exercised, because the exercise price of $100 exceeds the current stock price of $98. Therefore, we lose $3 on the exercise, which partially offsets our initial cash inflow of $6. This gives a $3 net profit.

Figure 3.4 shows the profits and losses on this trade for a range of stock prices. As the figure shows, we make at least $1, and we may make as much as $6. Because all outcomes show a profit with no investment, these transactions constitute an arbitrage. The chance to make this arbitrage profit stems from the fact that the call option prices differed by more than the difference between the exercise prices. In real markets, the difference between two call prices will usually be less than the difference in exercise prices. However, the difference in call prices cannot exceed the difference in exercise prices without creating an arbitrage opportunity.[4]

A Call Must be Worth at Least the Stock Price Less the Present Value of the Exercise Price—We have already noted that a call at expiration is worth the maximum of zero or the stock price less the exercise price. Before expiration, the call must be worth at least the stock price less the present value of the exercise price. That is, $C \geq S - Ee^{-rt}$.

To see why prices must observe this principle, we consider the following situation. Assume the stock trades for $103 and the current risk-free interest rate is 6 percent. A call with an exercise price of $100 expires in six months and trades for $2. These prices violate our rule, because the call option price is too low: $2 is less than the stock price less the present value of $100. These prices give rise to an arbitrage opportunity. To take advantage, we trade as follows:

Sell the stock	+$103
Buy the call option	-2
Buy a bond with remaining funds	-101
Net Cash Flow	0

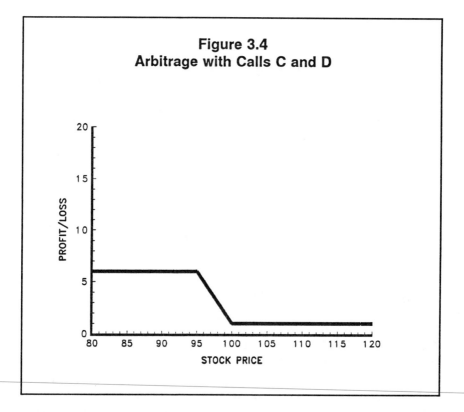

Figure 3.4
Arbitrage with Calls C and D

With these transactions, we owe one share of stock. However, with our call option and the money we have left from selling the stock, we can honor our obligations at any time and still have a profit. For example, at the beginning of the transactions, we can exercise our option, pay the $100 exercise price, return the stock, and keep $1.

Alternatively, we can wait until our option reaches expiration in six months. Then the bond we purchased with be worth $101e^{(.06)(.5)} = $104.08. Whatever the stock is worth at expiration, we can repay with profit. For example, if the stock price is higher than the exercise price, we exercise the option and pay $100 to get the stock. This gives a profit at expiration of $4.08. If the stock price is below the exercise price, we allow our option to expire. We then buy the stock in the open market and repay our debt of one share. For example if the stock price is $95 at expiration, our option expires, and we pay $95 for the share to repay our obligation. Our profit then is $104.08 - $95 = $9.08. Figure 3.5 graphs the profits from this transaction.

From this analysis, we can see that our option must cost at least $103 -$100e^{-(.06)(.5)} = $103 - $97.04 = $5.96. Any lower price allows an arbitrage profit. If the call is priced at $5.96, we have $97.04 to invest in bonds after

> **For a non–dividend paying stock, the call price must equal or exceed zero or the stock price minus the present value of the exercise price, whichever is greater.**
>
> $$C \geq MAX\{0, S - Ee^{-rt}\}$$

selling the stock at $103 and buying the option at $5.96. At expiration, our bond investment pays $100, which is the exercise price. If the option sold at $5.96, the profit line in Figure 3.5 would shift down to show a zero profit for any stock price of $100 or more. This would eliminate the arbitrage because there would be some stock prices that would give zero profits. However, in real markets the price of this call would generally be higher than $5.96. A price of $5.96 ensures against any loss and gives profits for any stock price below $100. If there is any chance that the stock price might be below $100 at expiration, then the call of our example should be worth more than $5.96.

The More Time Until Expiration, the Greater the Call Price—If we consider two call options with the same exercise price on the same underlying good, then the price of the call with more time remaining until expiration must equal or exceed the price of the call that expires sooner. Violating this principle leads to arbitrage, as the following example shows. Consider two options on the same underlying good.

	Exercise Price	Time Until Expiration	Option Price
Call E	$100	3 months	$6
Call F	$100	6 months	$5

These prices violate our principle, which implies that Call F must cost at least as much as Call E. To capture the arbitrage profits, we trade as follows:

Transaction	Cash Flow
Sell Call E	+$6
Buy Call F	−5
Net Cash Flow	+$1

With a net cash inflow at the time of contracting, the transactions clearly require no investment. Therefore, they meet the first condition for an arbitrage. Next, we

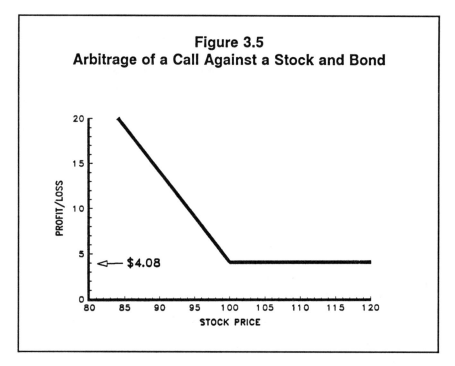

Figure 3.5
Arbitrage of a Call Against a Stock and Bond

need to show that the strategy produces a profit for all stock price outcomes.

First, we show how to protect the arbitrage profit if the options are American options. Any time that Call E is exercised against us, we can exercise Call F to secure the stock to give to the holder of Call E. For example, assume that Call E is about to expire and is exercised against us with the stock price at $105. In that case, we simply exercise Call F and surrender the stock to the holder of Call E, as the following transactions show.

Assuming Call E and Call F are American Options

Transaction	Cash Flow
Call E is exercised against us	
Receive $100 exercise price	+$100
Surrender stock worth $105	−105
Exercise Call F	
Receive stock worth $105	+105
Pay $100 exercise price	−100
Net Cash Flow	0

As these transactions show, if the call we sold is exercised against us, we can fulfill all our obligations by exercising our call. There will be no net cash flow on the exercise, and we keep the $1 profit from our original transaction.

Notice that our concluding transactions assumed that both Call E and Call F were American options. This allowed us to exercise our Call F before expiration. Had the options been European options, we could not exercise Call F when Call E was exercised against us. However, the principle still holds for European options—the European option with more time until expiration must be worth at least as much as the option with a shorter life. We can illustrate this principle for European options with the following transactions.

Assuming Call E and Call F are European Options

Transaction		Cash Flow
Call E is exercised against us		
Receive $100 exercise price		+$100
Surrender stock worth $105		−105
Sell Call F		
Receive $S - Ee^{-rt} \geq \$5$	at least	+5
	Net Cash Flow at least	0

As these transactions show, we will receive at least $5 for selling Call F. Earlier we used no arbitrage arguments to show that an in-the-money call must be worth at least the stock price minus the present value of the exercise price. The worst situation for these transactions occurs at very low interest rates. However, the arbitrage still works for a zero interest rate. Then, Call F must still be worth at least S - E = $105 - $100 = $5. If we get $5 from selling Call F, we still have a net zero cash flow when Call E is exercised against us. If we get more, any additional net cash flow at the time of exercise is just added to the $1 cash inflow we had at the time we initially transacted.

Do not Exercise Call Options on No–Dividend Stocks Before Expiration—In this section, we show that a call option on a non-dividend paying stock is always worth more than its mere exercise value. Therefore, such an option should never be exercised. If the trader wants to dispose of the option, it will always be better to sell the option than to exercise it.

For a call option, the **intrinsic value** or the **exercise value** of the option equals S - E. This is the value of the option when it is exercised, because the holder of the call pays E and receives S. We have seen that, prior to expiration, a call option must be worth at least $S - Ee^{-rt}$. Therefore, exercising a call before expiration discards at least the difference between E and Ee^{-rt}. The difference between the call price and the exercise value is the **time value** of the option. For example, consider the following values:

$S = \$105$
$E = \$100$
$r = .10$
$t = 6 \text{ months}$

The intrinsic value of this call option is \$5, or S − E. However, we know that the market price of the call option must meet the following condition:

$C \geq S - Ee^{-rt}$
$\quad \geq \$105 - \$100e^{-(.1)(.5)}$
$\quad \geq \$9.88$

Therefore, exercising the call throws away at least $E - Ee^{-rt} = \$100 - \$96.12 = \$4.88$. Alternatively it discards the difference between the lower bound on the call price and the exercise value of the call, \$9.88 − \$5.00 = \$4.88. For a non–dividend paying stock, early exercise can never be optimal. This means that the call will not be exercised until expiration. However, this makes an American option on a non–dividend paying stock equivalent to a European option. For a stock that pays no dividends, the American option will not be exercised until expiration and a European option cannot be exercised until expiration. Therefore, the two have the same price. Notice that this rule holds only for a call option on a stock that does not pay dividends. In some circumstances, it can make sense

> **A European and an American call on a non–dividend paying stock have the same value.**

to exercise a call option on a dividend paying stock before the option expires. The motivation for the early exercise is to capture the dividend immediately and to earn interest on those funds. We explore these possibilities in Chapter 5.

Relationships Between Put Option Prices

In Chapter 2, we saw that the value of a put at expiration is given by:

$P = MAX\{0, E - S\}$

Essentially, the put holder anticipates receiving the value of the exercise price and paying the stock price at expiration. Now we want to consider put values before expiration and the relationship between pairs of puts. As we did for calls, we illustrate these pricing relationships by invoking no–arbitrage conditions.

Before Expiration, an American Put Must be Worth at Least the Exercise Price less the Stock Price—The holder of an American put option can exercise any time. Upon exercising, the put holder surrenders the put and the stock and receives the exercise price. Therefore, the American put must be worth at least the difference between the exercise price and the stock price.

$$P_a \geq MAX\{0, E - S\}$$

where P_a is an American put.

We illustrate this principle by showing how to reap an arbitrage profit if the principle does not hold. Consider the following data:

$$S = \$95$$
$$E = \$100$$
$$P = \$3$$

With these prices, the put is too cheap. The put's price does not equal or exceed the $5 difference between the exercise price and the stock price. To take advantage of the mispricing, we transact as shown below. With these transactions, we capture an immediate cash inflow of $2. Also, we have no further obligations, so our arbitrage is complete. We net $2 with no investment. Notice that these transactions involve the immediate exercise of the put option. Therefore, this kind of arbitrage works only for an American put option. To prevent this kind of arbitrage, the price of the American put option must be at least $5. In actual markets, the price of a put will generally exceed the difference between the exercise price and the stock price.

Transaction	Cash Flow
Buy put	-$3
Buy stock	-95
Exercise option	+100
Net Cash Flow	+$2

Before Expiration, a European Put Must be Worth at Least the Present Value of the Exercise Price less the Stock Price—We have just seen that an

American put must be worth at least the difference between the exercise price and the stock price. The same rule does not hold for a European put, because we cannot exercise the European put before expiration to take advantage of the mispricing. However, a similar rule holds for a European put.

We can illustrate this price restriction for a European put by using our same stock and option, except we treat the put as a European put. Also, the risk-free interest rate is 6 percent and we assume that the option expires in 3 months.

$$S = \$95$$
$$E = \$100$$
$$P = \$3$$
$$t = 3 \text{ months}$$
$$r = .06$$

With these values, our principle states:

$$P \geq Ee^{-rt} - S = \$100e^{-(.06)(.25)} - \$95 = \$98.51 - \$95 = \$3.51$$

Because the put must be worth at least $3.51 but the actual price is only $3, we can reap an arbitrage profit by trading as follows:

Transaction	Cash Flow
Borrow $98 at 6 percent for 3 months	+$98
Buy put	−3
Buy stock	−95
Net Cash Flow	0

After making these initial transactions, we wait until the option is about to expire and we transact as follows:

Transaction	Cash Flow
Exercise option, deliver stock, and collect exercise price	+$100.00
Repay debt = $98e^{(.06)(.25)}$	−99.48
Net Cash Flow	+$.52

These transactions give an arbitrage profit of $.52 at expiration. Notice that there was a zero net cash flow when we first transacted, so there was no investment. These initial transactions guaranteed the $.52 profit at expiration. Therefore, we have an arbitrage—a riskless profit with no investment.

From these two examples, we can see that an American put must be worth at least as much as a European put. The lower bound for the price of an

American put is E - S, but the lower bound for the European put is $Ee^{-rt} - S$. Also, we know that the American put gives all the rights of the European put, plus the chance to exercise early. Therefore, the American put must be worth at least as much as the European put.

The Longer Until Expiration, the More Valuable an American Put-Consider two American put options that are just alike except that one has a longer time until expiration. The put with the longer time until expiration must be worth at least as much as the other. Informally, the put with the longer time until expiration offers every advantage of the shorter-term put. In addition, the longer-term put offers the chance for greater price increases on the put after the shorter-term put expires. Without this condition, arbitrage opportunities exist.

To illustrate the arbitrage opportunity, assume the underlying stock trades for $95 and we have two American puts with exercise prices of $100 as follows:

	Time Until Expiration	Put Price
Put A	3 months	$7
Put B	6 months	$6

These prices permit arbitrage, because the put with the longer life is cheaper. Therefore, we sell Put A and buy Put B for an arbitrage profit, as shown below.

Transaction	Cash Flow
Sell Put A	+$7
Buy Put B	−6
Net Cash Flow	+$1

After making these transactions, we must consider what happens if the Put A is exercised against us. Assume that Put A is exercised against us when the stock price is $90. In this situation, the following events occur.

Transaction	Cash Flow
On the exercise of Put A	
Receive stock worth $90	+$90
Pay exercise price of $100	−100
We exercise Put B	
Deliver stock worth $90	−90
Receive exercise price of $100	+100
Net Cash Flow	0

When the holder of Put A exercises against us, we immediately exercise Put B. No matter what the stock price may be, these transactions give a zero net cash flow. Therefore, the original transaction gave us $1, which represents an arbitrage profit of at least $1. The profit could be greater if Put A expires worthless. Then we have our $1 profit to keep, plus we still hold Put B which may have additional value. Therefore, the longer-term American put must be worth at least as much as the shorter-term American put. Notice that this rule holds only for American puts. Our arbitrage transactions require that we exercise Put B when the holder of Put A exercises against us. This we could only do with an American option.

For European put options, it is not always true that the longer-term put has greater value. A European put pays off the exercise price only at expiration. If expiration is very distant, the payoff will be diminished in value because of the time value of money. However, the longer the life of a put option, the greater its advantage in allowing something beneficial to happen to the stock price. Thus, the longer the life of the put, the better for this reason. Whether having a longer life is beneficial to the price of a European put depends on which of these two factors dominates. We will be able to evaluate these more completely in the next chapter.

The fact that a European put with a shorter life can be more valuable than a European put with a longer life shows two important principles. First, early exercise of a put can be desirable even when the underlying stock pays no dividends. This follows from the fact that a short-term European put can be worth more than a long-term European put. Second, American and European put prices may not be identical, even when the underlying stock pays no dividends. If early exercise is desirable, the American put allows it and the European put does not. Therefore, the American put can be more valuable than a European put, even when the underlying stock pays no dividend.

> **An American put can be worth more than a European put, even when the underlying stock pays no dividends.**
>
> **Early exercise of a put can be optimal, even when the underlying stock pays no dividend.**

The Higher the Exercise Price, the More Valuable the Put—For both American and European put options, a higher exercise price is associated with a higher price. A put option with a higher exercise price must be worth at least as much as a put with a lower exercise price. Violations of this principle lead to arbitrage.

To illustrate the arbitrage, consider a stock trading at $90 with the following two put options having the same time until expiration:

	Exercise Price	Put Price
Put C	$100	$11
Put D	$ 95	$12

These prices violate the rule, because the price of Put D is higher, even though Put C has the higher exercise price. To reap the arbitrage profit, we transact as follows:

Transaction		Cash Flow
Sell Put D		+$12
Buy Put C		−11
	Net Cash Flow	+$1

If the holder of Put D exercises against us, we immediately exercise Put C. Assuming the stock price is $90 at the time of exercise, we consider the appropriate transactions when we face the exercise of Put D:

Transaction		Cash Flow
Exercise of Put D against us:		
Receive stock worth $90		+$90
Pay exercise price		−95
Our exercise of Put C:		
Deliver stock worth $90		−90
Receive exercise price		+100
	Net Cash Flow	+$5

No matter what the stock price is at the time of exercise, we have a cash inflow of $5 if we both exercise. Further, Put D can be exercised only when it is profitable for us to exercise Put C. Notice that this principle holds for both American and European puts. Put C and Put D can be exercised either before expiration (for an American option) or at expiration only (for a European option). Figure 3.6 shows the profits for alternative stock prices. For any stock price of $100 or above, both puts expire worthless and we keep our initial $1 inflow. For a stock price between $95 and $100, we can exercise our option, but Put D cannot be exercised. For example, if the stock is at $97, we exercise and receive $100 for a $97 stock. This $3 exercise profit gives us a total profit of $4. If the stock price is below $95, both puts will be exercised. For example, with the

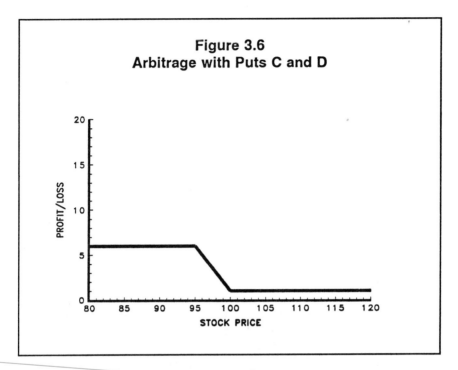

Figure 3.6
Arbitrage with Puts C and D

stock price at $90, the exercise profit on Put D is $5, as we have seen. However, our exercise profit on Put C is $10. Thus, we lose $5 on the exercise of Put D against us, but we make $10 by exercising Put C, and we still have our $1 initial inflow, for a net arbitrage profit of $6.

For Two American Puts, the Price Difference Cannot Exceed the Difference in Exercise Prices—The prices of two American puts cannot differ by more than the difference in exercise prices, assuming other features are the same. If prices violate this condition, there will be an arbitrage opportunity. To illustrate this arbitrage opportunity, consider the following puts on the same underlying stock:

	Exercise Price	Put Price
Put E	$100	$4
Put F	$105	$10

These prices violate our condition, because the price difference is $6, while the difference in exercise prices is only $5. To exploit this mispricing, we transact as follows:

Transaction		Cash Flow
Sell Put F		+$10
Buy Put E		−$4
	Net Cash Flow	+$6

With this initial cash inflow of $6, we have enough to pay any loss we might sustain when the holder of Put F exercises against us. For example, assume the stock trades at $95 and the holder of Put F exercises:

The exercise of Put F against us:		
Receive stock worth $95		+$95
Pay exercise price		−$105
Our exercise of Put E:		
Receive exercise price		+$100
Deliver stock worth $95		−$95
	Net Cash Flow	−$5

On the exercise, we lose $5. However, we already received $6 with the initial transactions. This leaves an arbitrage profit of at least $1. As Figure 3.7 shows, we could have larger profits, depending on the stock price. If the stock price exceeds $105, no exercise is possible and we keep the entire $6 of our initial transaction. For stock prices between $100 and $105, the holder of Put F can exercise against us, but we cannot exercise. For example, if the stock price is $103, we must pay $105 and receive a stock worth only $103, for a $2 exercise loss. However, with our initial cash inflow of $6, we still have a net profit of $4. For stock prices below $100, we can both exercise, as in the transactions we showed for a stock price of $95. In this case, we lose $5 on the exercise, but we still make a net profit of $1.

For Two European Puts, the Price Difference Cannot Exceed the Difference in the Present Value of the Exercise Prices—A similar principle holds for European puts, except the difference in put prices cannot exceed the difference in the present values of the exercise prices. If Puts E and F are European puts, the interest rate is 10 percent, and the options expire in six months, then the present values of the exercise prices are:

	Exercise Price	Present Value of Exercise Price
Put E	$100	$95.12
Put F	$105	$99.88

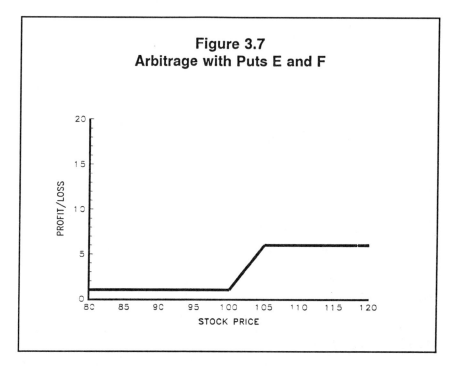

Figure 3.7
Arbitrage with Puts E and F

According to this principle, the price of Put F cannot exceed the price of Put E by more than $4.76 ($99.88-$95.12). With prices of $4 and $10 for Puts E and F, there should be an arbitrage profit.

To capture the profit, we sell Put F and buy Put E, as we did with the American puts. This gives a cash inflow of $6, which we invest for six months at 10 percent. The European puts cannot be exercised until expiration, at which time our investment is worth ($6e^{(.1)(.5)}) = $6.31. The most we can lose on the exercise is $5, the difference in the exercise prices. As we saw for the American puts, this happens when the stock price is $100 or less. However, we have $6.31 at expiration, so we can easily sustain this loss. If the stock price exceeds $105, neither option can be exercised, and we keep our entire $6.31. For the European puts, the graph of the arbitrage profit is exactly like Figure 3.7, except we add $.31 to every point. If the options had been priced $4.76 apart, our investment would have yielded $5 at expiration ($4.76e^{(.1)(.5)}). This $5 would protect us against any loss at expiration, but it would guarantee no arbitrage profit.

Summary

To this point, we have considered how call and put prices respond to stock and exercise prices and the time remaining until expiration. We have expressed all of these relationships as an outgrowth of our basic no-arbitrage condition: Prevailing option prices must exclude arbitrage profits. For call options, the story is very clear. The higher the stock price, the higher the call price. The higher the exercise price, the lower the call price. The longer the time until expiration, the higher the call price. For put options, the higher the stock price, the lower the put price. The higher the exercise price, the higher the put price. For time until expiration, the effects are slightly more complicated. For an American put, the longer the time until expiration, the more valuable the put. For a European put, a longer time until expiration can give rise to either a lower or higher put price.

We have also seen that no-arbitrage conditions restrict how call and put prices for different exercise prices can vary. For two call options or two American put options that are alike except for their exercise prices, the two option prices cannot differ by more than the difference in the exercise prices. For two European put options with different exercise prices, the option prices cannot differ by more than the present value of the difference in the exercise prices.

Throughout this discussion, we have been trying to tighten the bounds we can place on option prices. For example, Figure 3.1 gave the most generous bounds for call options. There we noted that the call price could never exceed the stock price as an upper bound. As a lower bound, the call price must always be at least zero or the stock price minus the exercise price, whichever is higher. The price relationships we considered in this section tighten these bounds by placing further restrictions on put and call prices. Figure 3.8 illustrates how we have tightened these bounds for call options. First, we showed that the call price must be at least zero or the stock price minus the present value of the exercise price. Figure 3.8 reflects this restriction by pulling in the right boundary. Now we know that the call price must lie in this slightly smaller area. Also, if we consider a call with a lower exercise price, we know that the call price must be at least as high for the call with the lower exercise price.

Further, we have considered price relationships between pairs of options that differ in some respects. For example, assume that option X in Figure 3.8 is priced correctly. We want to consider option Y, which is another call like X, except it has a longer time until expiration. With its longer time until expiration, the price of Y must equal or exceed the price of X. For example, Y in Figure 3.8 would have to lie on or above the dotted horizontal line abc that runs through X. Based on our information, Y in Figure 3.8 has a permissible location.

Consider another option, Z, which is just like X except Z has an exercise price that is $5 higher than X's. The price of Z can never fall below the stock price minus the present value of Z's exercise price. Therefore, the right boundary for the stock price minus the present value of Z's exercise price gives a floor for the price of Z. The price of Z must lie above the line eb. With a higher exercise price, the price of option Z cannot exceed the price of X. Therefore, the price of Z must lie on or below the line abc. Combining these two restrictions, we know that the price of Z must lie in the area given by abed.

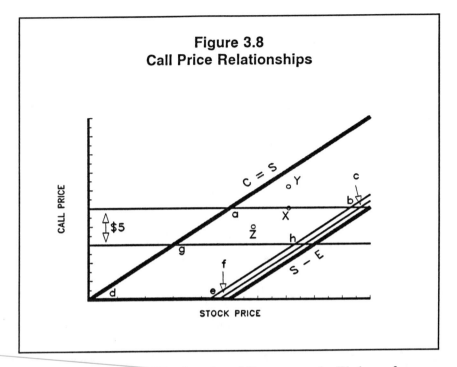

Figure 3.8
Call Price Relationships

However, we can locate the price of Z more exactly. We know from our discussion that two calls that differ only in their exercise prices must have prices that differ no more than their exercise prices. In our example, the exercise price of Z is $5 more than the exercise price of X. In Figure 3.8, line gh is $5 below line abc. Therefore, continuing to assume that the price of X is correct, Z must have a price that lies on or above gh. If it did not, the price of Z would be too low relative to X. Putting these principles together, we know that the price of Z must lie within the area defined by abhg. Z in Figure 3.8 conforms to these rules.

We cannot specify exactly where Z must lie within area abhg. Option prices also depend on two additional factors that we must now consider: interest rates and the way in which the stock price moves. After considering these additional factors in this chapter and in Chapter 4, we will be able to pinpoint the price that an option must have.

Option Prices and the Interest Rate

We now apply our no-arbitrage approach to examine the effect of interest rates on option prices. For a call option, the exercise price represents a potential liability the owner of a call option faces at expiration. Before expiration, the lower the present value of the liability associated with owning a call, the better for the call owner. Therefore, as we show below, call option prices increase with higher interest rates. The result may seem counter-intuitive because we generally associate higher asset prices with lower interest rates. This is not so for call options, as our no-arbitrage argument shows below. The owner of a put option may exercise and receive the exercise price in exchange for surrendering the stock, so the exercise price represents a potential asset for a put owner. The lower the interest rate, the higher the present value of that potential asset. Therefore, the lower the interest rate, the higher the price of a put. This section presents a no-arbitrage argument to show why the price of a put must fall as interest rates rise.

Call Prices and Interest Rates

We have already observed that the call price must equal or exceed the larger of zero or the stock price minus the present value of the exercise price:

$$C \geq MAX\{0, S - Ee^{-rt}\} \qquad\qquad 3.3$$

In equation 3.3, Ee^{-rt} is the present value of the exercise price. The larger the interest rate, r, the smaller that present value. A higher interest rate gives a larger value for $S - Ee^{-rt}$. This makes sense because the exercise price is a liability the call owner incurs if he exercises.

We can also show that the call price must rise if interest rates rise by the following no-arbitrage example. Consider a call option on a stock trading at $100. The exercise price of the call is $100. The option expires in six months and the current interest rate is 10 percent. From 3.3 the price of this call must equal or exceed $4.88:

$$C \geq MAX\{0, \$100 - \$100e^{-(.1)(.5)}\} \geq \$4.88$$

For convenience, we assume that the option is correctly priced at $4.88.[5]

Suddenly, interest rates jump from 10 to 12 percent, but the option price remains at $4.88. Now the option price does not meet the condition in 3.3. The option price is too low, so we want to transact to guarantee an arbitrage profit. Accordingly, we trade as follows:

Transaction	Cash Flow
Sell stock	+$100.00
Buy call	-4.88
Buy bond maturing in 6 months and yielding 12 percent	-95.12
Net Cash Flow	0

In six months, the option is at expiration and our bond matures. The bond will pay $101.

How we deal with the call and stock depends on the stock price relative to the option price. If the stock trades for $100, the call option is worthless. In this case, we buy the stock for $100 and return it, leaving a profit of $1. If the stock price is less than $100, our profit increases. For example, with a $95 stock price, the option is worthless and we buy the stock for $95. These transactions leave a total profit of $6. If the stock price exceeds $100, we exercise our call and pay the exercise price of $100. After exercising and returning the stock, we still have $1. Therefore, we have a profit at expiration with no investment. This arbitrage opportunity arose because the option price did not increase as the interest rate rose. With our example, the price of the call should have risen to at least $5.82 to exclude arbitrage:

$$C \geq MAX\{0, S - Ee^{-rt}\} \geq MAX\{0, \$100 - \$100e^{-(.12)(.5)}\} \geq \$5.82$$

Because the price did not respond, we were able to reap an arbitrage profit. To exclude arbitrage, the price of a call must be higher the higher the interest rate. Otherwise, a riskless profit without investment will be possible.

Put Prices and Interest Rates

Interest rates also affect put prices. When exercising, the holder of a put receives the exercise price. Therefore, for a put owner, the exercise price is a potential cash inflow. The greater the present value of that potential inflow, the higher will be the value of the put. As a consequence, the put price should be higher the lower the interest rate. If a put price fails to adjust to changing interest rates, there will be an arbitrage opportunity. This rule holds for both American and European puts.

To show how put prices depend on interest rates, consider a stock trading at $90. A European put option on this stock expires in six months and has an exercise price of $100. Interest rates are at 10 percent. We know that the European put price must meet the following condition:

$$P_e \geq MAX\{0, Ee^{-rt} - S\} \geq MAX\{0, \$100e^{-(.1)(.5)} - \$90\} \geq \$5.12$$

For convenience, we assume that the put is priced at $5.12.

Let us now assume that interest rates suddenly fall to 8 percent, but that the put price does not change. Our principle asserts that the put should be worth at least $6.08 now. With the put price staying at $5.12, when it should be $6.08, we trade as follows:

Transaction	Cash Flow
Borrow $95.12 at 8 percent	+$95.12
Buy stock	–90.00
Buy put	–5.12
Net Cash Flow	0

With these transactions in place, we wait until expiration in six months to reap our arbitrage profit. At expiration, we owe $99.00 on our borrowings. From the stock and the put, we must realize enough to cover that payment. Any remaining money will be profit. If the stock price at expiration is $100, we allow our put to expire and we sell the stock. We receive $100, from which we pay $99.00. This leaves a $1 profit. If the stock price at expiration is below $100, we exercise our put. For example, with a stock price of $95, we exercise our put, deliver the stock, and collect $100. This gives a $1 profit. We make exactly $1 at expiration for any stock price of $100 or less. For any stock price above $100, our put is worthless and our profit equals the difference between the stock price and our $99 debt. From these transactions, we see that we will make at least $1 at expiration. This we achieve with zero investment. Therefore, the failure of the put option price to adjust to changing interest rates generates an arbitrage opportunity. The put price must rise as interest rates fall.

Option Prices and Stock Price Movements

Up to this point, we have studied the way in which four factors constrain call and put prices. These factors are the stock price, the exercise price, the time remaining until expiration, and the interest rate. Even with these four factors, we cannot say exactly what the option price must be before expiration. There is a fifth factor to consider—stock price movements before expiration. If we consider a stock with options on it that expire in six months, we know that the stock price can change thousands of times before the option expires. Further, for two stocks, the pattern of changes and the volatility of the stock price changes can differ dramatically. However, if we can develop a model for understanding stock price movements, we can use that model to specify what the price of an option must be.

We now make a drastic simplifying assumption. Between the current moment and the expiration of an option, we assume that the stock price will rise by 10 percent or fall by 10 percent. With this assumption about the stock's price movement, we can use our no–arbitrage approach to determine the exact value of a European call or put. Therefore, knowing the potential pattern of stock price movements gives us the final key to understanding option prices. This chapter illustrates how to determine option prices based on this simplifying model of stock price movements. The next chapter shows how to apply more realistic models of stock price movements to compute accurate option prices.

Let us assume that a stock trades for $100. In the next year, the price can rise or fall exactly 10 percent. Therefore, the stock price next year will be either $90 or $110. Both a put and a call option have exercise prices of $100 and expire in one year. The current interest rate is 6 percent. We want to know how much the put and call will be worth. With these data, the call price is $7.55, and the put is worth $1.89. Other prices create arbitrage opportunities. This section shows that the options must have these prices. Chapter 4 explains why these no-arbitrage relationships must hold.

The Call Price

We have asserted that the call price must be $7.55 given our other data, if the call price is to exclude an arbitrage opportunity. If the option price is lower, we will enter arbitrage transactions that include buying the option. Similarly, if the option price is higher, our arbitrage transactions will include selling the call. We illustrate each case in turn. Let us begin by assuming that the call price is $7.00, which is below our no-arbitrage price of $7.55. If the call price is too low, we transact as follows:

Transaction	Cash Flow
Sell 1 share of stock	+$100.00
Buy 2 calls	-14.00
Buy bond	-86.00
Net Cash Flow	0

At expiration, the stock price will be either $110 or $90. If the stock price is $110, the calls will be worth $10 each—the stock price minus the exercise price. If the stock price is $90, the calls are worthless. In either case, the bond will pay $91.16. If the stock price is $90, we repurchase a share with our bond proceeds for $90. This leaves a profit of $1.16. If the stock price is $110, we sell our two options for $20. Adding this $20 to our bond proceeds, we have $111.16. From this amount, we buy a share for $110 to repay the borrowing of a share. This leaves a profit of $1.16. Therefore, we make $1.16 whether the stock price rises or falls. We made this certain profit with zero investment, so we have an arbitrage profit.

Now assume the call price is $8.00, exceeding $7.55. In this case, the call price is too high, so we sell the call as part of the following transactions.

Transaction	Cash Flow
Buy 1 share of stock	-$100.00
Sell 2 calls	+16.00
Sell a bond (borrow funds)	+84.00
Net Cash Flow	0

At expiration, we know we must repay $89.04. If the stock price at expiration is $90, the calls cannot be exercised against us. So we sell our stock for $90 and repay our debt of $89.04. This leaves a profit of $.96.

If the stock price goes to $110, the calls we sold will be exercised against us. To fulfill one obligation, we deliver our share of stock and receive the exercise price of $100. We then buy back the other call that is still outstanding. It costs $10, the difference between the stock price and the exercise price. This leaves $90, from which we repay our debt of $89.04. Now we have completed all of our obligations and we still have $.96. Therefore, with a call priced at $8.00, we will have a profit of $.96 from these transactions no matter whether the stock price goes up or down. We captured this sure profit with zero investment, so we have an arbitrage profit.

To eliminate arbitrage, the call must trade for $7.55. If that call price prevails, both transaction strategies fail. For example, we might try to transact as follows if the call price is $7.55.

Transaction	Cash Flow
Buy 1 share of stock	-$100.00
Sell 2 calls	+15.10
Sell a bond (borrow funds)	+84.90
Net Cash Flow	0

At expiration, we owe $90.00. If the stock price is $90, our calls are worthless. However, we can sell our share for $90 and repay our debt. Our net cash flow at expiration is zero. If the stock price is $110, the calls will be exercised against us. We deliver our one share and receive $100. From this $100 we repay our debt of $90. This leaves $10, the exact difference between the stock and exercise price. Therefore, we can use our last $10 to close our option position. Our net cash flow is zero. With a call price of $7.55, our transactions cost us zero and they yield zero. This is exactly the result we expect in a market that is free from arbitrage opportunities.[6]

The Put Price

Based on the same data, the put price must be $1.89 to avoid arbitrage. We can see that this must be the case in two ways. First, we show that put-call parity requires a price of $1.89. Second, we show how any other price leads to arbitrage opportunities similar to those that occurred when the call was priced incorrectly.

From Chapter 2 we know that put-call parity expresses the value of a put as a function of a similar call, the stock, and investment in the risk-free bond.

$$P = C - S + Ee^{-rt}$$

where Ee^{-rt} is the present value of the exercise price. For our example, we know that the correct call price is $7.55 and that the stock trades for $100. With one year remaining until expiration, the present value of the exercise price is $94.34. According to put-call parity for our example:

$$P = \$7.55 - \$100.00 + \$94.34 = \$1.89$$

If the put is not worth $1.89, arbitrage opportunities arise. This makes sense because the put-call parity relationship is itself a no-arbitrage condition.[7]

We now show how to reap arbitrage profits if the put does not trade for $1.89. We consider the transactions if the put price is above or below its correct price of $1.89. First, let us assume that the put price is $1.50. In this case, the put is too cheap relative to other assets. The other assets that replicate the put are too expensive, taken together. These are the call, stock, bond combination on the right-hand side of the put-call parity formula. The put-call parity relationship suggests that we should sell the relatively over-priced put and buy the relatively under-priced portfolio that replicates the put. To initiate this strategy we transact as follows:

Transaction	Cash Flow
Buy put	-$1.50
Sell call	+7.55
Buy stock	-100.00
Borrow $93.95 and invest at 6 percent for one year	+94.34
Net Cash Flow	0

In one year, our debt is $99.59 and the put and call are at expiration. The stock price will be either $90 or $110. We consider the value of our position for both possible stock prices. If the stock price is $90, we exercise our put and deliver our share of stock. This gives a cash flow of $100, from which we repay our debt of $99.59. We have no further obligations, yet $.41 remains. Thus, we make a profit with no initial investment.

If the stock price is $110, our put is worthless and the stock will be called away from us. When the call is exercised against us, we receive $100. From this $100, we repay our debt of $99.59. Again, this leaves us with $.41. No matter whether the stock goes to $90 or to $110, we make $.41. We achieved this profit with no initial investment. Consequently, we have a certain profit with zero investment, a sure sign of an arbitrage profit.

We now consider how to transact if the put price is higher than $1.89. Let us assume that the put trades for $2.00. With the put being too expensive, we sell the relatively over-priced put and purchase the relatively under-priced portfolio that replicates the put. In this case, our transactions are just the reverse of those we made when the put price was too low. We transact as follows:

Transaction	Cash Flow
Sell put	+$2.00
Buy call	-7.55
Sell stock	+100.00
Lend $94.45 at 6 percent for one year	-94.45
Net Cash Flow	0

In one year, our loan matures, so we collect $100.12. If the stock price is $90, our call is worthless and the put will be exercised against us. We must accept the $90 stock and pay the $100 exercise price. This leaves one share of stock and $.12. We use the share to cover our original sale of stock, and we have $.12 after meeting all obligations.

If the stock price goes to $110.00, the put we sold will expire worthless. We exercise our call, paying the $100 exercise price to acquire the stock. We now have $.12 and one share, so we cover our original share sale by returning the stock. Again, we have completed all transactions and $.12 remains. Therefore, no matter whether the stock goes to $90 or $110 over the one year investment horizon, we make $.12. We did this with zero investment, so we have an arbitrage profit.

These transactions illustrate why the put must trade for $1.89 in our example. Any other price allows arbitrage. If the put price is $1.89, both of the transactions we have just considered will cost zero to execute, but they will be sure to return zero when the options expire. In a market free of arbitrage opportunities, this is just what we expect.

Option Prices and the Riskiness of Stocks

As we have seen, option prices depend on several factors, including stock prices. In this section, we explore how stock price changes affect option prices. Specifically, we consider how the riskiness of the stock affects the price of the put or call. We use a simple model of the way a stock price changes to illustrate a very important result: The riskier the underlying stock, the greater the value of an option. This principle holds for both put and call options. While it may seem odd for an option price to be higher if the underlying good is riskier, we can use no-arbitrage arguments to show why this must be true.

Essentially, a call option gives its owner most of the benefits of rising stock prices and protects the owner from suffering the full cost of a drop in stock prices. Thus, a call option offers insurance against falling stock prices and holds out the promise of high profits from surging stock prices. The riskier the underlying stock, the greater the chance of an extreme stock price movement. If the stock price falls dramatically, the insurance feature of the call option comes into play. This limits the call holder's loss. However, if the stock price increases dramatically, the call owner participates fully in the price increase. The protection against large losses, coupled with participation in large gains, makes call options more valuable when the underlying stock is risky.

For put options, risk has a parallel effect. Put owners benefit from large stock price drops and suffer from price increases. However, a put protects the owner from the full force of a stock price rise. In effect, a put embodies insurance against large price rises. At the same time, the put allows its owner to benefit fully from a stock price drop. Because the put incorporates protection against rising prices and allows its owner to capture virtually all profits from falling prices, a put is more valuable the riskier the underlying stock.

In the preceding section, we used a very simple model of stock price movement to show how to price put and call options. In this section, we extend the same model and example to evaluate the effect of riskiness on stock prices. Earlier, we assumed a stock traded for $100 and that its price would go to either $90 or $110 in one year. We assumed that the risk-free rate of interest was 6 percent and that a call and put option both had exercise prices of $100 and expired in one year. Under these circumstances, the call was worth $7.55 and the put was worth $1.89. Any other price for the put or call led to arbitrage opportunities. To explore the effect of risk, we consider two other possible outcomes for the stock price. First, we assume that the stock is not risky. In this case, the stock price increases by the risk-free rate of 6 percent with certainty Second, we consider stock price movements in which the stock price goes to either $80 or $120.

Option Prices for Riskless Stock

If the stock is risk-free, its value grows at the risk-free rate. Otherwise, there would be an arbitrage opportunity between the stock and the risk-free bond.[8] Consequently, we consider prices of our example options assuming that the stock price in one year will be $106 with certainty. Under these circumstances, the call option will be worth $5.66 and the put will be worth zero.

The put will be worth zero one year before expiration because it is sure to be worth zero at expiration. If the stock price is sure to be $106 at expiration, the put only gives the right to force someone to accept a stock worth $106 for $100. Thus, the put is worthless, because there is no chance the stock price will be below the exercise price of the put.

The call has a certain payoff at expiration, because the stock price is certain. At expiration, the call is worth MAX{0,S - E} = $6. With a riskless stock, the call is also riskless. Investment in the call pays a certain return of $6 in one year, so the call must be worth the present value of $6, or $5.66. Any other price for the call creates an arbitrage opportunity. For example, if the option trades at $5.80, we sell the call and invest the $5.80 at 6 percent. In one year, our investment is worth $6.15 and the exercise of the call against us costs us $6. This yields a $.15 arbitrage profit. For any other price of either the put or the call, our familiar transactions guarantee an arbitrage profit.

Earlier, we placed the following bound on the call price before expiration:

$$C \geq MAX\{0, S - Ee^{-rt}\}$$

For a call option on a risk–free stock:

$$C = MAX\{0, S - Ee^{-rt}\}$$

Now we see that this relationship holds exactly if the stock is risk-free. In other words, the call price is on the lower boundary if the stock has no risk. Therefore, holding the other factors constant, any excess value of the call above the boundary is due solely to the riskiness of the stock.

Comparing our two examples of stock price movements, we saw that the risk-free stock implied a call price of $5.66. If the stock price was risky, moving up or down 10 percent in the next year, the call price was $7.55. This call price difference is due to the difference in the riskiness of the stock. As we now show, higher risk implies higher option prices.

Riskier Stocks Result in Higher Option Prices

In our model of stock price movements, we assumed that stock prices change over a year in a very specific way. When we assumed that stock prices could increase or decrease 10 percent, we found certain option prices. We now consider the same circumstances but allow for more radical stock price movements of 20 percent up or down. All other factors remain the same. In summary, a stock trades today at $100. In one year, its price will be either $80 or $120. The risk-free interest rate is 6 percent. A call and put each have an exercise price of $100 and expire in one year. Under these circumstances, the call price must be $12.26, and the put price must be $6.60. Any other prices create arbitrage opportunities. Therefore, we have observed the price effects of the following three stock price movements on option prices.

Stock Price Movement	Call Price	Put Price
Stock price increases by a certain 6 percent	$5.66	$0
Stock price rises or falls by 10 percent	7.55	1.89
Stock price rises or falls by 20 percent	12.26	6.60

In these examples, we held other factors constant. Each example used options with the same exercise price and time to expiration. Also, each example employed the same risk-free rate. As these examples illustrate, greater risk in the stock increases both put and call prices.

Summary

In this chapter we discussed the relationships that govern option prices. We began by considering general boundary spaces for calls and puts. By linking relationships between option features, such as time to expiration and exercise prices, we specified price relationships between options. For example, we saw that the price of a call with a lower exercise price must equal or exceed the price of a similar call with a higher exercise price. We discussed the five factors on which option prices depend: the exercise price, the stock price, the risk-free interest rate, the time to expiration, and the riskiness of the stock. We found that option prices have a definitive relationship to these factors, as Table 3.1 summarizes.

Understanding these factors helps us place bounds on call and put prices. However, to determine an exact price, we must specify how the stock price can move. To illustrate the important influence of stock price movements on option prices, we considered a very simple model of stock price movements. For example, we assumed that the stock prices can change 10 percent in the next year. With this assumption, we were able to find exact option prices. However, this assumption about the movement of stock prices is very unrealistic. A year from now, a stock may have a virtually infinite number of prices, not just two. With unrealistic assumptions about stock price movements, the option prices we compute are likely to be unrealistic as well. In the next chapter, we work toward more realistic assumptions about stock price movements and we develop a more exact option pricing model.

Table 3.1
The Response of Option Prices to the Underlying Variables

For an Increase in the:	The Call Price:	The Put Price:
Stock Price	Rises	Falls
Exercise Price	Falls	Rises
Time Until Expiration	Rises	May Rise or Fall[9]
Interest Rate	Rises	Falls
Stock Risk	Rises	Rises

Questions and Problems

1. What is the maximum theoretical value for a call? Under what conditions does a call reach this maximum value? Explain.

2. What is the maximum theoretical value for an American put? When does it reach this maximum? Explain.

3. Answer question 2 for a European put.

4. Explain the difference in the theoretical maximum values for an American and a European put.

5. How does the exercise price affect the price of a call? Explain.

6. Consider two calls with the same time to expiration that are written on the same underlying stock. Call 1 trades for $7 and has an exercise price of $100. Call 2 has an exercise price of $95. What is the maximum price that Call 2 can have? Explain.

7. Six months remain until a call option expires. The stock price is $70 and the exercise price is $65. The option price is $5. What does this imply about the interest rate?

8. Assume the interest rate is 12 percent and four months remain until an option expires. The exercise price of the option is $70 and the stock that underlies the option is worth $80. What is the minimum value the option can have based on the no-arbitrage conditions studied in Chapter 3? Explain.

9. Two call options are written on the same stock that trades for $70 and both calls have an exercise price of $85. Call 1 expires in six months and Call 2 expires in three months. Assume that Call 1 trades for $6 and that Call 2 trades for $7. Do these prices allow arbitrage? Explain. If they do permit arbitrage, explain the arbitrage transactions.

10. Explain the circumstances that make early exercise of a call rational. Under what circumstances is early exercise of a call irrational?

11. Consider a European and an American call with the same expiration and the same exercise price that are written on the same stock. What relationship must hold between their prices? Explain.

12. Before exercise, what is the minimum value of an American put?

13. Before exercise, what is the minimum value of a European put?

14. Explain the differences in the minimum values of American and European puts before expiration.

15. How does the price of an American put vary with time until expiration? Explain.

16. What relationship holds between time until expiration and the price of a European put?

17. Consider two puts with the same term to expiration (six months). One put has a exercise price of $110, the other has an exercise price of $100. Assume the interest rate is 12 percent. What is the maximum price difference between the two puts if they are European? If they are American? Explain the difference, if any.

18. How does the price of a call vary with interest rates? Explain.

19. Explain how a put price varies with interest rates. Does the relationship vary for European and American puts? Explain.

20. What is the relationship between the risk of the underlying stock and the call price? Explain in intuitive terms.

Notes

1. The price of an option depends on these five factors when the underlying stock pays no dividends. As we will discuss in Chapter 5, if the underlying stock pays a dividend, the dividend is a sixth factor that we must consider.

2. Like Chapter 2, the discussion of these rational bounds for option prices relies on a paper by Robert C. Merton, "Theory of Rational Option Pricing," *Bell Journal of Economics and Management Science*, 4, 1973, 141-183.

3. Scholars have tested market data to determine how well puts and calls meet these boundary conditions. Dan Galai was the first to test these relationships in his paper, "Empirical Tests of Boundary Conditions for CBOE Options," *Journal of Financial Economics*, 6 June/September 1978, 182-211. Galai found some violations of the no-arbitrage conditions in the reported prices. However, these apparent arbitrage opportunities disappeared if a trader faced a 1 percent transaction cost. Mihir Bhattacharya conducted similar, but more extensive, tests in his paper, "Transaction Data Tests on the Efficiency of the Chicago Board Options Exchange," *Journal of Financial Economics*, 1983, 161-185. Like Galai, Bhattacharya found that a trader facing transaction costs could not exploit apparent arbitrage opportunities. However, both studies found that a very low cost trader, such as a market maker, could have a chance for some arbitrage returns.

4. As we discuss in Chapter 5, differences between European and American call options require some slight revisions of these rules. In this section, we have said that the difference in the price of two calls cannot exceed the difference in exercise prices. Our arbitrage arguments for this principle assumed immediate exercise before expiration, thus implicitly assuming that the option is American. For a similar pair of European options, the price differential cannot exceed the present value of the difference between the two exercise prices. The arbitrage profit equals the excess difference

between the exercise prices. With European options, this excess differential is not available until expiration, when traders can exercise. Therefore, for European options, the arbitrage profit will be the excess difference in the exercise prices discounted to the present.

5. Assuming that the option is correctly priced at the lower bound implicitly assumes that the stock price has no risk. In other words, we implicitly assume that the stock price will not change before expiration. Making this assumption does not affect the validity of our example, because we are focusing on the single effect of a change in interest rates.

6. The next chapter explains why we need to buy one share of stock and sell 2 calls in this example. In brief, by combining a bond, a stock, and the right number of calls, we can form a riskless portfolio.

7. The put-call parity relationship was first addressed by Hans Stoll, "The Relationship Between Put and Call Option Prices," *Journal of Finance*, 24, May 1969, 801–824. Robert C. Merton extended the concept in his paper, "The Relationship Between Put and Call Option Prices: Comment," *Journal of Finance*, 28, 183–184. Robert C. Klemkosky and Bruce G. Resnick tested the put-call parity relationship empirically with market data. Their two papers are: "An Ex-Ante Analysis of Put-Call Parity," *Journal of Financial Economics*, 8, 1980, 363–372 and "Put-Call Parity and Market Efficiency," *Journal of Finance*, 34, 1979, 1141–1155. While they find that market prices do not agree perfectly with the put-call parity relationship, the differences are not sufficiently large to generate trading profits after considering all transaction costs.

8. If the stock earned a riskless rate above the risk-free rate, we would borrow at the risk-free rate and invest in the stock. Later, we could sell the stock, repay our debt, and have a certain return from the difference in the two riskless rates. If the stock earned a riskless rate below the risk-free rate, we would sell the stock and invest the proceeds in the higher rate of the risk-free bond. Therefore, for a given horizon, there is only one risk-free rate.

9. In Chapter 5 we explain this peculiar result more fully. In brief, it can sometimes be advantageous to exercise a put before expiration. Upon exercise, the owner receives a cash inflow. This cash inflow can earn interest between the time of exercise and the expiration date of the option. However, exercising early means that the owner receives only the intrinsic value of the option. Thus, early exercise of a put is wise when the value of the interest that can be earned outweighs the benefit of waiting to exercise.

Generally, this can happen only when the put is well in-the-money. With a European put, however, the owner cannot exercise until expiration. The longer the time until expiration, the longer the European put owner must wait to capture the intrinsic value of the option. Thus, the European put price can be lower with a longer time until expiration.

4

Option Pricing Models

Introduction

In Chapter 3 we showed how to compute call and put prices assuming that stock prices behave in a highly simplified manner. Specifically, we assumed that stock prices could rise by a certain percentage or fall by a certain percentage for a single period. After that single period, we assumed that the option expired. Under these unrealistic and highly restrictive assumptions, we found that calls and puts must each have a unique price; any other price leads to arbitrage. In this chapter, we develop similar option pricing models, but we use more realistic models of stock price movement.

To develop a more realistic option pricing model, this chapter first analyzes option pricing under the simple percentage change model of stock price movements. Now, however, we show how to find the unique prices that the no-arbitrage conditions imply. This framework is the **Single–Period Binomial Model**. Analyzing the single-period model leads to more realistic models of stock price movements. One of these more realistic models is the **Multi–Period Binomial Model**. By considering several successive models of stock price changes, we eventually come to one of the most elegant models in all of finance—the **Black-Scholes Option Pricing Model**.

OPTION! provides support for the diverse models that we study in this chapter. With **OPTION!**, we can compute the one-period and multi-period Binomial Model call and put values. In addition, with **OPTION!** we can compute the Black-Scholes Model prices. In each case, using the software can save considerable computational labor.

The Single–Period Binomial Model

In Chapter 3, we considered a stock priced at $100 and assumed that its price would be $90 or $110 in one year. In this example, the risk-free interest rate was 6 percent. We then considered a call and put on this stock, with both options having an exercise price of $100 and expiring in one year. The call was worth $7.55, and the put was worth $1.89. As we showed in Chapter 3, any other option price creates arbitrage opportunities.

Now we want to create a portfolio that exactly mimics the payoffs of the call option. The value of such a mimicking portfolio must equal the value of the call. Consider a portfolio comprised of one–half share of stock plus a short position in a risk–free bond that matures in one year and has an initial purchase price of $42.45. In one year, the portfolio's value depends on whether the stock price is $110 or $90. Depending on the stock price, the half–share will be worth $55 or $45. In either event, we will owe $45.00 to repay our bond. If the stock price rises, the portfolio will be worth $10. If the stock price falls, the portfolio will be worth zero. These are exactly the payoffs for the call option. Therefore, the value of the portfolio must be the same as the value of the call option. Figure 4.1 shows values for the stock, the call, the risk–free bond, and the portfolio value at the outset and one year later. The stock price moves to $110 or $90, and the call moves accordingly to $10 or zero. The risk–free bond increases at a 6 percent rate no matter what the stock does, so borrowing $42.45 generates a debt of $45 due in one year. Likewise, our portfolio of one–half share and a $42.45 borrowing will be worth $10 or zero in one year, depending on the stock price.

Because our portfolio and the call option have exactly the same payoffs in all circumstances, they must have the same initial value. Otherwise, there would be an arbitrage opportunity. This means that an investment of one–half share of stock, S, and a bond, B, of $42.45 must equal the value of the call.

$$C = .5S - \$42.45 = \$50 - 42.45 = \$7.55$$

Therefore, the call must be worth $7.55. This is the same conclusion we reached in Chapter 3. This result shows that a combined position in the stock and the risk–free bond can replicate a call option for a one–period horizon.

We now show how to find the replicating portfolio made of the stock and the risk–free investment. At the outset, time=0, the value of the portfolio, PORT, depends on the stock price, the number of shares, N, and the bond.

$$PORT = NS - B$$

At the end of the horizon, time=1, the debt equals the amount borrowed plus interest. The portfolio's value also depends on the stock price. If the stock price rises, the value of the portfolio will be:

$$PORT_u = NUS - RB$$

where:

$PORT_u$ = *value of the replicating portfolio if the stock price goes up*
$U = 1 +$ *percentage of stock price increase*
$R = 1 + r$

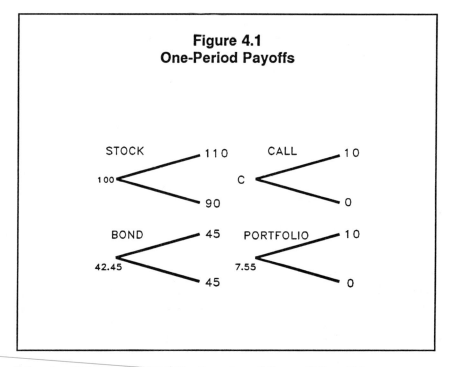

Figure 4.1
One-Period Payoffs

Likewise, if the stock price falls, the value of the portfolio will be:

$$PORT_d = NDS - RB$$

where:

    $PORT_d$ = value of the replicating portfolio if the stock price goes down
    D = 1 – percentage of stock price decrease

At the horizon, the value of the call also depends on whether the stock price rises or falls. For each circumstance, we represent the call's price as C_u and C_d.

    As our example showed, we can choose the number of shares to trade, N, and the amount of funds to borrow, B, to replicate the call. Replicating the call means that the portfolio will have the same payoff. Therefore, if the stock price rises:

$$PORT_u = NUS - RB = C_u$$

If the stock price falls:

$$PORT_d = NDS - RB = C_d$$

After these algebraic manipulations, we have two equations with two unknowns, N and B. Solving for the values of the unknowns that satisfy the equations, N* and B*, we find:

$$N^* = \frac{C_u - C_d}{(U - D)\ S}$$

$$B^* = \frac{C_u D - C_d U}{(U - D)\ R}$$

Therefore,

$$C = N^* S - B^* \qquad\qquad 4.1$$

This is the **Single-Period Binomial Call Pricing Model**. It holds for a call option expiring in one period when the stock price will rise by a known percentage or fall by a known percentage. The model shows that the value of a call option equals a long position in the stock, plus some borrowing at the risk-free rate. Applying our new notation to our example, we have:

$$C_u = \$10$$
$$C_d = \$0$$
$$US = \$110$$
$$DS = \$90$$
$$R = 1.06$$
$$B* = \frac{C_u D - C_d U}{(U - D)\ R}$$
$$= \frac{10\ (0.9) - 0\ (1.1)}{(1.1 - 0.9)\ (1.06)} = \$42.45$$
$$N* = \frac{C_u - C_d}{(U - D)\ S} = \frac{10 - 0}{(1.1 - 0.9)\ 100} = 0.5$$

The Role of Probabilities

In discussing the Single-Period Binomial Model, we have not used the concept of probability. For example, we have not considered the likelihood that the stock price will rise or fall. While we have not explicitly used probabilistic concepts, the array of prices does imply a certain probability that the stock price will rise,

---

Single–Period Binomial Call Pricing Model

The value of a call option equals the value of a portfolio of stock plus risk–free borrowing.

$$C = N^*S - B^*$$

where:
B^*	$= (C_u D - C_d U)/[U - D)R]$	
N^*	$= (C_u - C_d)/(U - D)S$	
C_u	= call price if stock price goes up	
C_d	= call price if stock price goes down	
U	= 1 + percentage increase if the stock price rises	
D	= 1 – percentage decrease if the stock price falls	
R	= 1 + risk–free rate of interest	

Restrictions: Call expires in one period.
The stock price can only increase or decrease by a known percentage.

---

if we are willing to assume that investors are risk-neutral.[1] We assume a risk-neutral economy in this section to show the role of probabilities. The option prices that we compute under the assumption of risk-neutrality are the same as those we found from strict no–arbitrage conditions without any reference to probabilities.

Assuming risk-neutrality and given the risk-free interest rate and the up and down percentage movements, we can compute the probability of a stock price increase. Using our definitions of N^* and B^*, we can express the value of the call as:

$$C = \left(\frac{C_u - C_d}{(U - D) S} \right) S - \frac{C_u D - C_d U}{(U - D) R}$$

Simplifying, we have:

$$C = \frac{C_u - C_d}{U - D} - \frac{C_u D - C_d U}{(U - D) R}$$

Isolating the C_u and C_d terms gives:

$$C = \frac{\left[\dfrac{R - D}{U - D}\right] C_u + \left[\dfrac{U - R}{U - D}\right] C_d}{R}$$

In this equation, the call value equals the present value of the future payoffs from owning the call. If the stock price goes up, the call pays C_u at expiration. If the stock goes down, the call pays C_d. The numerator of this equation gives the expected value of the call's payoffs at expiration. Therefore, the probability of a stock price increase is also the probability that the call is worth C_u. The probability of a stock price increase is (R-D)/(U-D), and the probability of a stock price decrease is (U-R)/(U-D).

For our continuing example, we have the following values: C_u = $10, C_d = $0, U = 1.1, D = 0.9, R = 1.06. Therefore, the probability of an increase in the stock price (π_u) is 0.8 and the probability of a decrease (π_d) is 0.2. The value of the call in our single period model is:

$$C_0 = \frac{\pi_u \times C_u + \pi_d \times C_d}{R}$$

$$= \frac{.8 \times 10 + .2 \times 0}{1.06}$$

$$= \$7.55$$

This result shows that the value of a call equals the expected payoff from the call at expiration, discounted to the present at the risk-free rate, assuming a risk-neutral economy.

> **For the Single–Period Binomial Call Pricing Model, the price of a call equals the expected value of the call at expiration discounted at the risk–free rate, assuming a risk–neutral economy.**

Summary

Our single-period model is a useful tool. We have seen how to replicate an option by combining a long position in stock with a short position in the risk-free asset. Also, we used the single-period model to show that the value of a call equals the present value of the call's expected payoffs at expiration. Nonetheless, our single-period model suffers from two defects. First, it holds only for a single period. We need to be able to value options that expire after many periods. Second, our assumption about stock price changes is still unrealistic. Obviously we do not really know how stock prices can change in one period. In fact, if we define one year as a period, we know that stock prices can take almost an infinite number of values by the end of the period. We now proceed to refine our model to consider these objections.

The Multi–Period Binomial Model

The principles that we developed for the single-period binomial model also apply to a multi-period framework.[2] Here we illustrate the underlying principles by considering a two-period horizon. Over two periods, the stock price must follow one of four patterns. For the two periods, the stock can go: up-up, up-down, down-up, or down-down. Assuming fixed down and up percentages, the up-down and down-up sequences result in the same terminal stock price. For each terminal stock price, a call option has a specific value. Figure 4.2 shows the possible outcomes for the stock and call. To clarify the notation, S_{uu} indicates the terminal stock price if the stock price goes up in both periods. C_{uu} is the resulting call price at expiration when the stock price rises in both periods. For the two period case, the notation π_{uu} indicates the probability of an up-up sequence of price movements, and π_{dd} indicates the probability of a down-down sequence of price movements. We define other patterns accordingly.

We can express the value of a call option two periods before expiration as:

$$C = \frac{\pi_{uu} C_{uu} + \pi_{ud} C_{ud} + \pi_{du} C_{du} + \pi_{dd} C_{dd}}{R^2}$$

In this equation, the call value equals the expected value of the payoffs at expiration discounted at the risk-free rate.

We continue to use our example of a $100 stock that can rise or fall by 10 percent. The probability that the stock price will increase is .8, so this gives a .2 probability of a price drop. Also, the probability of an increase in one period is independent from the probability of an increase in any other period. We now assume that the call is two periods from expiration and that the stock trades for

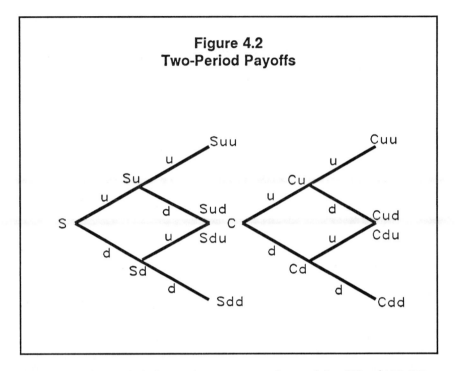

Figure 4.2
Two-Period Payoffs

$100. In the first period, the stock can go up or down, giving US = $110, DS = $90. After the second period, there are four possible patterns with three actually different stock prices: UUS = $121, DDS = $81, and UDS = DUS = $99. The probabilities of these different terminal stock prices are: π_{uu} = (.8)(.8) = .64, π_{ud} = (.8)(.2) = .16, π_{du} = (.2)(.8) = .16, and π_{dd} = (.2)(.2) = .04. The call price at expiration equals the terminal stock price minus the exercise price of $100, or zero, whichever is larger. Therefore, we have C_{uu} = $21, C_{dd} = 0, C_{du} = C_{ud} = 0.

To determine the call price two periods before expiration, we apply our formula for a call option two periods before expiration. In doing so, we compute the expected value of the call at expiration and discount for two periods:

$$C = \frac{.64\ (\$21) + .16\ (0) + .16\ (0) + .04\ (0)}{1.06^2} = \frac{\$13.44}{1.06^2} = \$11.96$$

If the call expires in two periods and the stock trades for $100, the call will be worth $11.96. Notice that our sample call pays off at expiration only if the stock price rises twice. Any other pattern of stock price movement in our example gives a call that is worthless at expiration. With one period until expiration and the stock trading at $100, we saw that the call was worth $7.55. With the same initial stock price and two periods until expiration, the call is worth $11.96. This price difference reflects the difference in the present value of the expected payoffs from the call.

In the single-period binomial model, there are two possible stock price outcomes. With two periods until expiration, there are four possible stock price patterns. In general, there are 2^n possible stock price patterns, where n is the number of periods until expiration. Thus, the number of stock and call outcomes increases very rapidly. For example, if the option is just 20 periods from expiration, there are more than 1 million stock price outcomes and the same number of call outcomes to consider.[3] It quickly becomes apparent that we need a more general formula for the multi-period binomial pricing model. Also, for options with many periods until expiration, we need a computer. **OPTION!** can compute binomial model call and put values.

We have explored the single-period and two-period binomial model in detail, and we have analyzed examples for each. The principles we have developed remain true no matter how many periods we consider. However, the computations become more numerous and cumbersome, as we just saw. Therefore, we now make a mathematical jump to present the formula, which we discuss in intuitive terms.

The Multi–Period Binomial Call Pricing Model

In this section, we begin by introducing the Multi-Period Binomial Call Pricing Model. As equation 4.2 shows, it is undeniably complex. However, a little study will show that the equation is not really so intimidating.

$$C = \frac{\sum_{j=0}^{n} \left(\frac{n!}{j!\,(n-j)!} \right) \left[\pi_u^{j}\, \pi_d^{n-j} \right] MAX \left[0,\, U^j D^{n-j} S - E \right]}{R^n} \qquad 4.2$$

To understand this formula, we need to break it into simpler elements. From our previous discussion, we know that the formula gives the present value of the expected payoffs from the call at expiration. The denominator R^n is the discount factor raised to n, the number of periods until expiration. The numerator gives the expected payoff on the call option. Thus, we need to focus on the numerator.

With the multi-period model, we are analyzing an option that expires in n periods. As a feature of the binomial model, we know that the stock price either goes up or down each period. Let us say that it goes up j of the n periods. Then the stock price must fall n-j periods. Our summation runs from j=0 to j=n, which includes every possibility. When j=0, we evaluate the possibility that the stock price never rises. When j=n, we evaluate the possibility that the stock price rises every period. The summation considers these extreme possibilities and every intermediate possibility.

For any random number of stock price increases, j, the numerator expresses three things about the call for the j stock price increases among the n periods. First, starting from the right, the numerator gives the payoff on the option if the stock price rises j times. This is our familiar expression beginning with max. The value of the call at expiration is either zero, or the stock price minus the exercise price, whichever is greater. The expression $U^j D^{n-j} S$ gives the stock price at expiration if the stock price rises j periods and falls the other n-j periods. Second, the numerator expresses the probability of exactly j stock price increases and n-j stock price decreases. Earlier, we saw how to find the probability of up and down movements. Therefore, $\pi_u^j \pi_d^{n-j}$ gives the probability of observing j up movements and n-j down movements. Third, more than one sequence of stock price movements can result in the same terminal stock price. For instance, in the two period model we saw that UDS gave the same terminal stock price as DUS. The numerator also computes the number of different combinations of stock price movements that result in the same terminal stock price. The expression

$$\frac{n!}{j! \, (n-j)!}$$

computes the number of possible combinations of j rises from n periods. In essence, the combination weights the possibility of exactly n rises and n-j falls by the number of different patterns that result in exactly j rises and n-j falls. For example, only one pattern results in n rises—the stock must rise in every period. By contrast, if j = n-j, there will usually be many patterns that can give j rises and n-j falls.

In the expression for the combination, n! is call n-factorial. It's value equals n multiplied by n-1 times n-2 and so on down to 1:

$$n! = n(n-1)(n-2)(n-3) \ldots (1)$$

To illustrate, if n = 5, then 5! = 5(4)(3)(2)(1) = 120. For example, with the two period model we could have the pattern up-down or down-up resulting in the same stock price. Thus, there are two combinations of one increase over two periods. The increase could be first or second. For any j value, the numerator computes the number of combinations of j increases from n periods, times the probability of having exactly j increases times the payoff on the call if there are j increases. The summation ensures that the numerator reflects all possible j values.

In our two-period example, the option pays off at expiration only if the stock price rises both times. In general, many stock price patterns leave the option out-of-the-money at expiration. For valuing the option, stock price patterns that leave the option out-of-the-money are a dead end, because they result in a zero option price. As a consequence, we do not need to fully evaluate stock price patterns that leave the option out-of-the-money at expiration. Instead, we only need to evaluate those values of j for which the option expires in-the-money. In our two period example, we do not need to compute the entire formula for j=0 and j=1. If the stock price never goes up or goes up only once, the option expires out-of-the-money. For our two-period example, we only need to consider what happens to the option when the stock price rises twice, that is, when j=2. Only then does the option finish in-the-money. Let us define m as the number of times the stock price must rise for the option to finish in-the-money. Thus, when the stock price rises exactly m times, it must fall n-m times. However, this pattern still leaves the option in-the-money, because the stock price rose the needed m times. Then we need only consider values of j=m to j=n. In our two-period example, m=2 because the stock price must rise in both periods for the option to finish in-the-money. Therefore, the following formula gives an alternative expression for the value of an option:

$$C = \frac{\sum_{j=m}^{n}\left(\frac{n!}{j!\,(n-j)!}\right)\left(\pi_u^{\,j}\,\pi_d^{\,n-j}\right)\left[U^j D^{n-j} S \quad E\right]}{R^n}$$

Notice that the summation begins with m, the minimum number of stock price increases needed to bring the option into-the-money. Because we consider only the events that put the option in-the-money, we no longer need to worry about the call being worth the maximum of zero or the stock price less the exercise price at expiration. With at least m stock price rises, the option will be worth more than zero because it necessarily finishes in-the-money. Now we divide the formula into two parts—one associated with the stock price and the other associated with the exercise price.

$$C = S\left[\sum_{j=m}^{n}\left(\frac{n!}{j!\,(n-j)!}\right)\left(\pi_u^{\,j}\,\pi_d^{\,n-j}\right)\frac{U^j D^{n-j}}{R^n}\right] - ER^{-n}\left[\sum_{j=m}^{n}\left(\frac{n!}{j!\,(n-j)!}\right)\left(\pi_u^{\,j}\,\pi_d^{\,n-j}\right)\right]$$

This version of the binomial formula starts to resemble our familiar expression for the value of the call as the stock price minus the present value of the exercise price. If the option is in-the-money and the stock price is certain to remain unchanged until expiration, the call price equals the stock price minus the present value of the exercise price. Our formula has exactly that structure except for the two complicated expressions in brackets. These two expressions reflect the riskiness of the stock. This uncertainty or riskiness about the stock gives the added value to the call above the stock price minus the present value of the exercise price.

The multi-period binomial model can reflect numerous stock price outcomes, if there are numerous periods. Just 20 periods gives more than 1 million stock price movement patterns. In our examples, we kept the period length the same and added more periods. This lengthened the total time until expiration. As an alternative, we could keep the same time to expiration and consider more periods of shorter duration. For example, we originally treated a year as a single period. For that year, we could regard each trading day as a period, giving about 250 periods per year. We could evaluate an option with the multi-period model by assuming that the stock price could change once a day.

The binomial model requires that the price move up a given percentage or down a given percentage. Therefore, if we shorten the period, we need to adjust the stock price movements to correspond to the shorter period. While up or down 10 percent might be reasonable for a period of one year, it certainly would not be reasonable for a period of one day. Similarly, a risk-free rate of 6 percent makes sense for a period of one year, but not for a period of one day.

By adjusting the period length, the stock price movement, and the interest rate, we can refine the binomial model as much as we wish. For example, we could assume that the stock price could move one-hundredth of a percent every minute of the year if we wished. Under this assumption, the model would have finer partitions than exist in the market for most stock. However, with the price changing every minute and a time to expiration of one year, we would have trillions of possible stock price outcomes to consider. While having so many periods would be computationally expensive, we could apply the model if we wished. Conceptually, we could make each period so short that the stock price would change continuously. However, if the stock price truly changed continuously, there would be an infinite number of periods to consider. While we cannot compute the binomial model for an infinite number of periods, mathematical techniques do exist to compute option prices when stock prices change continuously.

Binomial Put Option Pricing

In discussing binomial option pricing, we have used call options as an example. However, the model also applies to put options. To value put options, we follow the same reasoning process that we have considered in detail for call options. Rather than detail all of the reasoning leading to the formula, we begin with the formula for the price of a European put option. Our entire discussion in this section pertains to European puts. This formula matches our binomial call formula, except we substitute the expression for the value of a put at expiration, $E - U^j D^{n-j} S$, in place of the value of a call at expiration.

$$P = \frac{\sum_{j=0}^{n}\left(\frac{n!}{j!\,(n-j)!}\right)\left(\pi_u^{\,j}\ \pi_d^{\,n-j}\right) MAX\left[0, E - U^j D^{n-j} S\right]}{R^n} \qquad 4.3$$

In pricing the call option, we only considered stock price patterns that left the call in-the-money at expiration. The same is true for the put. The put finishes in-the-money if the stock price does not increase often enough to make the stock price exceed the exercise price. We defined m as the number of price increases needed to bring the call into the money. Therefore, if the price increases m-1 or fewer times, the put finishes in-the-money. Therefore, we can also write the formula for the put as follows:

$$P = \frac{\sum_{j=0}^{m-1}\left(\frac{n!}{j!\,(n-j)!}\right)\left(\pi_u^{\,j}\ \pi_d^{\,n-j}\right)\left[E - U^j D^{n-j} S\right]}{R^n}$$

Rearranging terms gives:

$$P = ER^{-n}\left[\sum_{j=0}^{m-1}\left(\frac{n!}{j!\,(n-j)!}\right)\left(\pi_u^{\,j}\ \pi_d^{\,n-j}\right)\right] - S\left[\sum_{j=0}^{m-1}\left(\frac{n!}{j!\,(n-j)!}\right)\left(\pi_u^{\,j}\ \pi_d^{\,n-j}\right)\frac{U^j D^{n-j}}{R^n}\right]$$

This formula for the put parallels our familiar expression for the put as equaling the present value of the exercise price minus the stock price. As with the call, the two bracketed expressions account for the risky movement of the stock price.

We can also value the put through put-call parity. We have the value of the call under the binomial model as given above. Put-call parity tells us that:

$$P = C - S + Ee^{-rt}$$

Both approaches must necessarily give the same answer.

Stock Price Movements

In actual markets, stock prices change to reflect new information. During a single day, a stock price may change many times. From the ticker, we can observe stock prices when transactions occur. When trading ceases overnight, however, we cannot observe the stock price for hours at a time. Where the price wanders during the night, no one can know. Our observations are also limited, because stock prices are quoted in eighths of a dollar. The true stock price need not jump from one eighth to the next, but the observed stock price does. Sometimes the observed price remains the same from one transaction to another. But just because we observe the same price twice in succession does not mean it remained at that price between the two observations. From these reflections, we see that we can never know exactly how stock prices change because we cannot observe the true stock price at every instant. Therefore, any model of stock price behavior deviates from an exact description of how stock prices move. Nonetheless, it is possible to develop a realistic model of stock price movements. In this section, we review a particular model that has been very successful in a wide range of finance applications.

Let us consider the random information that affects the price of a stock. We assume that the information arrives continuously and that each bit of information is small in importance. Under this scenario, we consider a stock price that rises or falls a small proportion in response to each bit of information. We know that finance depends conceptually on the twin ideas of expected return and risk. Thus, we might also think of a stock as having a positive expected rate of return. In the absence of special events, we expect the stock price to grow along the path of its expected rate of return. However, the world is risky. Information about the stock is sometimes favorable and sometimes unfavorable. As this random information becomes known, it pushes the stock away from its expected growth path. When the information is better than expected, the stock price jumps above its growth path. Negative information has the opposite effect; it pushes the stock price below its expected growth path. Thus, we might imagine the stock price growing along its expected growth path just as a drunk walks across a field. We expect the drunk to reach the other side of the field, but we also think he will wander and stumble in unpredictable short-term deviations from the straight path. Similarly, we expect a stock price to rise, because it has a positive expected return, but we also expect it to wander above and below its growth path, due to new information.

Finance uses a standard mathematical model that is consistent with the story of the preceding paragraph. It assumes that the stock grows at an expected rate μ with a standard deviation σ:

$$S_t - S_0 = S_0 \mu t + S_0 N(0,1) \sigma \sqrt{t} \qquad\qquad 4.4$$

where:

$S_t - S_0$ = *the stock price change during time t*

$S_0 \mu t$ = *expected value of the stock price change during time t*

$N(0,1)$ = *normally distributed random variable with $\mu = 0$, $\sigma = 1$*

$\sigma \sqrt{t}$ = *standard deviation of the stock price at t*

Equation 4.4 says that the stock price change between time zero and time t depends on two factors: the expected growth rate in the price and the variability of the growth. First, the expected growth in the stock price over a given interval depends on the mean growth rate, μ, and the amount of time, t. Therefore, if the stock price starts at S_0, the expected stock price increase after an interval of t equals $S_0 \mu t$. However, this is only the expected stock price increase after the interval. Due to risk, the actual price change can be greater or lower. Deviations from the expected stock price depend on chance and on the volatility of the stock. The equation captures risk by using the normal distribution. For convenience, the model uses the standard normal distribution, which has a zero mean and a standard deviation of 1. The standard deviation represents the variability of a particular stock. We multiply the standard deviation of the stock by a random drawing from the normal distribution to capture the riskiness of the stock. Also, the equation says that the variability increases with the square root of the interval. In other words, the farther into the future we project the stock price with our model, the less certain we can be about what the stock price will be.

Dividing both sides of equation 4.4 by the original stock price, S_0, gives the percentage change in the stock price during period t:

$$\frac{S_t - S_0}{S_0} = \mu t + N(0,1)\, \sigma \sqrt{t}$$

From this equation, it is possible to show that the percentage change in the stock price is normally distributed:

$$\frac{S_t - S_0}{S_0} \sim N\left[\mu t, \sigma \sqrt{t}\right] \qquad 4.5$$

Figure 4.3 shows two stock price paths over the course of a year, with both stock prices starting at $100. The straight line graphs a stock that grows at 10 percent per year with no risk. The jagged line shows a stock price path with an expected growth rate of 10 percent and a standard deviation of .2 per year. We generated the second price path by taking repeated random samples from a normal distribution to create price changes according to equation 4.4. As the jagged line in Figure 4.3 shows, a stock might easily wander away from its growth path due to the riskiness represented by its standard deviation.

To construct Figure 4.3, we used 1000 periods per year and a growth rate of 10 percent. To construct the straight line, we assumed that the stock price increased by .1/1000 each period. However, this gives an ending stock price of $110.51, not the $110 we expect if the stock prices grows at 10 percent per year. This difference results from using 1000 compounding intervals during the year.

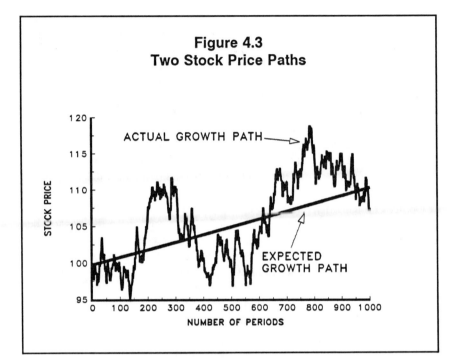

Figure 4.3
Two Stock Price Paths

ACTUAL GROWTH PATH

EXPECTED
GROWTH PATH

STOCK PRICE

NUMBER OF PERIODS

However, we hypothesize that information arrives continuously, so that the stock price could always change. To avoid worrying about the compounding interval, we now employ continuous compounding. Therefore, we focus on logarithmic stock returns. For example, consider a beginning stock price of $100 and an ending price of $110 a year later. The logarithmic stock return over the year is $\ln(S_t/S_0) = \ln(\$110/\$100) = \ln(1.1) = .0953$. The logarithmic stock return is just the continuous growth rate that takes the stock price from its original value to its ending value. Thus, $\$100e^{ut} = \$100e^{.0953(1)} = \$110$. We now need a continuous growth model of stock prices that is consistent with our model for the percentage change stock price model of equation 4.5. With some difficult math, it is possible to prove the following result:

$$\ln\left(\frac{S_t}{S_0}\right) \sim N\left[\mu t - .5t\sigma^2, \sigma\sqrt{t}\right] \qquad 4.6$$

This expression asserts that logarithmic stock returns are distributed normally with the given mean and standard deviation. For a later time, t, the expected stock price and the variance of the stock price are:

$$E(S_t) = S_0 e^{\mu t}$$

$$VAR(S_t) = S_0^2 e^{2\mu t}\left(e^{\sigma^2 t} - 1\right)$$

Thus the expected stock price at t depends on the original stock price, the expected growth rate, and the amount of time that elapses. Similarly, the variance of the stock price depends on the original stock price, the expected growth rate, and the elapsed time as well. The longer the time horizon, the larger will be the variance. The increasing variance reflects our greater uncertainty about stock prices far in the future.

As an example, consider a stock with an initial price of $100 and an expected growth rate of 10 percent. If the stock has a standard deviation of .2 per year, we can compute the expected stock price and variance for 6 months into the future. For this example, we have the following values:

$$S_0 = \$100$$
$$\mu = .1$$
$$\sigma = .2$$
$$t = .5$$
$$E(S_t) = \$100\, e^{.1(.5)} = \$105.13$$
$$VAR(S_t) = (\$100)(\$100)\left(e^{2(.1)(.5)}\right)\left(e^{(.2)(.2)(.5)} - 1\right) = \$223.26$$

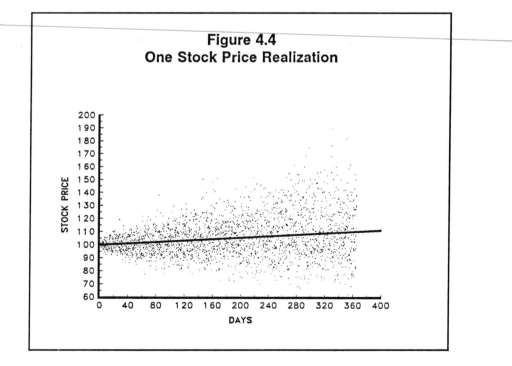

Figure 4.4
One Stock Price Realization

The standard deviation of the price over period t is $14.94. Figure 4.4 shows stock price realizations that are consistent with this example. We found these prices by drawing random values from a normal distribution and using our example growth rate and standard deviation. Each dot in the figure represents a possible stock price realization. Notice that the price tends to drift higher over time, consistent with a rising expected value. This is shown by the regression line that is fitted through the points. However, there is considerable uncertainty about what the price will be at any future date. The farther we go into the future, the greater that uncertainty becomes.

Research on actual stock price behavior shows that logarithmic stock returns are approximately normally distributed. So we say that, as an approximation, stock returns follow a **log–normal distribution**. Stock returns themselves are not normally distributed. As an example, Figure 4.5 shows a distribution of stock returns with a mean of 1.2 and a standard deviation of .6. It is easy to see that this distribution is not normal because it is skewed to the right. There is a greater chance of larger returns than one would expect with a normal distribution. Figure 4.6 shows the log-normal distribution that corresponds to the values in Figure

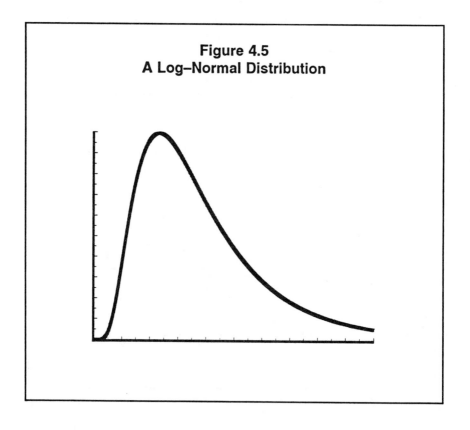

Figure 4.5
A Log–Normal Distribution

4.5. The values graphed in Figure 4.6 are the logarithms of the values used to construct Figure 4.5. The graph in Figure 4.6 shows a normal distribution. We will assume that stock returns are distributed as Figure 4.6 shows, except the mean and standard deviation differ from stock to stock.

While the log-normal distribution only approximates stock returns, it has two great virtues. First, it is mathematically tractable, so we can obtain solutions for the value of call options if stock returns are log-normally distributed. Second, the resulting call option prices that we compute are very good approximations of actual market prices. In the remainder of this chapter, we treat stock returns as log-normally distributed with a specified mean and variance.

The Binomial Approach to the Black-Scholes Model

We have seen how to generalize the binomial model to any number of periods. Increasing the number of periods allows for many possible stock price outcomes at expiration, thereby increasing the realism of the results. However, three problems remain. First, as the number of periods increases, computational difficulties begin to arise. Second, increasing the number of periods while holding the time until expiration constant means that the period length becomes shorter. We must adjust the up and down movement factors, U and D, and the risk-free rate to fit the time horizon. Obviously, we cannot use factors with a scale appropriate to a year when the period length is, say, one day, for example. Third, we have worked with more or less arbitrarily selected up and down factors. The price that the model gives can only be as good as its inputs. The example inputs we have been considering serve well as illustrations, but they are not appropriate for analyzing real options. Therefore, we need a better way to determine the up and down factors.

Modeling stock returns by a log-normal process solves these three problems simultaneously. If stock returns are log-normally distributed with the mean return given by μ and a standard deviation of σ for some unit of calendar time t, then we define the following binomial inputs as:

$$U = (r - .5\sigma^2)t + \sigma\sqrt{t}$$
$$D = (r - .5\sigma^2)t - \sigma\sqrt{t}$$

As we show in the next section, this approach allows us to compute the value of an option with an infinite number of periods until expiration. With the strict binomial model, we could never employ an infinite number of periods because it would take forever to add all the individual results. Notice that the

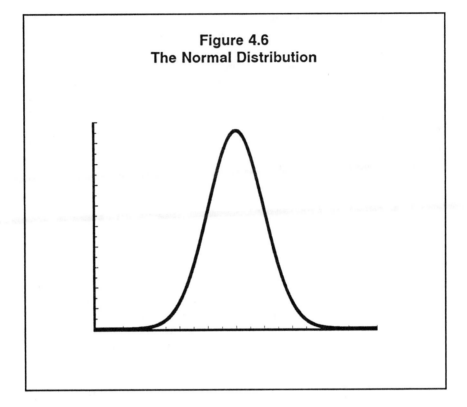

Figure 4.6
The Normal Distribution

values of R, U, and D adjust automatically as we consider more and more periods during the fixed calendar interval t. The absolute value of each becomes smaller, exactly as we would expect for a shorter time period. The values for U and D depend on the riskiness of the stock returns. The probability of a stock price increase depends upon the mean return on the stock. Thus, if we can estimate the standard deviation of stock returns, we have reasonable inputs to the binomial model. These can replace the arbitrary example values that we have been using.[4]

The Black-Scholes Option Pricing Model

To this point, we have developed the binomial option pricing model. We have discussed the log–normal distribution of stock returns and have presented up and down factors for the binomial model that are consistent with the log–normal distribution of stock returns. Also, we have seen how to adjust the precision of the binomial model by dividing a given unit of calendar time into more and more periods. As we deal with more periods, however, the calculations in the binomial model become cumbersome. As the number of periods in the binomial model becomes very large, the binomial model converges to the famous Black-Scholes Option Pricing Model.

Fischer Black and Myron Scholes developed their option pricing model under the assumptions that asset prices adjust to prevent arbitrage, that stock prices change continuously, and that stock returns follow a log–normal distribution.[5] Also, their model holds for European call options on stocks with no dividends. Further, they assume that the interest rate and the volatility of the stock remain constant over the life of the option. The mathematics they used to derive their result include stochastic calculus, which is beyond the scope of this text. In this section, we present their model and illustrate the basic intuition that underlies it. We show that the form of the Black-Scholes Model parallels the bounds on option pricing that we have already observed. In fact, the form of the Black-Scholes model is very close to the binomial model we have just been considering.

The Black-Scholes Call Option Pricing Model

The following expression gives the Black–Scholes Option Pricing Model for a call option:

$$C = SN(d_1) - Ee^{-rt}N(d_2) \qquad 4.7$$

where:

$N(\cdot)$ = cumulative normal distribution function

$$d_1 = \frac{\ln(\frac{S}{E}) + (r + .5\sigma^2)t}{\sigma\sqrt{t}}$$

$$d_2 = d_1 - \sigma\sqrt{t}$$

This model has the general form we have long considered—the value of a call must equal or exceed the stock price minus the present value of the exercise price:

$$C \geq S - Ee^{-rt}$$

To adapt this formula to account for risk, as in the Black-Scholes Model, we multiply the stock price and the exercise price by some factors to account for risk, giving the general form:

$$C = S \times \textit{Risk Factor \#1} - Ee^{-rt} \times \textit{Risk Factor \#2}$$

The binomial model shares this general form with the Black-Scholes model. With the binomial model, the risk adjustment factors were the large bracketed expressions of equation 4.2. With the Black-Scholes model, the risk factors are $N(d_1)$ and $N(d_2)$. In the Black-Scholes model, these risk adjustment factors are the continuous time equivalent of the bracketed expressions in the Binomial model.

The Black–Scholes Call Option Pricing Model

$$C = SN(d_1) - Ee^{-rt}N(d_2)$$

Computing Black-Scholes Option Prices

In this section, we show how to compute Black-Scholes option prices. Assume that a stock trades at \$100 and the risk-free interest rate is 6 percent. A call option on the stock has an exercise price of \$100 and expires in one year. The standard deviation of the stock's returns is .10 per year. We compute the values of d_1 and d_2 as follows:

$$d_1 = \frac{\ln\left(\dfrac{S}{E}\right) + \left(r + .5\sigma^2\right)t}{\sigma\sqrt{t}}$$

$$= \frac{\ln\left(\dfrac{100}{100}\right) + \left(.06 + .5\,(.01)\,\right)1}{.1\sqrt{1}} = .65$$

$$d_2 = d_1 - \sigma\sqrt{t}$$
$$= .65 - .1 \times 1 = .55$$

Next, we find the cumulative normal values associated with d_1 and d_2. These values are the probability that a normally distributed variable with a zero

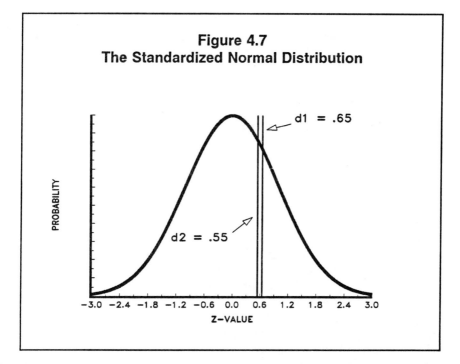

Figure 4.7
The Standardized Normal Distribution

mean and a standard deviation of 1.0 will have a value equal to or less than the d_1 or d_2 term we are considering. Figure 4.7 shows a graph of a normally distributed variable with a zero mean and a standard deviation of 1.0. It shows the values of d_1 and d_2 for our example. For illustration, we focus on d_1, which equals .65. In finding $N(d_1)$, we want to know which portion of the area under the curve lies to the left of .65. This is the value of $N(d_1)$. Clearly, the value we seek is larger than .5, because d_1 is above the mean of zero. We can find the exact value by consulting a table of the cumulative normal distribution for this variable. We present this table as Appendix A. Also, we can use **OPTION!** to find these values. For a value of .65 drawn from the border of the table, we find our probability in the interior: $N(.65) = .7422$. Similarly, $N(d_2) = N(.55) = .7088$. We now have:

$$C = \$100 \times .7422 - \$100 \times .9418 \times .7088 = \$7.46$$

We chose these values for our example because they parallel the values from our original binomial example. There we also assumed that the stock traded for $100 and that the risk-free rate was 6 percent. We assumed an up factor of 10 percent and a down factor of -10 percent. With a single-period binomial model and these values, we found that a call must be priced at $7.55. The two results are close. However, if we use more periods in the binomial model and use up and down factors that are consistent with a log-normal distribution of stock returns, the binomial model will converge to the Black-Scholes model price. The reader can explore this possibility by using **OPTION!**.

The Hedge Ratio

In our arbitrage discussions, we found that we could form a portfolio one period before expiration that would mimic a call option. With just one period until expiration, we saw that:

$$C = NS - Ee^{-rt}$$

In this equation, we mimic the call by borrowing the present value of the exercise price and by holding N shares. In this context, N is a **hedge ratio**, the number of shares to hold to form the mimicking portfolio. By holding N shares along with our borrowing, we create a portfolio that has the same payoffs as the call. If we hold the call and sell the mimicking portfolio, the entire set of investments will be worth zero at expiration. We will be perfectly hedged against any profits or losses.

A similar analysis applies to the Black-Scholes Model. For the Black-Scholes Model, $N(d_1)$ is the hedge ratio. However, the Black-Scholes Model operates in continuous time. Thus, we treat the hedge as holding for the next instant or for the next infinitesimal stock price change. If the stock price changes in the next instant, we will be hedged. However, a changing stock price will generally change the hedge ratio. Thus, $N(d_1)$ is an **instantaneous hedge ratio**. It holds for the next instant, after which we may need to slightly rebalance our mimicking portfolio to be fully hedged.

The hedge ratio also has considerable practical importance because it shows how the call price will change for a one unit change in the stock price. Thus, if we hold a call option on one share and sell $N(d_1)$ shares of stock, the resulting option/stock portfolio will not change in value when the stock price changes. As we will see, this principle holds for the next instant and for infinitesimal changes in stock prices. The resulting portfolio is risk-free, because its price does not change as the stock price changes. Therefore, the portfolio must earn the risk-free rate on the invested funds, which would equal $C - N(d_1) \times S$.

Because the hedge ratio relates the change in the price of the call to a change in the price of the stock, $N(d_1)$ is also known as the **delta** for the call. Earlier we computed a Black-Scholes price of $7.46 for our example data. There we found that $N(d_1) = .7422$. Based on this value, we expect an increase in the price of the call if the stock price rises by $1. If the stock price rose to $101, the Black-Scholes call price would be $8.22, for a $.76 difference. This is almost, but not quite, equal to the $.74 we expect. There is a reason for this difference.

The Black-Scholes Model operates on the assumption that stock prices can change at every instant. However, they can change by only a very small amount. We assumed an instantaneous one percent change. With the Black-Scholes Model, a one percent change would be accomplished by numerous smaller changes. Each of these smaller changes would require a re-balancing of the mimicking portfolio. For this reason, the hedge ratio gives only the approximate change in the price of the call if we assume a large change in the price of the stock. Nonetheless, it offers a very good approximation.

The Black-Scholes Put Option Pricing Model

Black and Scholes developed their option pricing model for calls only. However, we can find the Black-Scholes Model for European puts by applying put–call parity:

$$P = C - S + Ee^{-rt}$$

Substituting the Black-Scholes call formula in the put–call parity equation gives:

$$P = SN(d_1) - Ee^{-rt}N(d_2) - S + Ee^{-rt}$$

Collecting like terms simplifies the equation to:

$$P = S\left[N(d_1) - 1\right] + Ee^{-rt}\left[1 - N(d_2)\right]$$

If we consider the cumulative distribution of all values from $-\infty$ to $+\infty$, the maximum value is 1.0. For any value of d_1 we consider, part of the whole must lie at or below the value and the remainder must lie above it. For example, if $N(d_1)$ is .7422, for $d_1 = .65$, then .2578 of the total area under the curve must lie at values greater than .65. Now we apply a principle of normal distributions. The normal distribution is symmetrical, so the same percentage of the area under the curve that lies above d_1 must lie below $-d_1$. Therefore, for any symmetrical distribution and any arbitrary value, w:

$$N(w) + N(-w) = 1$$

Following this pattern and substituting for $N(d_1)$ and $N(d_2)$ gives the equivalent Black-Scholes value for a put option.

$$P = Ee^{-rt}N(-d_2) - SN(-d_1) \qquad 4.8$$

This equation has the familiar form that we have been exploring since Chapter 2. We emphasize that the Black-Scholes Model for puts holds only for European puts.

The Black–Scholes Put Option Pricing Model

$$P = Ee^{-rt}N(-d_2) - SN(-d_1)$$

Inputs for the Black-Scholes Model

We have seen that the Black-Scholes Model for the price of an option depends on five variables: the stock price, the exercise price, the time until expiration, the risk-free rate, and the standard deviation of the stock. Of these, the stock price is observable in the financial press or on a trading terminal. The exercise price and the time until expiration can be known with certainty. We want to consider how to obtain estimates of the other two parameters; the risk-free interest rate and the standard deviation of the stock.

Estimating the Risk–Free Rate of Interest

Estimates of the risk-free interest rate are widely available and are usually quite reliable.[6] There are still a few points to consider, however. First, we need to select the correct rate. Because the Black-Scholes Model uses a risk-free rate, we can use the Treasury-bill rate as a good estimate. Quoted interest rates for T-bills are expressed as discount rates. We need to convert these to regular interest rates and express them as continuously compounded rates. As a second consideration, we should select the maturity of the T-bill carefully. If the yield curve has a steep slope, yields for different maturities can differ significantly. With T-bills maturing each week, we choose the bill that matures closest to the option expiration.

We illustrate the computation with the following example. Consider a T-bill with 84 days until maturity. Its bid yield is 8.83 and its asking yield is 8.77. Letting B and A be the bid and asked yields, the following formula gives the price of a T-bill as a percentage of its face value:

$$P_{TB} = 1 - .01\left(\frac{B+A}{2}\right)\left(\frac{Days\ Until\ Maturity}{360}\right)$$

$$= 1 - .01\left(\frac{8.83+8.77}{2}\right)\left(\frac{84}{360}\right)$$

$$= .97947$$

In this formula, we average the bid and asked yields to estimate the unobservable true yield which lies between the observable bid and asked yields. For our example, the price of the T-bill is 97.947 percent of its face value. To find the corresponding continuously compounded rate, we solve the following equation for r:

$$e^{rt} = \frac{1}{P_{TB}}$$

$$e^{r(.23)} = 1/.97947$$

$$.23\,r = \ln(1.02096) = .0207$$

$$r = .0902$$

In the equation, t = .23 because 84 days is 23 percent of a year. Thus, the appropriate interest rate in this example is 9.02 percent.

Securing good estimates of the risk-free interest rate is fairly easy. However, having an exact estimate is not critical. As we show later in this chapter, the option price is not very sensitive to the interest rate.

Estimating the Stock's Standard Deviation

Estimating the standard deviation of the stock's returns is more difficult and more important than estimating the risk-free rate. The Black-Scholes Model takes as its input the current, instantaneous standard deviation of the stock. In other words, the immediate volatility of the stock is the riskiness of the stock that affects the option price. The Black–Scholes Model also assumes that the volatility is constant over the life of the option.[7] There are two basic ways to estimate the volatility. The first method uses historical data, while the second technique employs fresh data from the options market itself. This second method uses option prices to find the option market's estimate of the stock's standard deviation. An estimate of the stock's standard deviation that is drawn from the options market is called an **implied volatility**. We consider each method in turn.[8]

Historical Data—To estimate volatility using historical data, we compute the price relatives, logarithmic price relatives, and the mean and standard deviation of the logarithmic price relatives. Letting PR_t indicate the price relative for day t so that $PR_t = P_t/P_{t-1}$, we give the formulas for the mean and variance of the logarithmic price relatives as follows:

$$\overline{PR} = \frac{1}{T} \sum_{t-1}^{T} \ln PR_t$$

$$VAR\ (PR) = \frac{1}{T-1} \sum_{t-1}^{T} \left(\ln PR_t - \overline{PR} \right)^2$$

As an example, we apply these formulas to data in the following table, which gives eleven days of price information for a stock. With eleven price observations, we compute ten daily returns. The first column tracks the day, while the second column records the stock's closing price for the day. The third column computes the price relative from the prices in column 2. The fourth column gives the log of the price relative in column 3. The last column contains the result of subtracting the mean of the logarithmic price relatives from each observation and squaring the result.

Day	P_t	PR_t	$\ln(PR_t)$	$[\ln PR_t - PR_\mu]^2$
0	100.00			
1	101.50	1.0150	0.0149	0.000154
2	98.00	0.9655	-0.0351	0.001410
3	96.75	0.9872	-0.0128	0.000234
4	100.50	1.0388	0.0380	0.001264
5	101.00	1.0050	0.0050	0.000006
6	103.25	1.0223	0.0220	0.000382
7	105.00	1.0169	0.0168	0.000205
8	102.75	0.9786	-0.0217	0.000582
9	103.00	1.0024	0.0024	0.000000
10	102.50	0.9951	-0.0049	0.000053
		Sums	.0247	0.004294

Sample μ = .0247/10   = .00247
Sample σ^2 = .004294/9 = .000477
Sample σ = .021843

The mean, variance, and standard deviation that we have calculated are all based on our sample of daily data. We use the sample standard deviation as an input to the Black-Scholes Model.

Three inputs to the Black-Scholes Model depend on the unit of time. These inputs are the interest rate, the time until expiration, and the standard deviation. We can use any single measure we wish, but we need to express all three variables in the same time units. For example, we can use days as our time unit and express the time until expiration as the number of days remaining. Then we must also use a daily estimation of the standard deviation and the interest rate for a single day. Generally, one year is the most convenient common unit of time. Therefore, we need to convert our daily standard deviation into a comparable yearly estimate. We have estimated our daily standard deviation of ten days. However, these are ten trading days, not calendar days. Accordingly, we recognize that we are working in trading time, not calendar time. Deleting weekend days and holidays, each year has about 250–252 trading days. We use 250 trading days per year.

We have already seen that stock prices are distributed with a standard deviation that increases as the square root of time. Accordingly, we can adjust the time dimension of our volatility estimate by multiplying it by the square root of time. For example, we convert from our daily standard deviation estimate to an equivalent yearly value by multiplying the daily estimate times the square root of 250.[9]

$$Annualized\ \sigma\ =\ Daily\ \sigma\ \times \sqrt{250}$$

For our daily estimate of .021843, the estimated standard deviation in annual terms is .3454.

In our example, we have used ten days of data. In actual practice, we face a trade-off between using the most recent possible data and using more data. In statistics, we almost always get more reliable estimates by using more data. However, the Black-Scholes Model takes the instantaneous standard deviation as an input. This gives great importance to using current data. If we use the last year of historical data, then we have a rich data set for estimating the old volatility. Using just ten days, as we did in our example, emphasizes current data, but it is really not very much data for getting a reliable estimate.

To emphasize the importance of using current data, consider the Crash of 1987. On Bloody Monday, October 19, 1987, the market lost about 22 percent of its value. If we used a full year of daily data to estimate a stock's historical volatility the next day, our estimate would be too low. In the light of the Crash, the instantaneous volatility had surely increased.

Implied Volatility—To overcome the limitations inherent in using historical data to estimate standard deviations, some scholars have turned to techniques of implied volatility. In this section, we show how to use market data and the Black-Scholes Model to estimate a stock's volatility. There are five inputs to the Black-Scholes Model, which the model relates to a sixth variable, the call price. With a total of six variables, any five imply a unique value for the sixth. The technique of implied volatility uses known values of five variables to estimate the standard deviation. The estimated standard deviation is an implied volatility because it is the value implied by the other five variables in the model.[10]

To find implied volatilities, we begin with established values for the stock price, exercise price, interest rate, time until expiration, and the call price. We use these to find the implied standard deviation. However, the standard deviation enters the Black-Scholes Model through the values for d_1 and d_2, which are used to determine the values of the cumulative normal distribution. As a result, we cannot solve for the standard deviation directly. Instead, we must search for the volatility that makes the Black-Scholes equation hold. To do this, we need a computer. Otherwise, we would have to try an estimate of the standard deviation, make all of the Black-Scholes computations by hand, and adjust the standard deviation for the next try. This would be cumbersome and time consuming. Therefore, implied volatilities are almost always found using a computer. OPTION! has a module for finding implied volatilities.

For most stocks with options, several options with different expirations trade at once. Some researchers have argued that all of these options should be used to find the volatility implied by each. The resulting estimates are then given weights and averaged to find a single volatility estimate. The single estimate is known as a **weighted implied standard deviation**. In principle, this is a good idea because it uses more information. Other things being equal, estimates based on more information should dominate estimates based on less information. However, some options trade infrequently, which makes their prices less reliable for computing implied volatilities. In addition, options way out-of-the-money give somewhat spurious volatility estimates. Virtually all weighting schemes give the highest weight to options closest to-the-money. At-the-money options tend to give the least biased volatility estimates, and many option traders derive implied volatilities by focusing on at-the-money options.[11]

Consider the following example of an implied standard deviation based on a call option. We assume that $E = \$100$ and the option is at-the-money, so $S = \$100$. We also assume that the option has 90 days remaining until expiration and that the risk-free interest rate is 10 percent, so we have $t = 90$ and $R_f = .10$. The call price is 5.00. To find the implied standard deviation, we need to find the standard deviation that is consistent with these other values. To do this, we can compute the Black-Scholes Model price for alternative standard deviations. We adjust the standard deviation to make the option price converge to its actual price of 5.00. The sequence of standard deviations and call prices below shows this relationship. In our example, we first try $\sigma = .1$, which gives a call price of 3.41. This price is too low. Thus, we know the correct standard deviation must be larger, because the call price varies directly with the standard deviation. Next, $\sigma = .5$ results in a call price of 11.03, which is too high. Now we know that the standard deviation must be greater than $.1$, but less than $.5$. The task is to find the standard deviation that gives a call value equal to the specified 5.00. This

happens with σ = .187. Using the implied volatility module of **OPTION!**, we
find that the exact standard deviation is .186800.[12]

Standard Deviation	Corresponding Call Price	
.1	$ 3.41	too low
.5	11.03	too high
.3	7.16	too high
.2	5.24	too high
.15	4.31	too low
.175	4.78	too low
.18	4.87	too low
.185	4.97	too low
.19	5.06	too high
.188	5.02	too high
.187	5.00	success

Sensitivity of the Black-Scholes Model

We have seen that the Black-Scholes Model expresses the value of a call as a
function of five factors: the stock price, the exercise price, the time until
expiration, the risk-free rate, and the volatility of the stock. Also, we have just
seen that $N(d_1)$ shows how the call price changes for a change in the stock price.
In this section, we explore the sensitivity of call prices to the five parameters in
the Black-Scholes Model.

Sensitivity of Call Prices to the Stock Price—The Delta

Figure 4.8 graphs the relationship between the call price and the stock price. In
this graph, we hold the other factors constant. Specifically, we assume that the
exercise price is $100, the risk-free rate is .06, the option expires in one year,
and the standard deviation of the stock returns is .1. The curved line shows the
value of the call for various stock prices. When the stock price is $100, we know
that the call price is $7.46, for example.

The slope of the curved line in Figure 4.8 shows the sensitivity of the call's
price to a change in the stock price. In fact, the slope of the line at any point
equals the call's delta, $N(d_1)$. The delta is positive through the whole line—an
increasing stock price always gives an increasing call price. However, when the
stock price is low relative to the exercise price, the curved line is very flat. This
shows that the call price is not very responsive to stock price changes if the call

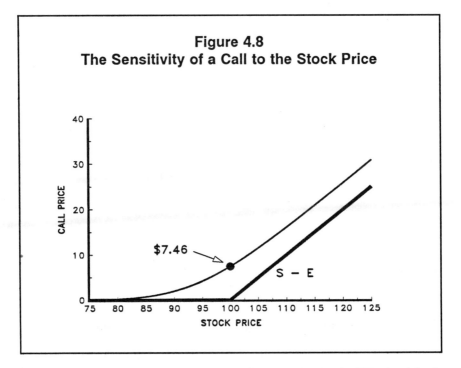

Figure 4.8
The Sensitivity of a Call to the Stock Price

is way out-of-the-money. For example, if the stock price is $50, the delta is only .0569. If the stock price increases by $1, the call price increases by less than $.06. For very large stock prices, however, the call price varies almost one-to-one with the stock price. For example, if the stock price is $120, the delta is .9933. An increase in the stock price of $1 gives an increase in the call price of $.9933. Thus, if the option is extremely far out-of-the-money, the delta will be near zero. For an option extremely far into-the-money, the delta approaches one.

What does it mean for the delta to be near one? We can address this issue by thinking about $N(d_1)$. The largest value that delta could possibly take is 1.0. That happens when the computed value of d_1 is so large that all other values fall to the left of it on the normal curve. If d_1 is 6.0, for example, $N(d_1)$ will be very close to 1.0. By examining d_1, we can see the factors that make it large. The larger the value of the stock price relative to the exercise price, the larger d_1 will be. We have already seen this from Figure 4.8. Deep in-the-money options have large deltas. Larger values for the interest rate and the standard deviation are also associated with larger values for d_1.[13]

The Sensitivity of Call Prices to Time Until Expiration

Options with a longer time remaining until expiration have higher values than those near expiration. Figure 4.9 compares options that are the same, except for time until expiration. For Figure 4.9, we consider call options with exercise prices of $100 on a stock with a standard deviation of .10. We assume interest rates are 6 percent, and we analyze options with six months, one year, and two years until expiration. Assuming the stock price is $100, a call option with one year until expiration will be worth $7.46. If the time until expiration is only six months, the option would trade for $4.51. If the option has two years until expiration, it would trade for $14.15.

In Figure 4.9, the less time remaining until expiration, the greater the curvature in the price lines. This makes sense because we know exactly what the price line for the call must look like when there is no time until expiration. When t=0, the call's value equals the maximum of zero, or the stock price minus the exercise price. Therefore, as the call approaches expiration, the price graph must bend more toward the point at which the stock price equals the exercise price.

Because options are worth more the longer the time until expiration, we expect the price of an option to fall over its life, if other factors are constant.

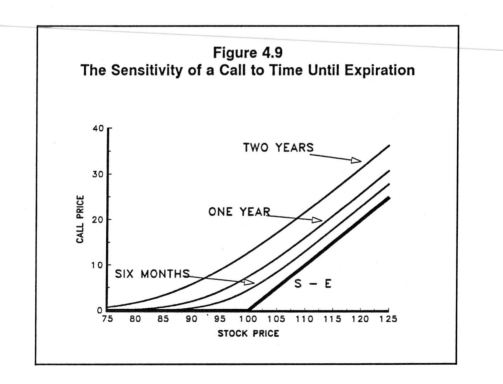

**Figure 4.9
The Sensitivity of a Call to Time Until Expiration**

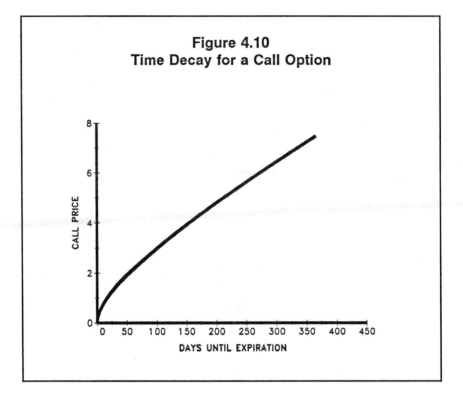

Figure 4.10
Time Decay for a Call Option

The tendency of option prices to fall due to approaching expiration is called **time decay**. For example, consider again our favorite option on a stock trading for $100 with an exercise price of $100, one year remaining until expiration, with interest rates at 6 percent, and the stock having a standard deviation of .1. This call is worth $7.46. If nothing else changes, except time passes, the call will be worth only $4.51 when it has six months until expiration. With three months to live, the option is worth $2.81. When the option has 30 days until expiration, the option is worth $1.40. If we buy our example call with one year until expiration, we will suffer time decay over the year unless some other factor affecting the value of the option changes. In this sense, an option is a wasting asset. Figure 4.10 graphs the fall in value as a call option approaches expiration. Assuming a stock and exercise price of $100, an interest rate of 6 percent, and a standard deviation of .1, the graph shows the option's values for the last year of its life.

The Sensitivity of Call Prices to the Interest Rate

Interest rates enter the Black-Scholes Model in the d_1 and d_2 terms and in the discount factor for the exercise price. Higher interest rates increase option values through all three channels. For our example option, the exercise price is $100, the standard deviation equals .1, one year remains until expiration, and the stock trades for $100. With interest rates at 6 percent, this call trades for $7.46. If interest rates were 4 percent, the call would be worth only $6.17. A rise in interest rates to 8 percent would drive the call price up to $8.84. Figure 4.11 graphs the call price for each interest rate. As the graph shows, the price is not very sensitive to changes in interest rates.

The Sensitivity of Call Prices to the Standard Deviation

A call option on a riskier stock is worth more than a similar option on a stock with lower risk. If the risk of the stock is very low, the call option is priced near the intrinsic value of the option. If the stock is riskless, then the option price equals the stock price minus the present value of the exercise price. Options on low risk stocks tend to have deltas very near one for options well into the money. Similarly, for out-of-the-money calls, the delta tends to be much lower. For options on high risk stocks, the delta is consistently high. This makes sense because, with enough risk, an out-of-the-money option can come into the money or an in-the-money option can go out-of-the-money.

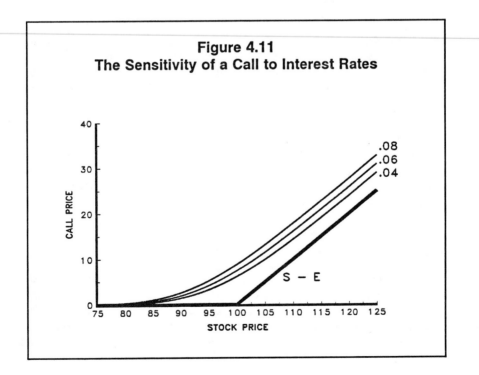

Figure 4.11
The Sensitivity of a Call to Interest Rates

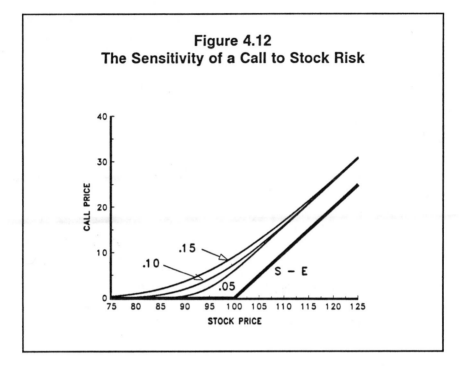

Figure 4.12
The Sensitivity of a Call to Stock Risk

Figure 4.12 graphs our standard option with an exercise price of $100, one year remaining until expiration, a 6 percent interest rate, and a standard deviation of .1. It also graphs similar calls with standard deviations of .05 and .15. As the graph shows, differences in risk affect price more strongly when options are near the money. For stock prices that put the options well into the money, the price differences almost disappear. For example, if the stock price is $120, the three call prices are $25.82, $25.85, and $26.18 for the low, medium, and high standard deviation stocks. This entire price range is less than 1.5 percent of the value of the cheapest option. By contrast, if the stock price is $95, the three prices are $2.33, $4.20, and $6.08. The most expensive costs 2.6 times as much as the cheapest.

The Sensitivity of Call Prices to the Exercise Price

Unlike the other parameters in the option pricing model, the exercise price remains fixed for a given option. However, several different exercise prices are usually available for options on a given stock. Figure 4.13 graphs prices for calls that are alike except for the exercise price. For each call, the time until expiration is one year, the standard deviation of the underlying stock is .1, and the risk-free

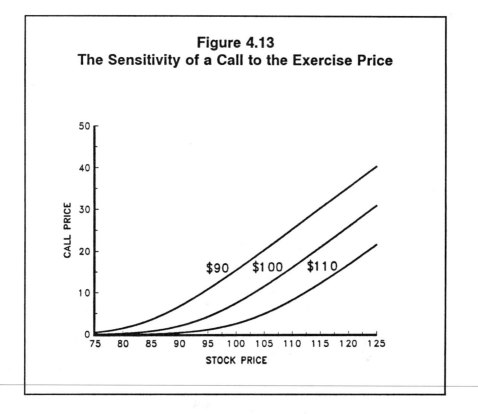

Figure 4.13
The Sensitivity of a Call to the Exercise Price

interest rate is 6 percent. The figure graphs the prices of calls with exercise prices of $90, $100, and $110.

In Chapter 2 we considered bounds on calls with different exercise prices. There we showed that the price difference between two similar calls cannot exceed the present value of the difference in exercise prices. For example, the call with an exercise price of $100 is worth $7.46. With the arbitrage restriction, the call with an exercise price of $90 cannot sell for more than $7.46 + $10 $e^{-.06(1)}$ = $16.88. In fact, with the stock price at $100, the call with an exercise price of $90 sells for $15.43.

Tests of the Option Pricing Model

If the Black–Scholes Option Pricing Model correctly captures the factors that affect option prices, the price computed according to the model should correspond closely to the price observed in the market. Otherwise, either the model is inadequate or prices in the market are irrational. Therefore, each of the tests that we will consider in this section test a joint hypothesis—adequacy of the option pricing model and market rationality. If we find a discrepancy between the two, we can account for this divergence by claiming that the model is inadequate or by allowing that market participants are foolish. Note, however, that the Black–Scholes Model was derived under the assumption that prices should not permit arbitrage. Accordingly, any major discrepancy between the model price and the market price would be serious indeed.

The Black–Scholes Study

The first empirical study of option pricing was conducted by Black and Scholes.[14] In this 1972 test, they examined over-the-counter option prices, because listed options did not yet trade. Black and Scholes computed a theoretical option price based on their model. If the market price exceeded their theoretical price, they assumed that they sold the option. Similarly, if the market price was below the price they computed, they assumed that they bought the option. In both cases, they assumed that they held a stock position in conjunction with the option that gave a riskless position. (In other words, if they were long the call option, they would hold $-N(d_1)$ shares of stock as well.) This risk-free position should earn the risk-free rate if option prices in the market and their model are identical. They maintained this position until expiration, adjusting the portfolio as needed to maintain its riskless character. Their results showed significant profit opportunities. In other words, actual market prices differed significantly from the theoretical price given by the model. However, this difference was statistically significant, but not economically important. When Black and Scholes considered transaction costs, they found that the costs of trading would erode any potential profit. Therefore, option traders could not follow their strategy and make a profit. This result helped to show the strong correspondence between market prices and option prices computed from theoretical models, such as the Black-Scholes model.

The Galai Studies

As in the Black-Scholes study, Galai created hedged portfolios of options and stock and used these portfolios to study the correspondence between the Black-Scholes Model price and actual market prices for options.[15] In contrast to the Black-Scholes study, Galai used listed option data from the Chicago Board Options Exchange. With options trading on an exchange, Galai had access to daily price quotations. Therefore, he was able to compute the rate of return on the hedged option-stock portfolio for each option for each day. He also adjusted the hedge ratio each day to maintain the neutral hedge—neutral in the sense that a change in the stock price would not change the overall value of the combined option-stock position. Comparing market prices to Black–Scholes Model prices, Galai assumed that he sold overpriced options and bought underpriced options each day.

Galai's results showed that this strategy could earn excess returns. In other words, his initial results seemed to be inconsistent with an efficient market. However, this apparent result disappeared when Galai considered transaction costs. If transaction costs were only 1 percent, the apparent excess returns disappeared. Most traders outside the market face transaction costs of 1 percent or higher. However, market makers can transact for less than 1 percent transaction costs. This suggests that market makers could have followed Galai's strategy to earn excess returns. Yet even market makers face some additional transaction costs implied by their career choice. For instance, the market maker must buy or lease a seat on the exchange and the market maker must forego alternative employment. When Galai brought these additional implicit transaction costs into the analysis, the market maker's apparent excess returns diminished or disappeared. At any rate, Galai's results showed that Black–Scholes Model prices closely match actual market prices for options.

The Bhattacharya Study

Mihir Bhattacharya used an approach like the Black–Scholes and Galai studies to analyze the correspondence between actual market prices and theoretical prices.[16] Bhattacharya discussed the adherence of market prices to theoretical boundaries implied by no-arbitrage conditions. We focus on one of his three boundaries. As we discussed in Chapter 3, a call option should be worth more than its exercise value if time remains until expiration. Bhattacharya compiled a sample of 86,000 transactions and examined them to determine if immediate exercise was profitable. He found 1100 such exercise opportunities, meaning that the stock price exceeded the exercise price plus the call price. As we argued in Chapter 3, such a price relationship should not exist. However, these exercise opportunities assumed that the exercise could be conducted without transaction costs. When Bhattacharya considered transaction costs, these apparently profitable exercise opportunities disappeared. The apparent violation of the boundary condition was observed only because transaction costs were not considered. This means that traders could not exploit the deviation from the boundary condition to make a profit.

The Macbeth–Merville Study

James MacBeth and Larry Merville used the Black–Scholes Model to compute implied standard deviations for the underlying stocks.[17] They assumed that the

Black–Scholes Model correctly prices at-the-money options with at least 90 days until expiration correctly. Based on these assumptions and the estimated standard deviation, they evaluated how well the Black–Scholes Model prices options that are in-the-money or out-of-the-money and how well the model prices options that have fewer than 90 days until expiration. They found some systematic discrepancies between market prices and Black–Scholes Model prices. First, the Black–Scholes prices tended to be less than market prices for in-the-money options and the Black–Scholes prices tended to be higher than market prices for out-of-the-money options. Second, this first effect is larger the farther the options are from the money. However, it is smaller the shorter the time until expiration. Therefore, we expect to find the greatest discrepancy between market prices and the Black–Scholes Model price for options with a long time until expiration and options that are way in- or way out-of-the-money.

The Rubinstein Study

Mark Rubinstein compared market prices with theoretical option prices from the Black–Scholes Model and other models of option prices.[18] Some other models out-performed the Black–Scholes Model in some respects, yet none did so consistently. Further, Rubinstein confirmed some of the biases noted by MacBeth and Merville for the Black–Scholes Model. However, none of the other models was consistently free of bias either. In general, Rubinstein was unable to conclude that there was a single model superior to the others.

Summary

Testing of the option pricing model is far from complete. Recently, attention has turned to the information inherent in option prices that might not be reflected in stock prices or that might be reflected first in option prices and later in stock prices. For example, Joseph Anthony finds that trading volume in call options leads trading volume in the underlying stock by one day.[19] While this lead–lag relationship does not necessarily imply any inefficiency in either market, it does seem to suggest that information that reaches the market affects options first.[20] In recent years the proliferation of many new kinds of options has attracted attention away from options on individual stocks. The kinds of studies on options on individual stocks that were conducted by Black and Scholes, Galai, Bhattacharya, and Rubinstein have recently been conducted for these new kinds of options. (We mention some of these very briefly in Chapter 5.) In large part, these new results corroborate the earlier results that were found for options on individual stocks. In this section, it has been possible to discuss only some of the most famous studies. There are many other worthwhile studies that have been conducted and many more still that remain to be conducted.

Summary

We began this chapter by developing the binomial model. We showed that the Single–Period Binomial Model emerges directly from no–arbitrage conditions that govern all asset prices. We extended the single–period model to the Multi–Period Binomial Model. With this model, we found that we could apply our no–arbitrage principles to value options with numerous periods remaining until expiration. Throughout this development, we considered price movements that were somewhat arbitrary.

Researchers have studied the actual price movements of stocks in great detail. We found that logarithmic stock returns are distributed approximately normally and that this model of stock price movements has proven to be very useful as a working approximation of stock price behavior. Using this model of stock price behavior, a binomial model with many periods until expiration approaches the Black-Scholes Model. The Black-Scholes Model gives an elegant equation for pricing a call option as a function of five variables: the stock price, the exercise price, the risk-free rate, the time until expiration, and the standard deviation of the stock. Only two of these variables, the interest rate and the standard deviation, are not immediately observable. We showed how to estimate these two parameters.

We also considered the sensitivity of option prices to changing values for the parameters. For example, we considered how the price of a call option responds to a changing stock price. For each variable in the Black-Scholes Model, we analyzed the call's sensitivity and presented graphs showing how the option price differs for different input values.

OPTION! is a useful tool for analyzing the concepts we developed in this chapter. A module for the binomial model allows the user to specify one or many periods for analysis. In this module, the user specifies the up and down percentage factors. A separate module uses up and down factors that are consistent with the Black-Scholes Model. With this module, we can study the convergence of the binomial price to the Black-Scholes price. Another module of OPTION! allows us to compute Black-Scholes call and put values. A separate module finds the implied volatility of the stock based on the Black-Scholes Model. Another module computes values of the cumulative normal distribution for input values of d_1 or d_2. Finally, OPTION! also includes a module to generate random price paths consistent with initial values that the user specifies.

Questions and Problems

1. What is binomial about the Binomial Model? In other words, how does the Model get its name?

2. If a stock price moves in a manner consistent with the Binomial Model, what is the chance that the stock price will be the same for two periods in a row? Explain.

3. Assume a stock price is $120 and in the next year it will either rise by 10 percent or fall by 20 percent. The risk-free interest rate is 6 percent. A call option on this stock has an exercise price of $130. What is the price of a call option that expires in one year? What is the chance that the stock price will rise?

4. Based on the data in question 3, what would you hold to form a risk-free portfolio?

5. Based on the data in question 3, what will the price of the call option be if the option expires in two years and the stock price can move up 10 percent or down 20 percent in each year?

6. Based on the data in question 3, what would the price of a call with one year to expiration be if the call has an exercise price of $135? Can you answer this question without making the full calculations? Explain.

7. A stock is worth $60 dollars today. In a year, the stock price can rise or fall by 15 percent. If the interest rate is 6 percent, what is the price of a call option that expires in three years and has an exercise price of $70? What is the price of a put option that expires in three years and has an exercise price of $65? (Use **OPTION!** to solve this problem.)

8. Consider our model of stock price movements given in equation 4.4. A stock has an initial price of $55 and an expected growth rate of .15 per year. The annualized standard deviation of the stock's return is .4. What is the expected stock price after 175 days?

9. A stock sells for $110. A call option on the stock has an exercise price of $105 and expires in 43 days. If the interest rate is .11 and the standard deviation of the stock's returns is .25, what is the price of the call according to the Black–Scholes Model? What would be the price of a put with an exercise price of $140 and the same time until expiration?

10. For the call option in problem 9, what is the hedge ratio?

11. Use the option in problem 9 and the hedge ratio found in problem 10 to form a riskless hedge. Now assume that the stock price jumps to $115 and that 43 days still remain until expiration. How does the value of the hedge portfolio change? Why isn't the hedge completely risk-free?

12. Consider a Treasury-bill with 173 days until maturity. The bid and asked yields on the bill are 9.43 and 9.37. What is the price of the T-bill? What is the continuously compounded rate on the bill?

13. Consider the following sequence of daily stock prices: $47, $49, $46, $45, $51. Compute the mean daily logarithmic return for this share. What is the daily standard deviation of returns? What is the annualized standard deviation?

14. A stock sells for $85. A call option with an exercise price of $80 expires in 53 days and sells for $8. The risk-free interest rate is 11 percent. What is the implied standard deviation for the stock? (Use **OPTION!** to solve this problem.)

Notes

1. A risk-neutral investor considers only the expected payoffs from an investment. For such an investor, the risk associated with the investment is not important. Thus, a risk-neutral investor would be indifferent between an investment with a certain payoff of $50 or an investment with a 50 percent probability of paying $100 and a 50 percent probability of paying zero.

2. The development of the binomial model stems from two seminal articles: R. Rendleman and B. Bartter, "Two-State Option Pricing," *Journal of Finance*, 34, December 1979, 1093-1110 and J. Cox, S. Ross, and M. Rubinstein, "Option Pricing: A Simplified Approach," *Journal of Financial Economics*, 7, September 1979, 229-263. J. Cox and M. Rubinstein develop and discuss the binomial model in their book *Option Pricing*, Prentice-Hall, 1973 and their paper "A Survey of Alternative Option Pricing Models," which appears in *Option Pricing*, edited by M. Brenner, Lexington: D. C. Heath, 1983, 3-33.

3. Not every one of these stock price outcomes will be unique. Even in the two-period model we saw that UDS = DUS. Strictly speaking, with 20 periods, there are more than 1 million stock price paths.

4. To this point, we have considered the Binomial Model in some detail and we have considered the log–normal model of stock prices. In essence, each different assumption about stock price movements leads to a different class of option pricing models. For instance, we have already observed that assuming stock prices can either rise or fall by a given amount in a period leads to the Binomial Model. The log–normal assumption that we have just been considering assumes that the stock price path is continuous. In other words, for the stock price to go from $100 to $110, the price must pass through every value between the two. Another entire class of assumption about stock price movements assumes that the stock price follows a jump process—the stock price jumps from one price to another without taking on each of the intervening values. A quick test to distinguish these two models is to determine whether the stock price path can be drawn without lifting pen from paper. If so, then the stock price path is continuous. The following papers analyze option pricing under alternative assumptions about stock price movements: John Cox and Stephen Ross, "The Valuation of Options for Alternative Stochastic Processes," *Journal of Financial Economics*, 3, January–March 1976, 145–166; Robert Merton "Option Pricing when Underlying Stock Returns are Discontinuous," *Journal of Financial Economics*, 3, January–March 1976, 125–144; Frank Page and Anthony Saunders, "A General Derivation of the Jump Process Option Pricing Formula," *Journal of Financial and Quantitative Analysis*, 21:4, December 1986, 437–446; Clifford Ball and Walter Torous, "On Jumps in Common Stock Prices and Their Impact on Call Option Pricing," *Journal of Finance*, 40:1, March 1985, 155–173; and Edward Omberg, "Efficient Discrete Time Jump Process Models in Option Pricing," *Journal of Financial and Quantitative Analysis*, 23:2, June 1988, 161–174.

5. Fischer Black and Myron Scholes, "The Pricing of Options and Corporate Liabilities," *Journal of Political Economy*, May 1973, 637–659 provides the classic statement of the model. In his paper, "Fact and Fantasy in the Use of Options," *Financial Analysts Journal*, 1975, May/June, 31:4, pp. 36–41 and 61–72, Fischer Black develops many of the same ideas in a more intuitive manner. More recently, Fischer Black has told the story of how Myron Scholes and he discovered the option pricing formula. See Fischer Black, "How We Came Up With the Option Formula," *Journal of Portfolio Management*, Winter 1989, 4–8.

6. In imperfect markets, there may not be a single interest rate, but traders may face a borrowing rate and a lending rate. John Gilster and William Lee consider this possibility in their paper, "The Effects of Transaction Costs and Different Borrowing and Lending Rates on the Option Pricing Model: A Note," *Journal of Finance*, 39:4, September 1984, 1215-1221. They also consider transaction costs and show that considering both imperfections in the debt market and transaction costs results in two offsetting influences. As such, they conclude, neither has a strong effect on the estimation of the option price and Black-Scholes option prices conform well to actual prices observed in the market. Thus, neither market imperfection is too important because the two imperfections tend to cancel each other.

7. Of course, it is possible that the stock volatility could change over the life of the option. But shifting volatilities present difficulties in finding an option pricing model. John Hull and Alan White, "The Pricing of Options on Assets with Stochastic Volatilities," *Journal of Finance*, 42:2, June 1987, 281-300, address this issue. While Hull and White acknowledge that no formula for an option price assuming changing volatility has been found, they develop techniques for approximating the value of an option with changing volatility. In doing so, they assume that changes in volatility are correlated with changes in the stock price. This problem has also been studied by Louis Scott, "Option Pricing when the Variance Changes Randomly: Theory, Estimation, and an Application," *Journal of Financial and Quantitative Analysis*, 22:4, December 1987, 419-438. Scott uses simulation techniques to approximate option prices, but concedes that no formula for an option price under shifting volatilities has been found. Finally, James Wiggins explores this problem as well in his paper, "Option Values Under Stochastic Volatility: Theory and Empirical Estimates," *Journal of Financial Economics*, 19:2, December 1987, 351-372. He also acknowledges that an actual formula for the price of an option under shifting volatilities is lacking. Wiggins applies a numerical estimation technique to develop estimates of option prices assuming that volatility follows a continuous process. Under this assumption, Wiggins is able to compute estimated option prices.

8. There is a third potentially useful method that we do not consider in this book. Michael Parkinson, "The Random Walk Problem: Extreme Value Method for Estimating the Variance of the Displacement," *Journal of Business*, 53, January 1980, 61-65, showed that focusing on high and low prices for a few days could give as good an estimate as using historical data for five times as many days. His model assumes that stock prices are distributed log-normally. Compared with the use of historical data on the closing price for a given day, Parkinson's method uses both the high and

low prices for the day. This method would allow a good estimate from more recent historical data than simply focusing on the history of closing prices. Mark Garman and Michael Klass, "On the Estimation of Security Price Volatilities from Historical Data," *Journal of Business*, 53:1, 1980, 67-78 pointed out some difficulties with Parkinson's approach. First, his method is very sensitive to any errors in the reported high and low prices. Further, if trading during the day is sporadic, Parkinson's method will generate biased estimates of volatility. In particular, with discontinuities in the trading, the reported high will almost certainly be lower than the high that would have been observed with continuous trading. Similarly, the reported low will be higher than the value that would have been achieved under continuous trading. Garman and Klass also show how to improve Parkinson's type of estimate.

9.   Similarly, assume that we estimate the standard deviation with weekly data. We would convert this raw data to annualized data by multiplying the weekly standard deviation times the square root of 52. Similarly, if we begin with monthly data, we annualize our monthly standard deviation by multiplying it times the square root of 12.

10.   In principle, we can take any five of the values as given and solve for the sixth. For example, Menachem Brenner and Dan Galai, "Implied Interest Rates," *Journal of Business*, 59, July 1986, 493-507, find that interest rates implied in the options market correspond to other short-term rates of interest. These implied rates are nearer to the borrowing rate than to the lending rate. Further, in situations where early exercise is imminent, the interest rates implied in the option markets can differ widely from short-term rates on other instruments. Steve Swidler takes this approach a step further in his paper, "Simultaneous Option Prices and an Implied Risk-Free Rate of Interest: A Test of the Black-Scholes Model," *Journal of Economics and Business*, 38:2, May 1986, 155-164. Swidler uses two options, which allow him to estimate two parameters simultaneously—two equations in two unknowns. Swidler estimates the implied interest and the implied standard deviation. While the standard deviation can differ from stock to stock, there should be a common interest rate for all options on a given date. For most of the stocks he examines, Swidler finds that a single interest rate can be found. Accordingly, he regards his evidence as supporting the reasonableness of the Black-Scholes Model.

11.   For a discussion of these weighting techniques, see Henry A. Latane and Richard J. Rendleman, Jr., "Standard Deviations of Stock Price Ratios Implied in Option Prices," *Journal of Finance* 31, 1976, 369-382; Donald P. Chiras and Steven Manaster, "The Information Content of Option Prices

and a Test of Market Efficiency, *Journal of Financial Economics*, 6, 1978, 213-234; and Robert E. Whaley, "Valuation of American Call Options on Dividend Paying Stocks: Empirical Tests," *Journal of Financial Economics*, 10, 1982, 29-58. In his paper, Stan Beckers, "Standard Deviations Implied in Option Prices as Predictors of Future Stock Price Variability," *Journal of Banking and Finance*, 5, 1981, 363-382, concludes that using the option with the highest sensitivity to the standard deviation provides the best estimate of future volatility.

12. **OPTION!** searches for the correct standard deviation in a way similar to the sequence of standard deviations and prices shown here. However, it uses a somewhat more sophisticated procedure for choosing the next standard deviation to try.

13. In the equation for d_1, the time until expiration and the standard deviation both appear in the numerator and denominator. However, an increase in the value of either contributes more to the numerator than to the denominator. Therefore, increasing time until expiration or increasing standard deviation both make d_1 bigger and make the option more valuable.

14. Fischer Black and Myron Scholes, "The Valuation of Option Contracts and a Test of Market Efficiency," *Journal of Finance*, 27:2, 1972, 399-417.

15. Dan Galai, "Tests of Market Efficiency of the Chicago Board Options Exchange," *Journal of Business*, 50:2, April 1977, 167-97 and "Empirical Tests of Boundary Conditions for CBOE Options," *Journal of Financial Economics*, 6:2/3, June–September 1978, 182-211.

16. Mihir Bhattacharya, "Transaction Data Tests on the Efficiency of the Chicago Board Options Exchange," *Journal of Financial Economics*, 12:2, 1983, 161-185.

17. James D. MacBeth and Larry J. Merville, "An Empirical Examination of the Black–Scholes Call Option Pricing Model," *Journal of Finance*, 34:5, 1979, 1173-1186.

18. Mark Rubinstein, "Nonparametric Tests of Alternative Option Pricing Models Using All Reported Trades and Quotes on the 30 Most Active CBOE Option Classes from August 23, 1976 Through August 31, 1978," *Journal of Finance*, 40:2, 1985, 455-480. The other models tested were extensions of the Black–Scholes Model based on changing assumptions about how stock prices move. For instance, they included option models

based on the assumption that stock prices jump from one price to another, rather than moving continuously through all intervening prices as the stock price moves from one price to another. Rubinstein tested the following models: the Black–Scholes Model, the jump model, the mixed diffusion-jump model, the constant elasticity of variance model and the displaced diffusion model.

19. Joseph H. Anthony, "The Interrelation of Stock and Options Market Trading-Volume Data," *Journal of Finance*, 43:4, September 1988, 949-964.

20. Option prices may react before stock prices due to the trading preferences of informed traders. We have already seen that option markets often offer lower transaction costs that the market for the underlying good. For traders with good information, the options market may be the preferred market to exploit their information. On this scenario, we would expect to see option prices and volume change before stock prices and volume. The trading of the informed traders would move option prices, and the arbitrage linkages between options and stocks would lead to an adjustment of the corresponding stock prices.

5

Applications of Option Pricing Models

Introduction

In this chapter we apply the capital developed in preceding chapters. To this point, we have restricted our attention to European options. However, most options that trade are actually American options—they can be exercised any time before expiration. Options also trade on other instruments besides stock. This chapter considers the special issues that arise for options on foreign currencies and options on futures contracts. In addition, principles of option pricing apply to other financial instruments and to corporate decisions. As this chapter shows, the option pricing framework we have developed is incredibly rich and diversified.

We begin this chapter by considering the pricing differences between American and European options. Focusing on European options has been convenient because it avoids the general problem of early exercise. Under some circumstances, it can be optimal to exercise a call or put before expiration. We want to understand when a trader should exercise early, and we want to know the effect the chance for early exercise has on the price of an option.

Considering early exercise will lead us into a discussion of options on other instruments. Two important classes of instruments with options are foreign currencies and futures. For both of these, early exercise is potentially important. We extend the pricing principles that we have already developed to understand these other types of options.

The development of option pricing has led to a deeper understanding of some old financial instruments, such as stocks and bonds. For example, this chapter shows how a share of common stock resembles a call option on the firm. Like stock, bonds often have options imbedded within them. We show why risky corporate debt resembles a combination of a risk-free bond and a short position in a put option. By considering some key applications of option concepts to stocks, bonds, and corporate decision making, we point the way to even further extensions of the option pricing mode of thought.

European versus American Options

Because a European option can only be exercised at expiration, we have not needed to consider early exercise. Most options that trade in actual markets are American options that permit early exercise. Compared to European options, the early exercise feature of American options creates some special complications. In this section, we consider calls and puts separately to determine the effects of early exercise. The most important effect of the right to exercise an American option before expiration is that American and European option prices may differ. This section also explores the source of those pricing differences and analyzes the conditions under which a price differential will arise.

European and American Calls

Typically, early exercise is unwise for a call option. However, certain circumstances can arise that justify early exercise. We begin by showing that early exercise of a call on a non-dividend paying stock is a mistake. If we exercise a call, we receive the intrinsic value of the call S - E. However, we know that a call must meet the following condition to avoid arbitrage:

$$C \geq S - Ee^{-rt}$$

If a trader exercises a call early, he receives only the intrinsic value, S - E. However, the call value will always exceed the intrinsic value if time remains until expiration and the interest rate is not zero. We assume throughout that the interest rate is positive. Therefore, for an in-the-money option with time remaining until expiration:

$$C \geq S - Ee^{-rt} > S - E \qquad\qquad 5.1$$

This equation shows that the price of a call will be greater than its intrinsic value if time remains until expiration. This extra value in equation 5.1 depends on the time remaining until expiration and the interest rate, because these two factors reduce the present value of the exercise price.

The inequality of 5.1 holds even without considering the Black–Scholes Model. However, we know that the excess value of the call over the stock price minus the present value of the exercise price is due to the riskiness of the underlying stock. In terms of the Black–Scholes Model, recall that:

$$d_2 = d_1 - \sigma \sqrt{t}$$

Therefore, d_1 will always exceed d_2 when time remains until expiration, when the interest rate is positive, and when the stock has any risk. As a consequence,

$N(d_1)$ exceeds $N(d_2)$ in the same conditions. Therefore, the following relationship must hold before expiration:

$$C = Sn(d_1) - Ee^{-rt}N(d_2) \geq S - Ee^{-rt} > S - E$$

This relationship holds for a call on any no-dividend stock before the call expires. It says that the call value will equal or exceed its intrinsic value any time the call has time remaining until expiration. Also, when the stock is risky and time remains until expiration, the Black-Scholes Model shows that the call price will have extra value. If a trader exercises a call before expiration, he discards the extra value that the call has from its time value and the risk of the stock. Exercising gives the trader only S - E, so he loses all other value. Therefore, when the stock is risky and time remains until expiration, the inequalities in the preceding expression are strict inequalities.

We illustrate this principle with the following example. Consider the following values.

S = 115
E = 100
r = .10
t = 3 months
σ = .3

The Black-Scholes call price for this option is $18.55. If a trader exercises the call, he receives only the intrinsic value of $15. Clearly, early exercise is a mistake. The trader will have more money if he sells the call and captures the excess value over the intrinsic value. Therefore, on a non-dividend paying stock, early exercise is always a mistake.

> **For an American call option on a dividend paying stock, early exercise can be rational, but only immediately before an ex–dividend date.**

We now consider how dividends can justify the early exercise of a call. Assume that the stock underlying our example option pays a dividend and the stock is about to go ex-dividend with a $5 dividend.[1] When the stock pays its $5 dividend, the stock price will drop by the amount of the dividend.[2] After the stock goes ex-dividend, S = $110, and the Black-Scholes call value is $14.32.

Typically, dividend payments are known well in advance, so the owner of a call must decide whether to exercise before the ex-dividend date or to let the stock go ex-dividend without exercising. If the owner does not exercise, he still holds the call, which will be worth $14.32 after the stock goes ex-dividend. On the other hand, the call owner could exercise and transact as follows:

Transaction	Cash Flow
Exercise call	-$100
Receive dividend	+$5
Receive stock worth $110 after dividend	+$110
Net Cash Flow	+$15

If he exercises, the call owner has $15. If he does not exercise, he only has the call worth $14.32. Therefore, the call owner should exercise.

Exercising is not always the correct strategy, however. With a standard deviation for the stock of .4, the call is worth $19.89 before the stock goes ex-dividend. When the stock goes ex-dividend, the call drops from $19.89 to $15.93. In this case, the trader should not exercise. Exercising yields a total of $15, but not exercising leaves the trader holding a call worth $15.93. Exercising in this situation throws away $.93.

In our example, a standard deviation of .344 makes the trader indifferent about exercising. With this volatility, the unexercised option is worth $15 after the stock goes ex-dividend. If the stock's volatility exceeds .344, the trader should not exercise. With any lower volatility, the trader should exercise the call. Generally, early exercise of a call is more attractive when the underlying stock is low risk, when the dividend is large, or when little time remains until expiration.

The Value of Calls on Dividend Paying Stocks

Valuing call options on dividend paying stocks is difficult, because the payment of dividends affects the value of the underlying stock. However, different approximation methods exist to simplify the process. In this section, we consider three different methods. First, we assume that the dividend payment date and amount are known in advance. We show that we can approximate the value of the American call by subtracting the present value of the dividend from the stock price and applying the Black–Scholes Model to this adjusted stock price. Second, we consider a more sophisticated method that includes the first technique and adds more refinements for a better estimate. Third, we treat the dividend as being paid continuously. That is, we ignore the date of the dividend and assume that the stock pays out its dividend continuously. All three techniques provide useful adjustments to the Black–Scholes Model.

Approximate Call Values with Known Dividends

In this section we show one way to adjust the Black–Scholes Model to account for known dividends. With this technique, we can apply a slightly adjusted Black–Scholes Model to value American call options even when early exercise is feasible.

In the last section we saw that it is sometimes wise to exercise an American option just before the stock goes ex-dividend. For our example of early exercise, a trader exercises to capture the $5 dividend and receive a total payoff of $15. Because exercising the American option gives an immediate payoff of $15 and because exercise is optimal, the American option must be worth $15. For the European option, early exercise is prohibited. However, we know that the stock price will drop from $115 to $110 after the stock goes ex-dividend with the $5 dividend. To value the option right after the ex-dividend date, we subtracted the dividend from the stock price and applied the Black–Scholes Model with the adjusted stock price. This gave an option value of $14.32.

> To apply the Black–Scholes Model to an option on a stock with known dividends, adjust the stock price by subtracting the present value of the dividends to be paid before the option expires. Use the adjusted stock price to compute the Black–Scholes price in the normal way.

Now we extend this approach to value a call before the ex-dividend date. Instead of adjusting the stock price by subtracting the full dividend, we now subtract the present value of the dividend from the stock price and apply the Black–Scholes Model in the usual way. This is exactly the adjustment to the Black–Scholes Model to account for known dividends: Subtract the present value of the dividend from the stock price, and compute the Black–Scholes Model price as usual. In our early exercise example, the stock was at the ex-dividend date, so the present value of the dividend was the dividend itself. Before the ex-dividend date, we need to consider the discounted value of the dividend. Subtracting the present value of the dividend from the stock price also reduces the values of d_1 and d_2. Thus, in our example we had the following three call values:

American call value with early exercise optimal	$15.00
European call value ignoring the dividend problem	18.55
European call value adjusted for the dividend	14.32

By subtracting the present value of the dividend and applying the Black–Scholes Model, we created a fairly decent approximation of the American call's true value. The error in our estimate is less than 5 percent. Ignoring the dividend and applying the Black–Scholes Model gave an error of 24 percent. The adequacy of this adjustment has been studied and the typical error is about 2 percent.[3] We can apply this method no matter how many dividends remain. Using the following data, we give a complete example of this technique.

$$S = \$85$$
$$E = \$80$$
$$r = .09$$
$$t = 90 \ days$$
$$\sigma = .4$$
$$D = \$2 \ to \ be \ paid \ in \ 90 \ days$$

The present value of the dividend is $De^{-rt} = \$2e^{-(.09)(90/365)} = \$1.96$. Therefore, we adjust the stock price to $\$85 - \$1.96 = \$83.04$ and apply the Black–Scholes Model. This gives an estimated American call price of $\$13.21$.

Pseudo–American Call Options

Fischer Black developed a more sophisticated technique to value American call options. It has come to be known as the **pseudo–American call**.[4] Essentially, the valuation technique requires four steps. First, from the current stock price, subtract the present value of all dividends that will be paid before the option expires. So far, this is the same procedure we followed for known dividends. Second, for each dividend date, reduce the exercise price by the present value of all dividends yet to be paid, including the dividend that is about to go ex-dividend. Third, taking each dividend date and the actual expiration date of the option as potential expiration dates, compute the value of a European call using the adjusted stock and exercise prices. Fourth, select the highest of these European call values as the estimate of the value of the American call.

Each step has a clear rationale. In the first step, we adjust the stock price to reflect its approximate value after it pays the dividends. In the second step, we effectively add back the value of dividends to be received from the stock if we exercise. This is accomplished by reducing the liability of the exercise price by the present value of the dividends we will capture if we exercise. In the third step, we evaluate different exercise decisions. If we exercise, we will do so just before a dividend payment. This will allow us to capture the dividend from the stock. Thus, in the third step we consider the payoffs from each potential exercise date. Finally, in the fourth step, we compare the different payoffs associated with each exercise strategy that we computed in the third step.

Assuming that we plan to follow the best exercise strategy, we approximate the current American call price as the highest of these computed European call prices.

As an example, consider the following data.

S = $60
E = $60
t = 180 days
r = .09
σ = .2
D_1 = $2, to be paid in 60 days
D_2 = $2, to be paid in 150 days

What is the pseudo-American call worth? We compute the present value of the dividends as:

$$D_1e^{-rt} + D_2e^{-rt} = \$2e^{-(.09)(60/365)} + \$2e^{-(.09)(150/365)} = \$3.90$$

We subtract this amount from the stock price, so we use $56.10 as our stock price in all subsequent calculations. We will use this adjusted stock price to compute call values assuming the option expires at three different times: the actual expiration date, the date of the last dividend, and the date of the first dividend. Three inputs remain constant for each computation: S = $56.10, r = .09, and σ = .2. The time until expiration will vary, and we must adjust the exercise price for different dividend amounts.

We begin with the actual expiration date. Applying the Black-Scholes Model with t = 180 days and E = $60 gives a call value of $2.57. (This is the same as our approach with known dividends.) Next, we deal with each dividend date, starting with the final dividend. The dividend is just about to be paid, so we adjust the exercise price by subtracting $2. Thus, for E = $58 and t = 150, the call value is $2.97. Next, we consider the date of the first dividend. The present value of the dividends at that time consists of the dividend that is just about to be paid, $2, plus the present value of the second dividend that will be paid in 90 days, $2e^{-(.09)(90/365)} = $1.96. Together, these dividends have a present value of $3.96, so we adjust the exercise price to $56.04. Therefore, for E = $56.04 and t = 60, the call price is $2.28.

Now we have three estimated call prices corresponding to each dividend date and the actual expiration date of the option. The estimates are $2.28 for the first dividend date, $2.97 for the second date, and $2.57 for the actual expiration date. Therefore, we take the largest value, $2.97, as the estimate of the pseudo-American call value. Notice that this answer is not the same as the known dividend adjustment. According to Whaley, the average error for this pseudo-American model is about 1.5 percent.[5]

Approximate Call Values With Continuous Dividends

We now consider a third and final dividend adjustment. In this model, we assume that the dividends on a stock are earned continuously. In other words, we ignore the typical quarterly payment pattern and assume that stocks pay dividends continuously. This adjustment leads to a slight modification of the Black–Scholes Model. As we show later in this chapter, this modified model applies to options on currencies and some other instruments with a high degree of accuracy.

> **To adjust the Black–Scholes Model for continuous dividends, subtract the percentage dividend rate from the interest rate in d₁ and d₂ and discount the stock price to the present at the continuous dividend rate.**

Essentially, the adjustment for continuous dividends treats the dividend rate as a negative interest rate. We have already seen that dividends reduce the value of a call option, because they reduce the value of the stock that underlies the option. In effect, we have a continuous leakage of value from the stock that equals the dividend rate. We let the Greek letter delta, δ, represent this rate of leakage.[6] The Black–Scholes Model with the continuous dividend adjustment is:

$$C^* = e^{-\delta t} S N(d_1) - E e^{-rt} N(d_2)$$

$$d_1^* = \frac{\ln\left(\dfrac{S}{E}\right) + \left(r - \delta + .5\sigma^2\right)t}{\sigma\sqrt{t}}$$

$$d_2^* = d_1^* - \sigma\sqrt{t}$$

To adjust the regular Black–Scholes Model, we subtract the continuous dividend rate, δ, from the regular interest rate, r, wherever r occurs. The role of this dividend rate is clearest where it is used to discount the stock price. As we have seen, we can treat the dividend as a continuous reduction in the value of the stock price.

As an example, we apply the continuous dividend adjustment to the same option we considered for the pseudo-American call. A $2 quarterly dividend on a $60 stock gives a continuous dividend rate of 13.33 percent. Our data are:

$$S\ =\ \$60$$
$$E\ =\ \$60$$
$$r\ =\ .09$$
$$\sigma\ =\ .2$$
$$t\ =\ 180\ days$$
$$\delta\ =\ .1333$$

We compute the adjusted call price, C^*, as follows:

$$d_1 = \frac{\ln\left(\frac{60}{60}\right) + [.09 - .1333 + .5\,(.2)\,(.2)]\left(\frac{180}{365}\right)}{.2\sqrt{\frac{180}{365}}}$$

$$= \frac{0 - .01149}{.14045} = -.08181$$

$$d_2 = -.08181 - .2\sqrt{\frac{180}{365}} = -.2223$$

$$N(d_1) = .4674$$

$$N(d_2) = .4120$$

$$C^* = e^{-.1333\,(.4932)}\,(60)\,(.4674) - e^{-.09\,(.4932)}\,(60)\,(.4120)$$

$$C^* = 26.26 - \$23.65 = \$2.61$$

The corresponding adjusted option price, $C^* = \$2.61$, falls in the range of our other estimates. **OPTION!** allows the direct estimation of American call values using the continuous dividend adjustment.

Summary

Only dividends can justify the early exercise of a call option. When it is attractive to exercise early, exercise of a call can reasonably occur only immediately before an ex-dividend date. We have considered three ways to deal with dividends: the known dividend adjustment, the pseudo-American call, and the continuous dividend adjustment. As we show in later sections, the continuous dividend model also applies to securities other than stocks.

American and European Puts

The rules for the rational early exercise of puts are more complicated than those for calls. Unlike calls, dividends enhance the value of a put. Dividend payments tend to reduce the value of a stock, but the stock is a potential liability for the put owner. Therefore, put holders have an incentive to delay exercise until after dividend payments. On the other hand, put holders receive a cash inflow upon exercise, just the opposite of call holders. When the exercise price is large, put holders have an incentive to exercise. From this line of reasoning, we see that early exercise of put options on non-dividend stocks can be rational. These differences justify a price difference between American and European puts.

American and European Puts with No Dividends

An American put can be more valuable than a European put, even when the stock pays no dividends. The difference in value stems from the right to exercise early that is inherent in an American style option. If the put is American, exercise yields an immediate cash flow of E - S. At the same time, the Black-Scholes Model price for a European put is:

$$P = Ee^{-rt}N(-d_2) - SN(-d_1)$$

We know that the N(.) terms reflect the riskiness of the stock, so we focus on our no-arbitrage principle:

$$P \geq Ee^{-rt} - S$$

Therefore, the put value will equal or exceed the present value of the exercise price minus the stock price. Any excess value will be associated with the riskiness of the stock. By contrast, the value of the put, if it can be exercised immediately, will be at least E - S. This intrinsic value is a minimum value, because it might still be better not to exercise. However, since exercise pays E - S, the value of an American put cannot be less than the intrinsic value. By implication, the value of a European put can be less than the intrinsic value. This happens because the holder of a European put does not have immediate access to the intrinsic value. Instead, the holder of a European put must wait until expiration to exercise and capture whatever is the intrinsic value of the put at that time.

Differences in American and European put values on no-dividend stocks will be greater when the stock price is low relative to the exercise price, when the risk of the stock is low, and when the interest rate is high. In that case, the difference between E and Ee^{-rt} can be enough to override the benefit that the riskiness of the stock provides. The exact exercise decision depends upon a

> **Early exercise of an American put can be rational even if the underlying stock pays no dividends. Early exercise of a put immediately captures the cash inflow, E – S.**

combination of these factors. In general, early exercise can only be rational when the intrinsic value of the put, E - S, exceeds the Black–Scholes put value. However, just because the intrinsic value exceeds the Black–Scholes value for a European put, exercise is not warranted. We know that exercise can never be warranted unless the intrinsic value exceeds the Black–Scholes put value.

As an example, consider the following data:

S = $100
E = $110
t = 91 days
r = .1
σ = .2

With these values, the Black–Scholes put price is $8.76. However, this is below the intrinsic value of $10. In this situation, we know that the American put must be worth at least $10, though it may be worth more. Figure 5.1 graphs the value of the European put for alternative stock price and shows that the European put value falls below the intrinsic value of $10 when the stock price is $98.39 or higher.

Unfortunately, there is no closed-form solution for the value of an American put. Early exercise of an American put is possible at any time with the right combination of low stock price, high interest rate, and low stock risk. Various numerical techniques have been developed to approximate American put values with an extremely high degree of accuracy. Unfortunately, their mathematical complexity puts them beyond the scope of this text. One of the most popular such numerical techniques employs the binomial model we have examined. In Chapter 4, we developed the Multi-Period Binomial Model to price a European put. Researchers apply a similar technique to value an American put. However, the analysis must consider the exercise decision in every period covered by the binomial model.

Dividends and Put Values

Put values depend largely on the intrinsic value of the put, E - S. Because dividends reduce the value of the stock that underlies the put, they generally

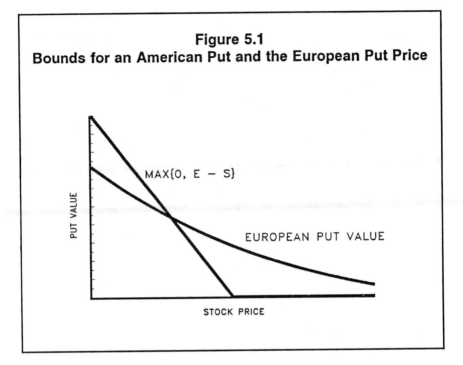

Figure 5.1
Bounds for an American Put and the European Put Price

increase put values. From the point of view of the put holder, the stock is a potential liability, so the lower its value the better. For a European put, we can take account of continuous dividends by the same method we employed for calls. For these circumstances, we have:

$$P^* = Ee^{-rt}N(-d_2) - Se^{-\delta't}N(-d_1)$$

$$d_1^* = \frac{\ln(S/E) + (r - \delta + .5\sigma^2)t}{\sigma\sqrt{t}}$$

$$d_2^* = d_1 - \sigma\sqrt{t}$$

However, we emphasize that this expression pertains to the value of a European put on a dividend-paying stock.

Dividends tend to increase American put values as well. Because most stocks pay dividends quarterly, the decision to exercise an American put is usually the decision whether to exercise immediately after a stock goes ex-dividend. The incentive to exercise an American put early is the desire for faster access to the intrinsic value E - S. However, if a dividend is about to be paid, the stock price will likely fall when the stock goes ex-dividend. The falling stock price will increase the intrinsic value of the option. Typically, across all stocks, annual dividends average about 4 percent of the stock price. Thus, we might expect a typical quarterly dividend to be about 1 percent of the stock price. In practice, this amount usually warrants postponing exercise until the stock goes ex-dividend, so exercise of American puts is most likely to occur immediately after a stock goes ex-dividend or just before the put expires.[7] The temptation to exercise an American put before expiration is greatest after the last ex-dividend date before the option expires. At this time, the American put owner has no further dividends to drive down the stock price. After this final dividend, the American put becomes a put on a non-dividend stock.

Options on Stock Indexes

In recent years, options on stock indexes have become extremely popular and controversial. These instruments are essentially like the stock options we have considered through this text, except the underlying asset is a stock index instead of a single stock. In the United States, the two most popular stock index options have the S&P 500 and the S&P 100 indexes as the underlying asset. The option value depends on the index value in just the same way that the value of a stock option depends on the underlying stock.[8]

The S&P 500 index is based on 400 industrial firms, 40 utilities, 20 transportation firms, and 40 financial institutions, most of which are listed on the New York Stock Exchange. Together, these 500 firms comprise approximately 80 percent of the total value of the stocks listed on the New York Stock Exchange. Each stock in the index has a different weight in the calculation of the index. For each stock, the weight is proportional to the total market value of the stock (the price per share times the number of shares outstanding). The value of the index is reported relative to the value during the period of 1941-1943, which was assigned an index value of 10. The index value at any time t is given by:

$$Index_t = \frac{\sum_{i-1}^{500} N_{i,t} P_{i,t}}{OV} \times 10$$

where:

OV = *original valuation 1941–43*
$N_{i,t}$ = *number of shares outstanding for firm i*
$P_{i,t}$ = *price of shares for firm i*

Because each firm receives a weighting based on its market value, the weights of each stock change as the stock price fluctuates relative to other firms represented in the index. Firms such as Exxon, AT&T, and IBM represent large shares of the index, while other firms have only a minuscule impact. The index is computed on a continuous basis throughout the trading day and reported to the public. Many portfolio owners measure the performance of their portfolio managers relative to the S&P 500. As a consequence, the S&P 500 serves as an industry standard for many purposes. The S&P 500 index excludes dividends. This naturally means that the indexes do not reflect the full appreciation that the market has enjoyed over any given period. The omission of dividends is also very important for understanding the pricing of the option as well. The S&P 100 index has a similar construction, but includes only 100 of the very largest firms.

Options on these two indexes trade on the Chicago Board Options Exchange, with options on the S&P 100 having considerably more trading interest. Options on the S&P 100 Index are American, while options on the S&P 500 index are European. For each option, the contract value is 100 times the Index value. For example, an index value of 325 implies an underlying value of $32,500 for the index. Settlement for these options is accomplished by cash payment, rather than by actual delivery. For example, if a call option is exercised, the index price must lie above the striking price. To settle, the seller of the call pays the owner of a call the difference between the index value and the striking price.[9]

> **An option on a stock index can be analyzed as an option on a dividend paying stock, where the stock index takes the role of the stock.**

As we saw for options on individual stocks, dividends create significant pricing complications for options on stock indexes. For a single stock, it is often easy to predict the amount and timing of the dividend payment. For 100 or 500 stocks, this is not so simple. On the other hand, for a single stock the dividend stream tends to be lumpy, because most firms pay dividends only quarterly. For a stock index, the dividend stream is much smoother, because different firms are on different dividend cycles.[10] The smoothness of the dividend stream suggests that we value the option using the continuous dividend model, where δ is the annual dividend rate:

$$C^* = e^{-\delta t} \, Index \, N(d_1) - E e^{-rt} N(d_2)$$

$$d_1^* = \frac{\ln(Index/E) + (r - \delta + .5\sigma^2)t}{\sigma \sqrt{t}}$$

$$d_2^* = d_1^* - \sigma \sqrt{t}$$

As an example, we consider the following data for the S&P 100 option:

Index = *320.10*
E   = *315*
t   = *43 days*
r   = *.09*
σ   = *.23*
δ   = *.04*

For these values, the call price is 13.76 and the put price is 6.84. Because the contract value is for 100 units of the index, the dollar prices of the options will be $1,376.00 and $684.00 per contract.[11]

Options on Foreign Currency

Options also trade on foreign currencies. For example, a call option on the Swiss Franc gives the owner of the option the right to purchase a certain number of Francs at a certain price in dollars for a certain period of time. Currency options trade on the Philadelphia Exchange and are offered with expirations on the March–June–September–December cycle. Options trade on the Swiss Franc, German Mark, Japanese Yen, Australian Dollar, British Pound, and Canadian Dollar. The amount of the contract differs according to currency. For example, one Swiss Franc contract is for 62,500 Francs, but the Pound contract specifies 31,250 Pounds. These differences reflect the varying value of the currencies in U.S. dollar terms. However, all of the pricing principles are the same. Therefore, we illustrate our discussion using the Swiss Franc.

A foreign currency resembles a stock that pays a continuous dividend. In this analogy for a foreign currency, the dividend rate is the risk-free rate of interest in the foreign currency. The Swiss Franc and U.S. dollar rates of interest need not be the same. Interest rate differentials between currencies are determined by a relationship known as **interest rate parity**. Essentially, the interest rate parity theorem is a no-arbitrage condition that expresses the relationship between exchange rates and interest rates.[12] For our purposes, we do not need to explore interest rate parity. It is enough to know that interest rates can differ across currencies.

An option on a foreign currency can be analyzed as an option on a stock that pays a continuous dividend, where the dollar value of the foreign currency takes the role of the stock price and the continuous dividend on the stock equals the risk–free rate on the foreign currency.

Therefore, we can price foreign currency options using our model for the price of an option on a stock that pays a continuous dividend.[13] The foreign currency takes the place of the stock. The exercise price is the dollar price that the owner of the call must pay for the currency if he exercises. The volatility measure is the standard deviation of the logarithmic changes in the currency's dollar value. Taking the role of the dividend rate, δ equals the risk-free interest rate on the foreign currency. In choosing a value for δ we need to be sure to use a rate that is risk-free and pertains to an instrument that matches the maturity of the option as closely as possible. As an example, consider the following data for an option on the Swiss Franc:

$$S = .67$$
$$E = .65$$
$$t = 56 \ days$$
$$r = .085$$
$$\sigma = .11$$
$$\delta = .06$$

For these data, we treat the Swiss Franc as a share of stock with a value of $.67. The striking price is $.65 per Franc. The option expires in 56 days, and the U.S. risk-free interest rate is 8.5 percent. The standard deviation of the Swiss Franc's dollar value is 11 percent per year, and the Swiss risk-free interest rate is 6 percent. With these values, we apply the Black–Scholes Model adjusted for continuous dividends to find the option prices. The call is worth $.0257 and the put value is $.0034. These are the prices of the option per Swiss Franc. However, a Swiss Franc contract specifies 62,500 Francs. Therefore, the dollar price of the call option contract is $1,606.25 and the put contract trades for $212.50.[14]

Options on Futures

To this point, we have considered options that are written directly on a substantial underlying good. We now consider options on futures. Futures are themselves a derivative instrument. Futures prices, like option prices, depend on the price of some other good. In a futures contract, a buyer and seller agree at the time of contracting to perform in certain ways in the future. The buyer of a futures contract agrees to pay a specific amount on a future date in exchange for the delivery of the good that underlies the futures contract. The seller promises to deliver the good in exchange for the payment. At the time of contracting, the futures buyer and seller establish a price that will be paid when the futures contract matures and the delivery takes place. While agricultural commodities were originally the good on which futures contracts were written, much has changed in the futures market since the 1970s. In 1973, futures on foreign currencies began to trade. These first financial futures were quickly followed by futures on debt instruments and futures on stock indexes.

As an example, the Chicago Board of Trade lists a wheat futures contract. The contract calls for the delivery of 5,000 bushels of wheat of a certain quality and type.[15] Assume that a trader buys a wheat futures contract in March for delivery in December of the same year at a futures price of $3.50. By buying this contract, the trader promises to accept delivery of 5,000 bushels of wheat in December and to pay $3.50 per bushel at that time.[16] Like the options market, the futures market is a zero-sum game. For the buyer to buy, there must be a seller. The seller in this example promises to deliver 5,000 bushels of wheat in December in exchange for the payment of $3.50 per bushel.

In considering a futures contract, it is critical to note that the futures price prevailing at the time of contracting determines the futures traders' profits and losses. Also, most futures contracts are not satisfied by delivery. Instead, most futures contracts are settled by an offsetting trade. For example, someone who bought a wheat futures contract at $3.50 might later sell a wheat contract for the same maturity at $3.60. The long trader's profit in this case would be $.10 per bushel or $500 on a 5,000 bushel contract.

When a trader buys a call option on a futures contract, he pays the option price. In return, the call owner receives the right to exercise his option and assume a long position in the futures contract. For the call owner, exercise makes sense only if the futures price exceeds the exercise price on the option. If the call owner exercises, he receives a long position in the futures contract and a cash payment that equals the difference between the futures price at the time of exercise and the exercise price. The seller of a call is subject to the exercise decision of the call holder. If the call holder exercises, the call seller receives a short position in the futures contract and pays the call holder the difference between the current futures price and the exercise price. As an example, assume that a trader buys a call option on the December wheat futures with an exercise price of $3.50. Later, the futures price is $3.75, and the call holder exercises. Upon exercise, the call holder receives a long position in the futures contract with a contract price of $3.75. In addition, the call holder receives $.25 per bushel, or $1250 on one contract. The seller of this call must pay the call holder $1250 and accept a short position in the futures contract with a contract price of $3.75.

At this point, both traders have completed all transactions related to the futures option. However, the call owner holds a long position in the futures and the call seller holds a short position in the futures, both at a contract price of $3.75. At this point, neither trader has a profit or loss on the futures. They can both offset their futures position to avoid any future obligations. Alternatively, they can maintain their positions and hope to profit from subsequent movements in the futures price.

For a put, the buyer of a futures option acquires the right to force the seller of the put to assume a futures position and to pay the long put trader the difference between the exercise price of the option and the futures price at the time of exercise. As an example, assume a trader buys a put option with an exercise price of $3.80. Later, when the futures price is $3.75, the put owner can exercise. The seller then receives a long position in the futures at the current futures price of $3.75. In addition, the seller pays the put owner the difference between the futures price and the exercise price. In this example, the futures price is $3.75 and the exercise price is $3.80. Therefore, the put seller pays the put buyer $.05 per bushel, or $250 on a 5,000 bushel contract. The buyer of a put receives a short position in the futures. Both the long and short put traders now hold futures positions at $3.75, the market price prevailing at the time of exercise. They may offset their futures positions to avoid further profits or losses, or they may maintain the futures position in pursuit of profit.[17]

To understand the pricing of options on futures, we first need to understand the pricing of futures contracts. The best model of futures pricing is the **Cost–of–Carry Model**. The Cost–of–Carry Model holds that the futures price equals the cash or spot price of the commodity plus the cost of carrying the commodity forward to the delivery date. The model does not hold for all commodities with equal precision. Essentially, the model holds well for goods that are easily storable and have large supplies. In addition, the model requires that the good underlying the futures contract can be sold short.

The cost–of–carry equals the total cost of carrying a commodity forward in time. It consists of three elements: storage costs, transportation costs, and financing costs. Storage costs include the cost of warehousing the commodity in the appropriate facility and the cost of insuring the good in storage. Transportation costs cover the costs of getting the good to the delivery point for the futures. The most significant carrying charge in the futures market is the financing cost. The carrying charge reflects only the charges involved in carrying a commodity from one time or one place to another. The carrying charges do not include the value of the commodity itself. So, if gold costs $400 per ounce and the financing rate is 1% per month, the financing charge for carrying the gold forward is $4 per month (1% x $400).

The carrying charges just described are important because they play a crucial role in determining pricing relationships between spot and futures prices. For present purposes, we assume that the only carrying charge is the financing cost or an interest rate of 10 percent per year. As an example, consider the following prices:

Spot price of gold	$400
Future price of gold (for delivery in one year)	$450
Interest rate	10%

With these prices, a trader could trade as follows right now:

Transaction	Cash Flow
Borrow $400 for one year at 10 percent interest	+$400
Buy 1 ounce of gold in the spot market	-400
Sell the futures contract for delivery in one year	0
Net Cash Flow	0

These transactions guarantee a profit that can be realized in one year. After a year, trade as follows:

Transaction	Cash Flow
Deliver gold against the futures contract and collect the futures price	+$450
Repay debt plus interest	-440
Net Cash Flow	+$10

These transactions represent a successful arbitrage. At the outset, the transactions guaranteed the trader a riskless profit without investment. There was no investment because there was no initial cash flow. The trader merely borrowed funds to purchase the gold and to carry it forward. The profit in these transactions was certain once the trader made the initial transactions. As these transactions show, to prevent arbitrage, the following rule must hold:

The futures price must be less than or equal to the spot price of the commodity plus the carrying charges necessary to carry that spot commodity forward to delivery:

$$F_{0,t} \leq S_0 e^{ct} \qquad\qquad 5.2$$

where: $F_{0,t}$ = *the futures price at t=0 for delivery at time=t,*
       S_0 = *the spot price at t=0,*
       c = *the percentage cost of carry*

As we have seen, if this condition does not hold, a trader can borrow funds, buy the spot commodity with the borrowed funds, sell the futures contract, and carry the commodity forward to deliver against the futures contract. These transactions would generate a certain profit without investment. Therefore, they represent an arbitrage opportunity. The sale of the futures contract guarantees the certain profit. Also, there is no investment because the trader borrowed the funds needed to carry out the strategy and we included the cost of using those funds in the carrying charge. Such opportunities cannot exist in a rational market.

Consider now the following set of prices for gold:

Spot price of gold	$420
Future price of gold (for delivery in one year)	$450
Interest rate	10%

Faced with these prices, the smart trader would transact as follows:

Transaction	Cash Flow
Sell one ounce of gold short	+$420
Lend $420 for one year at 10 percent	−420
Buy the futures contract for delivery in one year	0
Net Cash Flow	0

These transactions guarantee a profit that can be realized in one year. After a year, trade as follows:

Transaction	Cash Flow
Collect debt	+$462
Accept delivery of one ounce on the futures contract	−450
Return one ounce of gold to complete the short transaction	0
Net Cash Flow	$12

In these transactions, the trader sold the gold short. As in the stock market, a short seller borrows the good from another trader and must repay it later. After borrowing the good, the short seller sells it and uses the money from the sale.

(The transaction is called short selling because the trader sells a good that he or she does not actually own.) In this example, the short seller can use all of the proceeds from the short sale, which he invests at 10 percent. The trader also buys a futures contract to ensure that he can acquire the gold needed to repay the lender when the futures contract expires in one year.

These transactions constitute an arbitrage opportunity. The initial transactions ensure a profit of $12 in one year. The trader had no initial cash flow, so there was no investment. To prevent this arbitrage opportunity, the spot and futures prices must obey the following rule:

The futures price must equal or exceed the spot price plus the cost of carrying the good to the futures delivery date:

$$F_{0,t} \geq S_0 e^{ct} \qquad\qquad 5.3$$

If prices do not meet this condition, an arbitrage opportunity exists.

To prevent arbitrage, we have seen that the two following rules must hold:

$$F_{0,t} \leq S_0 e^{ct}$$
$$F_{0,t} \geq S_0 e^{ct}$$

Together, these imply the Cost-of-Carry Model:

The futures price must equal the spot price plus the cost of carrying the spot commodity forward to the delivery date of the futures contract:

$$F_{0,t} = S_0 e^{ct} \qquad\qquad 5.4$$

We derived this relationship under the following assumptions: Markets are perfect, i.e., they have no transaction costs and no restrictions on the use of proceeds from short sales. In many markets, restrictions on short-selling keep the arbitrage from working perfectly. Also, goods under storage sometimes provide cash throw-offs that complicate the calculation of the cost-of-carry. Finally, some goods cannot be stored, so they cannot be carried forward to delivery.

As a consequence of these limitations, our analysis of options on futures focuses on futures contracts that can be adequately described by the Cost-of-Carry Model. For the most part, this model works well for precious metal futures and financial futures. By contrast, the model does not describe agricultural and energy futures very well. To see this, note that the Cost-of-Carry Model implies that the futures price must always exceed the cash price. This condition is often violated by agricultural goods and by energy products, such as oil.[18]

When the Cost-of-Carry Model applies, we can treat a futures contract as an asset that pays a continuous dividend at the risk-free rate.[19] In terms of our notation for the continuous dividend version of the Black-Scholes Model, $\delta = r$. In this case, the futures rate equals the cost-of-carry. The only cost of carrying the commodity is the interest cost. Applying the continuous dividend version of the Black-Scholes Model to a futures contract, F, gives the value of a call option on a futures, C^f:

$$C^f = e^{-rt}\left[FN(d_1^f) - EN(d_2^f)\right]$$

$$d_1^f = \frac{\ln(F/E) + (.5\,\sigma^2)t}{\sigma\sqrt{t}}$$

5.5

$$d_2^f = d_1^f - \sigma\sqrt{t}$$

> **An option on a futures contract can be analyzed as an option on a stock that pays a continuous dividend, where the futures price takes the role of the stock price and the continuous dividend rate equals the risk–free rate.**

To see why this model is correct, assume for the moment that there is no risk. From our previous discussions, we know that the N(.) terms drop out from the Black-Scholes Model under conditions of certainty. In that case, the payoff at expiration is just the difference between the futures price at the time the call is purchased and the exercise price of the call:

$$C^f = \left[S - E\right]e^{-rt}$$

The value of the call at time zero must be the present value of the certain payoff at expiration.

Now we introduce risk and consider an example of a European futures option. Assume a wheat futures contract trades at $3.50 per bushel and the corresponding futures options have a striking price of $3.45 and expire in 47 days. The standard deviation of the futures price is .23. The interest rate is 9 percent, which equals the cost-of-carry. With these values, the call price is $.1395 and the put price is $.0901 per bushel. With a contract size of 5,000 bushels, the two contracts cost $697.50 and $450.50, respectively.

Thus far, we have considered only European futures options. Because futures options are generally American, they can be exercised any time. This makes them extremely difficult to price. Essentially, an American futures option consists of an infinite series of European options. In essence, the American futures option has an exercise price equal to the explicit amount that must be paid, plus the sacrifice of the remaining European options in the series. Because the American futures option is analyzed as an infinite series of European options, there is no closed-form solution for the value of the American futures option. Instead, we must approximate the value of the American futures option. The value of an American futures option is given by:

$$C = F \times W_1 - E \times W_2 \qquad\qquad 5.6$$

where:

$W_1, W_2 =$ *"weighting factors comprised of infinite sums of the products of discount factors and conditional probability terms that reflect, at each instant, the present value of the exercise value conditioned on the probability that exercise did not occur at a previous instant."*[20]

Because W_1 and W_2 are sums of an infinite series, the value of the call must be estimated instead of being computed exactly. However, we can compute the estimate to a very high degree of accuracy. In every instance, the value of the American futures option should equal or exceed the value of the corresponding European futures option.

With futures options, there is always the prospect of early exercise, whether the good on which the futures contract is written pays dividends or not. For a call option on a non-dividend paying stock, early exercise never makes sense. If the owner exercises, he or she receives the intrinsic value, S - E. In effect, this means that the owner throws away the time value of the option. If the underlying stock pays a dividend, early exercise is sometimes reasonable. When a stock pays a dividend, the value of the share drops by the amount of the dividend. In this case, value is "leaking out" of the underlying good, so it may be wise to exercise before expiration.

Similarly, it may be wise to exercise futures options before expiration. Consider a call option with an exercise price E = $50 and a futures contract with a price F = $100. Assume for the moment that the futures price will not change anymore, and consider whether the call owner should exercise early or wait until expiration. With these data, the owner should exercise early. By doing so, the owner receives $50 immediately. After exercising, the trader can earn interest on $50 until the expiration date. In short, the benefit of early exercise on a futures option is that exercise provides an immediate payment of F - E. The value of the early exercise is the interest that can be earned between the time of exercise and the expiration date:

$$[F - E]e^{rt}$$

In this example, we have assumed that the futures price does not change. In that circumstance, it was clearly wise to exercise early to capture the interest on the mark to market payment F - E. However, in the normal event, the futures price can fluctuate. Therefore, early exercise discards the option's value over and above the intrinsic value F - E. As a consequence, early exercise of a futures option has a benefit and a cost:

Benefit: Use of the funds F - E until expiration
Cost: Sacrifice of option value over and above intrinsic value F - E

Figure 5.2 illustrates the differences between the pricing of American and European futures call options.[21] Consider a futures call with exercise price E. Figure 5.2 shows how the prices of otherwise identical American and European options vary as a function of the futures price, F. We already observed that the minimum price for a European futures call option is $(F - E)e^{-rt}$. In Figure 5.2, the European option attains this minimum when its price touches the line designated as $(F - E)e^{-rt}$. This happens when the futures price reaches F', which is equivalent to $N(d_1^f)$ and $N(d_2^f)$ both equaling 1.0 in equation 5.5. In economic terms, this situation arises when it is certain that the option will remain in-the-money. In that case, the option will pay F - E at maturity. Before maturity, its price must equal the present value of F - E, or $(F - E)e^{-rt}$.

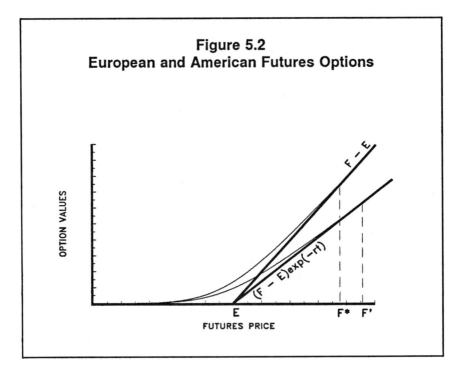

Figure 5.2
European and American Futures Options

The American futures option price must equal or exceed the corresponding European futures call price shown in Figure 5.2.[22] The difference between the American and European futures option prices is the early exercise premium. It is the extra value the American futures option has because it can be exercised before expiration. In the figure, the American futures option attains an important level of F^*, at which the American futures option has no excess value above its intrinsic value. When the futures price is F^*, the intrinsic value of the American futures option is $F^* - E$ and its market value should be the same.

Following Whaley, we call F^* the critical futures price.[23] This is a critical price because it is the point at which the option price hits reaches a price that justifies immediate exercise. We can compute the critical price using various sophisticated methods. For any futures price above F^*, the value of the American futures option equals its intrinsic value. Therefore, the owner of the call option should exercise the option at any futures price above F^* and invest the proceeds to earn interest. For any futures price below F^*, the option should not be exercised because the option will still have value above its intrinsic value. At F^*, the owner is indifferent about exercising.[24]

The Option Approach to Corporate Securities

Since the Black–Scholes Model first appeared in the early 1970s, research on options has expanded rapidly. Option theory has given insight into several areas of finance, one of the most fruitful being corporate finance. In this section, we explore the insights that option theory brings to understanding corporate securities. By thinking of corporate securities as embracing options, we can build a deeper understanding of the value of securities such as stocks and bonds.[25]

Common Stock as a Call Option

Consider a firm with a very simple capital structure. We assume the firm has common stock and a single bond issue outstanding. To keep the analysis simple, we assume the bond issue is a pure discount bond, with face value FV. Let the current time be t=0 and let the maturity date of the bond be t=m. Between the present and t=m, the firm operates, generating cash flows. Also, during this period, new information about the prospects of the firm becomes available. At any time, the value of the firm equals the present value of the firm's future cash flows. The firm value also equals the total value of its outstanding securities. Therefore, at t=0, the firm's value, V_0, is:

$$V_0 = S_0 + B_0$$

where:

S_0 = *entire value of all stocks outstanding at time zero*
B_0 = *entire value of all bonds outstanding at time zero*

The value of the bonds equals the present value of the face value, discounted at the appropriate risky discount rate r' for m periods.

$$B_0 = FVe^{-r'm}$$

Common stock can be analyzed as a call option on the entire firm that expires when the firm's debt is due and that has an exercise price equaling the face amount of the outstanding debt.

When the bond matures, the firm can either pay the indebtedness, FV, or default. If the firm defaults, the bondholders take over the firm to salvage whatever they can. If the firm has a value greater than its indebtedness, FV, the firm will pay the bondholders and the firm will then belong entirely to the stockholders. Thus, the stockholders' payoff at t=m, S_m, is either zero (if they default) or the value of the firm minus the debt to the bondholders (V_m - FV). In other words, the stock is just like a call, with a payoff that equals:

$$S_m = MAX(0, V_m - FV)$$

Therefore, the stock is a call option on the firm with an exercise price equal to the debt obligation, FV. Figure 5.3 shows the position of the stockholders. If the firm value at expiration is less than or equal to FV, then the stockholders do not have enough to pay the bondholders. Accordingly, they default and receive nothing. If the firm value exceeds FV, the stockholders pay the bondholders and keep any excess value.

From our analysis of stock options, we know the call value must equal or exceed the stock price minus the present value of the exercise price. Applying that principle to our treatment of stock itself as an option, we have:

$$S_0 \geq V_0 - FVe^{-r't}$$

This formula emphasizes another principle of option pricing. We know that call prices increase for higher risk in the underlying good. In analyzing common stock as an option on the value of the firm, we see that increasing the risk of the

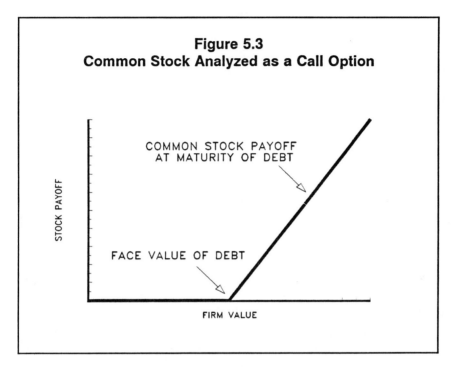

**Figure 5.3
Common Stock Analyzed as a Call Option**

firm will make the stock more valuable. This is true even if the increasing risk does not increase the expected value of the firm at the expiration of the bond. The reason for this increase in value is the same that we saw for stock options. The stockholders have an incentive to increase risk. If the higher risk pays off, the stockholders keep all the benefits. If the risk does not pay off, the limited liability feature of stock protects the stockholders from losing more than their investment. Therefore, increasing risk gives a better chance for a very positive outcome for the stockholders, while the option protects against very negative outcomes. However, increasing the risk of the firm without increasing its expected value cannot increase the value of the firm as a whole. The increase in the value of the stock must come at the expense of the bondholders. Increasing the risk of the firm without increasing the firm's expected value transfers wealth from bondholders to stockholders. Bondholders are aware of this incentive for the stockholders. As a result, bond covenants often prevent the borrower from increasing the risk of the firm.

The Option Analysis of Corporate Debt

Let us now examine the same firm from the perspective of the debt holder. The stockholders have promised to pay FV to the debt holders at t=m. However, the

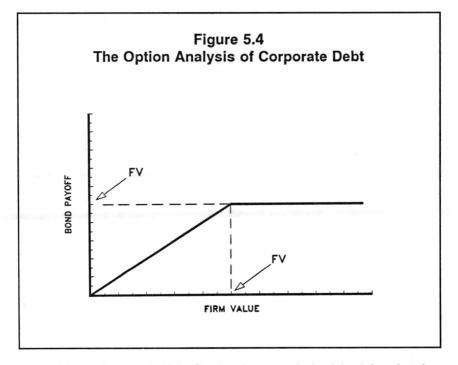

Figure 5.4
The Option Analysis of Corporate Debt

stockholders will pay only if the firm's value exceeds the debt. Otherwise, they will let the bondholders have the firm. Therefore, the payoff for the bondholders at t=m, B_m, will be the lesser of the firm's value or FV. Figure 5.4 graphs the payoffs that the bondholders receive. As the figure shows, the bondholders receive the entire value of the firm for all firm values less than the debt obligation. However, the bondholders never receive more than the promised payment FV. Thus, the payoff to the bondholders, B_m, is the lesser of the firm's value, V_m, or FV.

$$B_m = MIN(V_m, FV)$$

We have already seen the payoff to the stockholders at t=m and we know that the value of the bonds and stocks must equal the value of the firm. Therefore,

$$B_m = V_m - MAX(0, V_m - FV)$$

This equation shows that the bondholders have effectively purchased the entire firm and written a call option to the stockholders. The call option is on the entire firm. The face value of the debt, FV, is the exercise price. This conclusion exactly complements our analysis of the stock as a call option on the value of the firm.

> **We may analyze corporate debt as ownership of the entire firm and a short position in a call option on the firm. The shareholders hold the call option that expires when the debt is due and has an exercise price equaling the face amount of the debt.**

A closer analysis of Figure 5.4 shows that it has the same payoff shape that we studied in Chapter 2. In essence, the bondholders' payoff consists of two imbedded positions. The general shape matches that of a short position in a put. However, the entire position can never be worth less than zero. The bondholders effectively hold a short position in a put with an exercise price of FV, in addition to a long position in a risk-free bond paying FV. To see why this is so, assume that the firm's value at maturity exactly matches the obligation to the bondholders, $V_m = FV$. From Figure 5.4, we see that the bondholders receive FV for this terminal firm value. With $V_m = FV$, the put option the bondholders issued expires worthless.

Now consider any lower value for the firm at maturity. If the firm value is lower than FV, the stockholders exercise their put option forcing the firm upon the bondholders. Now the bondholders receive their risk-free payment of FV, but they lose an amount equal to the shortfall in the firm's value below FV. In our notation, the bondholders receive FV. They also lose either zero, if the firm's value exceeds FV, or they lose $FV-V_m$, if the debt obligation exceeds the value of the firm:

$$B_m = FV - MAX(0, FV-V_m)$$

As this equation shows, the bondholders receive a payoff equal to a long position in a riskless bond and a short position in a put with an exercise price of FV.

Subordinated Debt

Now let us consider a firm with three securities: stock, senior debt, and subordinated debt. Subordinated debt is a bond issue that receives payment only after the firm fully meets senior debt obligations. Let the two debt issues be pure discount bonds that both mature at t=m. The face values on the two obligations are FV_s for the senior debt and FV_j for the junior or subordinated debt. We want to analyze the subordinated debt in option terms.

The holders of the subordinated debt receive payment only after the firm fully meets the claims of the senior debtholders. Therefore, for any firm value V_m that is less than FV_s, the junior debtholders receive zero. If the firm value exceeds FV_s, the junior debtholders receive at least some payment. The subordinated debtholders receive full payment if the firm's value equals or exceeds the entire amount due on both debt issues, $V_m \geq FV_s + FV_j$. Figure 5.5 shows the payoffs for the senior and junior debt. The payoffs on the junior debt match a portfolio of a long call with a striking price of FV_s and a short call with a striking price of FV_j, as Figure 5.6 shows. The stockholders in this firm own a call on the value of the firm with a striking price equal to $FV_s + FV_j$. For the call option represented by the stock to come into the money, the value of the firm must exceed the total payoff of the two debt issues. Therefore, the payoff on the call in this situation is:

$$S_m = MAX[0,\ V_m - (FV_s + FV_j)]$$

As always, the value of the firm must equal the value of all outstanding securities. However, the different classes of securities offer different ways to

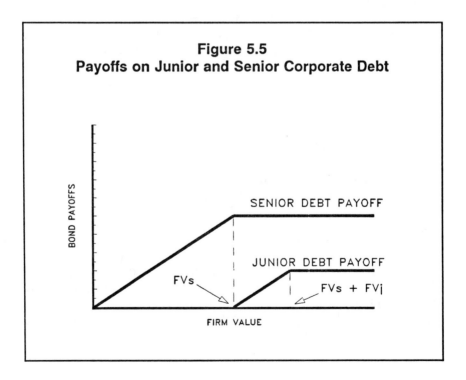

Figure 5.5
Payoffs on Junior and Senior Corporate Debt

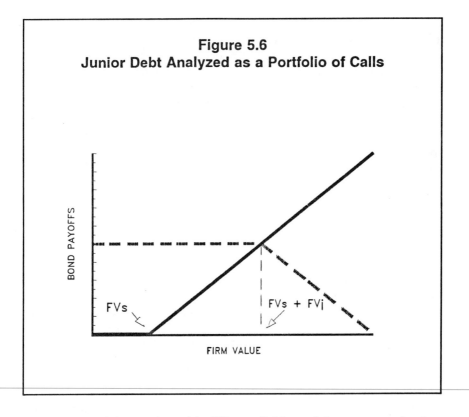

Figure 5.6
Junior Debt Analyzed as a Portfolio of Calls

create various options and provide different divisions of the corporate pie when the bonds mature.

Summary

This chapter began by offering a more complete analysis of the difference between American and European options. We then discussed the effects of dividends and the incentives for early exercise. We found that there is no reason to exercise a call early if the underlying stock pays no dividends. If the stock does pay dividends, the values of a European and an American call option can differ. We considered several different methods for adjusting the Black–Scholes Model to reflect the impact of dividends. We saw that we could approximate American call option values by adjusting for known dividends, by employing a pseudo–American call option, or by using a continuous dividend adjustment. For puts, we found that early exercise can sometimes be justified even if the underlying stock pays no dividend.

In recent years, markets have developed to trade options on a number of different goods in addition to individual stocks. We analyzed options on stock indexes, foreign currencies, and futures contracts. In each of these three cases, the continuous dividend adjustment to the Black–Scholes Model proved to be important in developing pricing models for the options.

Finally, we explored corporate securities and showed how they can be analyzed as different kinds of options. Common stock, for example, performs like a call option on the value of the firm, with a striking price that equals the promised payment to debtholders. Debt itself can be analyzed in option terms. We saw that risky corporate debt can be analyzed as consisting of risk-free debt and a short position in a put option. The advent of the Black–Scholes Model has created a revolution in finance. This revolution shows no signs of abating and we can expect further extensions of the option framework to solve even more challenging problems.

Questions and Problems

1. For two otherwise identical call options, under what circumstances can a European and American option have different prices? Explain.

2. For two otherwise identical put options, under what circumstances can a European and American option have different prices? Explain.

3. For known dividends, we approximate an American call value with the Black–Scholes Model by subtracting the present value of the dividends from the stock price. Explain what else is required and explain the rationale for this procedure.

4. Explain the difference between the known dividend adjustment and the pseudo-American dividend model.

5. For the continuous dividend adjustment, consider two situations for the same stock. First, the next quarterly dividend will be paid in two days. Second, the next quarterly dividend will be paid in 85 days. For which circumstances is the continuous dividend adjustment better suited? Explain.

6. Explain the circumstances that can justify the early exercise of a call option. If early exercise is warranted, explain when it will occur.

7. Consider a call option with an exercise price of $110 written on a stock that now trades at $116. The standard deviation of the stock is .2 and the risk-free interest rate is 9 percent. The option expires in 60 days and the

stock will pay an $8 dividend in 20 days. Using the Black–Scholes Model, what is the call value? Using the known dividend adjustment, what is the call value? (Use **OPTION!** to solve this problem.)

8. A stock trades for $80 and has a standard deviation of returns of .35. The risk-free interest rate is 11 percent. The stock will pay a dividend of $1.50 in 47 days and another dividend of $1.50 in 135 days. Assuming a common striking price of $75 for all of the options, compute the value of the following calls. (Use **OPTION!** to solve this problem.)

   a. A call that expires in 45 days
   b. A call that expires in 60 days, with the continuous dividend adjustment
   c. A call that expires in 60 days, with the known dividend adjustment
   d. A call that expires in 60 days, with the pseudo–American Model
   e. A call that expires in 150 days, with the continuous dividend adjustment
   f. A call that expires in 150 days, with the known dividend adjustment
   g. A call that expires in 150 days, with the pseudo–American Model

9. Evaluate the following claim: Because early exercise discards the time value of a put option, early exercise of a put on a non-dividend stock is always irrational. Therefore, otherwise identical American and European puts on a non-dividend stock must have the same price.

10. Explain what is true and what is false in the following claim: Early exercise of a call and put becomes attractive only if the underlying stock pays a dividend. Early exercise of a call will occur just before an ex-dividend date, if it occurs at all. The attraction of exercising a call just before the dividend is to capture the dividend. Similarly for a put, early exercise will occur just before a stock goes ex-dividend for the same reason.

11. Consider options on stock indexes and foreign currencies. In what ways can we treat these alike? Evaluate the suitability of the Black–Scholes Model for evaluating these two kinds of options. What adjustments to the Black–Scholes Model might be required? Do the adjustments differ in the two cases? Explain.

12. Considering the Black–Scholes Model and its various adjustments, which best suits the analysis of options on futures? Explain.

13. Explain the conditions that could make early exercise of a call on a futures contract attractive.

14. Assume that we are using the continuous dividend adjustment to the Black–Scholes Model to value a call option on a futures contract. Futures pay no dividends. Explain what value we should use in the model for the continuous dividend rate.

15. Explain why common stock is itself like a call option. In the option analysis of common stock, what plays the role of the exercise price and what plays the role of the underlying stock?

16. Consider a firm that issues a pure discount bond promising to pay $1,000,000 in one year. Analyze the payoffs that the bondholders will receive in option pricing terms.

Notes

1. When the stock goes ex–dividend, the current stock owner receives the dividend.

2. Some research shows that the stock price does not drop by the full amount of the dividend, due largely to tax effects. See, for example, E. J. Elton and M. J. Gruber, "Marginal Stockholders' Tax Rates and the Clientele Effect," *Review of Economics and Statistics*, February 1970, 68-74. This continues to be a controversial topic. For example, Giovanni Barone-Adesi and Robert E. Whaley use options data to estimate the drop in the stock price as a percentage of the dividend in their paper, "The Valuation of American Call Options and the Expected Ex-Dividend Stock Price Decline," *Journal of Financial Economics*, 17:1, September 1986, 91-111. They find that the expected decline in the stock price does not differ meaningfully from 100 percent. By contrast, Costas P. Kaplanis examines the same issue and finds that the expected stock price decline is about 55-60 percent of the dividend in his paper, "Options, Taxes, and Ex-Dividend Day Behavior," *Journal of Finance*, 41:2, June 1986, 411-424. The importance of this issue for options arises in part because of potential inefficiency in option pricing that may result. Avner Kalay and Marti G. Subrahmanyam find evidence of inefficient pricing of in-the-money calls around ex-dividend dates in their paper, "The Ex-Dividend Day Behavior of Option Prices," *Journal of Business* 57, 1984, 113-128. Rick Castanias, Ki-Young Chung, and Herb Johnson explicitly dispute this result in their paper, "Dividend Spread," *Journal of Business*, 61:3, July 1988, 299-319. Recent research indicates that the entire issue of the ex-dividend day behavior of stock prices may

not be important for option market efficiency in any case. David C. Heath and Robert A. Jarrow show that the stock price can drop by less than the full amount of the dividend without generating any arbitrage opportunities anyway. See their paper, "Ex-Dividend Stock Price Behavior and Arbitrage Opportunities," *Journal of Business*, 61:1, January 1988, 95-108. Beyond this note, we do not explicitly consider this issue in our discussion. However, one way of dealing with the problem is to assume throughout the book that the dividend value is the amount the stock will fall on the ex-dividend date. The problem is knowing whether to expect a share price drop equal to, or less than, the dividend.

3.   R. E. Whaley, "Valuation of American Call Options on Dividend Paying Stocks: Empirical Tests," *Journal of Financial Economics*, 10, March 1982, 29-58.

4.   Fischer Black first proposed this idea in his paper "Fact and Fantasy in the Use of Options," *Financial Analysts Journal*, July/August 1975, 36-72.

5.   R. E. Whaley, "Valuation of American Call Options on Dividend Paying Stocks: Empirical Tests," *Journal of Financial Economics*, 10, March 1982, 29-58.

6.   This is not the same as capital delta, Δ, which stands for the sensitivity of the call option price to a change in the stock price.

7.   Robert Geske and Kuldeep Shastri explore this issue in detail in their paper, "The Early Exercise of American Puts," *Journal of Banking and Finance*, 9:2, June 1985, 207-219. They found that 93 percent of firms paid dividends that were large enough to affect the early exercise decision. Specifically for puts, the approaching dividend tended to be large enough to warrant postponing the exercise. Also, Geske and Shastri found that managerial policy about changing dividend payments can also affect the probability of early exercise.

8.   James F. Meisner and John W. Labuszewski provide an overview of option pricing models for stock indexes and a variety of other instruments in their paper, "Modifying the Black-Scholes Option Pricing Model for Alternative Underlying Instruments," *Financial Analysts Journal*, 40:6, November/December 1984, 23-30. For an extended treatment of stock index futures and options, see Frank J. Fabozzi and Gregory M. Kipnis, *The Handbook of Stock Index Futures and Options*, Homewood: Richard D. Irwin, Inc., 1989. This book includes 26 articles on all aspects of stock index futures and options.

9. Options also trade on the Value Line Index. The Value Line Index, in contrast to the S&P indexes, is a geometric index. Instead of adding terms pertaining to individual stocks, these individual terms are multiplied in computing the Value Line Index. This leads to significant pricing differences between the different types of indexes. T. Hanan Eytan and Giora Harpaz explore these issues in their article, "The Pricing of Futures and Options Contracts on the Value Line Index," *Journal of Finance*, 41:4, September 1986, 843-855. Oddly, Eytan and Harpaz show that the price of a call option on the Value Line Index can fall even when the volatility of the index increases.

10. Even though the portfolio of stocks included in an index has a dividend stream that is much more regular than that of an individual stock, there is still considerable variability in the amount of dividends paid through the year. Many firms tend to be on similar dividend cycles so there are peak dividend days and periods through the year.

11. There is considerable evidence that option expirations are associated with increases in stock market volatility. For example see Hans Stoll and Robert Whaley, "Expiration Day Effects of Index Options and Futures," *Financial Analysts Journal*, March-April 1987, 16-28 and Robert Whaley, "Expiration Day Effects of Index Futures and Options: Empirical Results," *Review of Research in Futures Markets*, 5, 1986, 292-304. Not surprisingly, this same result is reflected in implied volatilities estimated through options on stock indexes. Theodore E. Day and Craig M. Lewis study this issue in "The Behavior of the Volatility Implicit in the Prices of Stock Index Options," *Journal of Financial Economics*, 22:1, October 1988, 103-122.

    Studies have also explored the efficiency of the stock index options market. These results tend to follow earlier results found for options on individual stocks. Don M. Chance "Boundary Condition Tests of Bid and Ask Prices of Index Call Options," *Journal of Financial Research*, 11:1, Spring 1988, 21-31, conducts tests of no-arbitrage conditions. For example, he tests whether immediate exercise offers arbitrage profits. Summarizing all of his tests, Chance concludes that violations are infrequent and short-lived. Also, violations were relatively infrequent when the market was new. Warren Bailey and Rene M. Stulz address the issue of over- and under-pricing by the model for options away from the money, "The Pricing of Stock Index Options in a General Equilibrium Model," *Journal of Financial and Quantitative Analysis*, 24:1, March 1989, 1-12. They find that the model tends to underprice deep-in-the-money options and to overprice deep-out-of-the-money options.

12. For an accessible treatment of interest rate parity, see Chapter 9 of Robert W. Kolb, *Understanding Futures Markets*, Miami: Kolb Publishing Co., 1991.

13. Several studies explore the performance of the foreign currency options market. Alan L. Tucker, "Empirical Tests of the Efficiency of the Currency Option Market," *Journal of Financial Research*, 8:4, Winter 1985, 275-285, conducts several tests for violation of boundary conditions. He finds that there is little or no opportunity for abnormal profits. James N. Bodurtha, Jr. and Georges R. Courtadon, "Efficiency Tests of the Foreign Currency Options Market," *Journal of Finance*, 41:1, March 1986, 151-162, find violations of the parity conditions. However, Bodurtha and Courtadon point out that these violations are of such small magnitude that the transactions costs incurred to exploit them would more than offset the potential profits. Thus, after considering transaction costs, the two studies generally agree. Two other papers support these conclusions: Kuldeep Shastri and Kishore Tandon, "Valuation of Foreign Currency Options: Some Empirical Tests," *Journal of Financial and Quantitative Analysis*, 21:2, June 1986, 145-160; and Joseph P. Ogden and Alan L. Tucker, "Empirical Tests of the Efficiency of the Currency Futures Options Market," *Journal of Futures Markets*, 7:6, December 1987, 695-705.

14. While the continuous dividend adjustment does a good job of pricing foreign currency options, more advanced models may perform even better. For example, Kuldeep Shastri and Kishore Tandon, "On the Use of European Models to Price American Options on Foreign Currency," *Journal of Futures Markets*, 6:1, Spring 1986, 93-108 find that the European model closely approximates call prices. However, it does not perform as well for puts. Paul D. Adams and Steve B. Wyatt, "Biases in Option Prices: Evidence from the Foreign Currency Option Market," *Journal of Banking and Finance*, 11:4, December 1987, 549-562 find similar results using actual market data. American currency option pricing models have some biases, according to James N. Bodurtha and Georges R. Courtadon, "Tests of an American Option Pricing Model on the Foreign Currency Options Market," *Journal of Financial and Quantitative Analysis*, 22:2, June 1987, 153-167. They find that the model underprices out-of-the-money options and that the model has a time-to-maturity bias. Kuldeep Shastri and Kishore Tandon, "Valuation of American Options on Foreign Currency," *Journal of Banking and Finance*, 11:2, June 1987, 245-269 find similar divergences between market and model prices. Alan L. Tucker, David R. Peterson and Elton Scott find that alternative descriptions of currency price movements lead to better models in their paper, "Tests of the Black-Scholes

and Constant Elasticity of Variance Currency Call Option Valuation Models," *Journal of Financial Research*, 11:3, Fall 1988, 201-213. Kuldeep Shastri and Kulpatra Wethyavivorn consider four different models of currency price changes, "The Valuation of Currency Options for Alternate Stochastic Processes," *Journal of Financial Research*, 10:4, Winter 1987, 283-293. They find that a mixed jump-diffusion model gives prices that most closely approximate market prices.

15. Many futures contracts allow different items to be delivered in completion of the futures contract. For example, the Chicago Board of Trade wheat futures contract allows the short trader to select one of several different types of wheat to deliver. The short trader may also select one of several locations for the delivery and may choose the business day within the delivery month for the delivery to occur. Because of these choices, futures contracts often contain embedded options. The choice of which grade of commodity to deliver is the **quality option**. The choice of delivery point gives the short trader **a location option,** and the right to choose the day of delivery affords the short trader **a timing option.** These implicit options were first studied by Gerald D. Gay and Steven Manaster, "The Quality Option Implicit in Futures Contracts," *Journal of Financial Economics*, 13:3, September 1984, 353-370 and studied further in their paper, "Implicit Delivery Options and Optimal Delivery Strategies for Financial Futures Contracts," *Journal of Financial Economics*, 16:1, May 1986, 41-72. Gay and Manaster find that the quality option has a significant value and that its presence affects the price at which the futures trades. In addition, for their 1977-1983 sample period, Gay and Manaster found that wise exercise of these options could generate excess returns. See also Phelim Boyle, "The Quality Option and Timing Option in Futures Contracts," *Journal of Finance*, 44:1, March 1989, 101-113. The options inherent in the Treasury bond futures contract have attracted the most attention. In addition to the options mentioned above, the Treasury bond futures contains two others. First, there is an **end-of-the-month** option. Trading of the futures ceases on the eighth-to-last business day of the delivery month, but the short trader can wait until the second-to-last business day to choose which bond to deliver. Thus, the short position has an option to substitute a more advantageous bond in the delivery depending on what happens to bond prices in the six days between the end of trading and choosing the bond to deliver. Second, there is an option called the **wild-card option.** The price for delivery is established when the market closes at 2:00 p.m. on a given delivery day. However, the short trader can choose to make a given day a delivery day by notifying the exchange of his intention to deliver by 8:00 p.m. Therefore, the short trader has a valuable option that can be exploited if bond prices move in the six-hour interval between the market's close and

8:00 p.m. These various options have been studied in a number of papers: Alex Kane and Alan J. Marcus, "The Quality Option in the Treasury Bond Futures Market: An Empirical Assessment," *Journal of Futures Markets*, 6:2, Summer 1986, 231-248; Marcelle Arak and Laurie S. Goodman, "Treasury Bond Futures: Valuing the Delivery Options," *Journal of Futures Markets*, 7:3, June 1987, 269-286; Theodore M. Barnhill and William E. Seale, "Optimal Exercise of the Switching Option in Treasury Bond Arbitrages," *Journal of Futures Markets*, 8:5, October 1988, 517-532; Alex Kane and Alan J. Marcus, "Valuation and Optimal Exercise of the Wild Card Option in the Treasury Bond Futures Market," *Journal of Finance*, 41:1, March 1986, 195-207; and Shantaram P. Hegde, "An Empirical Analysis of Implicit Delivery Options in the Treasury Bond Futures Contract," *Journal of Banking and Finance*, 12:3, September 1988, 469-492.

16. In the actual futures market, traders make cash flows on a daily basis that reflect the change in their positions on that day. As a consequence, they do not simply wait until the expiration of the futures but they have paid the difference between the futures price when they contracted and the futures price that prevails at the expiration date. They paid it in daily increments in a process called **marking-to-market**. For a discussion of the actual procedure in futures markets, see Robert W. Kolb, *Understanding Futures Markets*, 3rd. Edition, Miami: Kolb Publishing Company, 1991.

17. For a more extensive discussion of options on futures, see Robert W. Kolb, *Understanding Futures Markets*, 3rd. ed., Miami: Kolb Publishing Co., 1991, Chapters 11-12. Two books discuss options on futures in great detail: John W. Labuszewski and Jeanne Cairns Sinquefield, *Inside the Commodity Options Market*, New York: John Wiley, 1985 and John W. Labuszewski John E. Nyhoff, *Trading Options on Futures*, New York: John Wiley, 1988.

18. If we define the net cost-of-carry to include all benefits that come from holding the commodity, we can specify a revised Cost-of-Carry Model that fits more commodities. These benefits of holding the physical good are known as the **convenience yield**. However, this strategy merely saves the model by stipulating that apparent discrepancies in the model equal the unobservable convenience yield. For applying the option model, we would then need to measure the convenience yield, which appears difficult at best.

19. Fischer Black, "The Pricing of Commodity Contracts," *Journal of Financial Economics* 3, 1976, 167-179, was the first to develop a pricing model for options on futures. Other discussions of pricing models are: Avner Wolf,

"Options of Futures: Pricing and the Effect of an Anticipated Price Change," *Journal of Futures Markets*, 4:4, Winter 1984, 491–512; George S. Oldfield and Carlos E. Rovira, "Futures Contract Options," 4:4, Winter 1984, 479–490; Krishna Ramaswamy and Suresh M. Sundaresan "The Valuation of Options on Futures Contracts," *Journal of Finance*, 40:5, December 1985, 1319–1340; Edward O. Thorp, "Options on Commodity Forward Contracts," *Management Science*, 31:10, October 1985, 1232-1236; and Menachem Brenner, Georges Courtadon, and Marti Subrahmanyam, "Options on the Spot and Options on Futures," *Journal of Finance*, 40:5, December 1985, 1303–1317.

20. K. Shastri and K. Tandon, "An Empirical Test of a Valuation Model for American Options on Futures Contracts," *Journal of Financial and Quantitative Analysis*, 21:4, December 1986, 377-392.

21. Several papers consider alternative valuation models for options on futures and provide tests of these models. Jin W. Choi and Francis A. Longstaff, "Pricing Options on Agricultural Futures: An Application of the Constant Elasticity of Variance Option Pricing Model," *Journal of Futures Markets*, 5:2, Summer 1985, 247-258, find that the constant elasticity of variance model is superior to the Black model for valuing agricultural futures options. Kuldeep Shastri and Kishore Tandon, "Options on Futures Contracts: A Comparison of European and American Pricing Models," *Journal of Futures Markets*, 6:4, Winter 1986, 593-618, find that the European model works well for options near the money and near expiration. Black's European model has obviously desirable properties of simplicity. William W. Wilson, Hung-Gay Fung, and Michael Ricks, "Option Price Behavior in Grain Futures Markets," 8:1, February 1988, 47–65 find a lack of correspondence between actual futures option prices and prices from the Black model. Most strikingly, actual option prices sometimes decreased as futures market volatility increased. James V. Jordan, William E. Seale, and Nancy C. McCabe, "Transactions Data Tests of the Black Model for Soybean Futures Options," *Journal of Futures Markets*, 7:5, October 1987, 535-554, find a very close correspondence between market prices and model prices. For puts the average discrepancy was one-tenth of a cent per bushel, and for calls the average discrepancy was four-hundredths of a cent per bushel. By contrast, Edward C. Blomeyer and James C. Boyd, "Empirical Tests of Boundary Conditions for Options on Treasury Bond Futures Contracts," *Journal of Futures Markets*, 8:2, April 1988, 185-198, find violations of boundary conditions on the futures option prices. However, these opportunities were relatively rare. Warren Bailey, "An Empirical Investigation of the Market for Comex Gold Futures Options,"

Journal of Finance, 42:5, December 1987, 1187-1194, finds no attractive arbitrage opportunities due to violations of the boundary conditions.

22. In Figure 5.2, we indicate the special number "e" by the notation "exp."

23. R. Whaley, "Valuation of American Futures Options: Theory and Empirical Tests," *Journal of Finance*, March 1986, pp. 127-150. Figure 5.2 is based on a figure in Whaley's paper. See also Robert E. Whaley, "On Valuing American Futures Options," *Financial Analysts Journal*, 42:3, May-June 1986, 49-59.

24. Giovanni Barone-Adesi and Robert E. Whaley, "Efficient Analytical Approximation of American Option Values," *Journal of Finance*, 42:2, June 1987, 301-320, show how to find the critical futures price efficiently. Two articles explore the actual exercise of options on futures, both focusing on Treasury bond futures and both relying on the Barone-Adesi and Whaley approximation. James A. Overdahl, "The Early Exercise of Options on Treasury Bond Futures," *Journal of Financial and Quantitative Analysis*, 23:4, December 1988, 437-449, finds that the model of exercise developed by Whaley and Barone-Adesi underestimates the critical futures price of calls and overestimates the critical futures price for puts. Gerald D. Gay, Robert W. Kolb, and Kenneth Yung, "Trader Rationality in the Exercise of Futures Options," *Journal of Financial Economics*, 23:2, August 1989, 339-362, examine the correspondence between actual exercise behavior and the guidance provided by the Barone-Adesi and Whaley model. In general, Gay, Kolb, and Yung find that there are very few instances in which traders exercise when they should not. However, in many instances traders should have exercised but did not. There are rare occasions of traders exercising when they should not have with these exercises resulting in large losses.

25. Of course the original Black-Scholes paper, "The Pricing of Options and Corporate Liabilities," *Journal of Political Economy*, 81, 1973, 637-659, already focused on the option characteristics of stocks and bonds.

6

OPTION! Software

Introduction

In this chapter, we explain how to use **OPTION!**, the software that accompanies this book. **OPTION!** operates on virtually any IBM PC or compatible. If the computer has a graphics capability, **OPTION!** can graph many of the option pricing relationships explained in previous chapters. The program has been written for easy use. Many readers will only need to skim the next section to be able to use all the features of the software. However, this chapter explains how to use each separate module. Figure 6.1 shows the main menu for **OPTION!**. After explaining how to install the software, we discuss each module.

Installation and Quick Start

The installation of **OPTION!** varies for a computer system with a hard disk or a system with only floppy disks. Use the installation instructions that correspond to your computer system.

Installation on a Floppy Drive System

1. Make a back-up copy of the original **OPTION!** diskette. Place the original diskette in drive A. (If you have a second drive B:, place a formatted blank diskette in the B: drive.) Give the following command: "DISKCOPY A:*.* B:". (If you have only a single disk system, the computer will tell you when to remove the **OPTION!** diskette and insert a blank diskette.)

2. Place the original diskette in a safe location.

3. Place the working copy of **OPTION!** in drive A: and make drive A: the logged drive by giving the following command: "A:".

4. Installation is complete. You may run the program by typing "OPTION!" and pressing return.

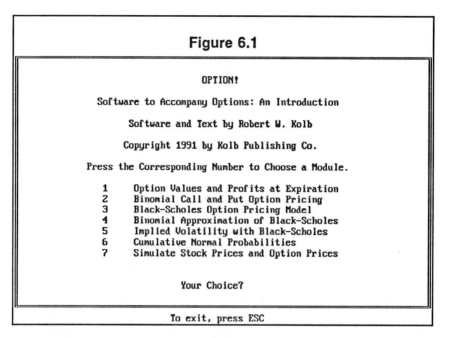

Figure 6.1

OPTION!

Software to Accompany Options: An Introduction

Software and Text by Robert W. Kolb

Copyright 1991 by Kolb Publishing Co.

Press the Corresponding Number to Choose a Module.

1   Option Values and Profits at Expiration
2   Binomial Call and Put Option Pricing
3   Black-Scholes Option Pricing Model
4   Binomial Approximation of Black-Scholes
5   Implied Volatility with Black-Scholes
6   Cumulative Normal Probabilities
7   Simulate Stock Prices and Option Prices

Your Choice?

To exit, press ESC

Installation on a Hard Drive System

1. Make a directory to hold the files for **OPTION!**. Assuming the system has a hard disk named drive C: and you want to install the software in a sub-directory called "OPTION," use the Make Directory command as follows:
    "MD C:\OPTION".

2. Place the original diskette for **OPTION!** in the A: drive.

3. Copy all the files from the original diskette to the sub-directory on the hard disk created in step 1, by using the following command:
    "COPY A:*.* C:\OPTION".

4. To run **OPTION!**, be sure that the logged drive and sub-directory hold the **OPTION!** files. To do this you can use the following two commands:
    "C:" and "CD \OPTION".

5. Installation is complete. Place the original diskette in a safe location. You may start the program with the following command: "OPTION!" and press return.

To use **OPTION!**, be sure that the logged drive or sub-directory is the location for all of the **OPTION!** files. To start the program, type "OPTION!" and press ENTER. The program then shows the main menu of Figure 6.1. The program contains seven modules. To start a given module from the main menu, press the corresponding number. To exit a given screen at any time, press ESC. Pressing ESC when the main menu is showing exits the program and returns to DOS. From any screen, pressing ESC repeatedly will exit the program.

In general, the modules function by entering data and then pressing a function key to perform some analysis. For example, the program uses the F1 key to request solution. F2 is the key for graphics. Watch the bottom line of the screen for special instructions.

Module 1
Option Values and Profits at Expiration

Figure 6.2 shows the menu for Module 1, which computes option values and profits at expiration, as Chapter 2 explained. Consistent with our discussion in Chapter 2, the program distinguishes value and profit. The module allows us to analyze any combination of the following instruments: three calls, three puts, a stock, and a risk-free bond. The program assumes that all options have the same expiration and the same underlying stock.

Figure 6.2

Option Values and Profits at Expiration

Use this screen to calculate option position values and profits at expiration. Provide data for any combination of options and securities you wish. All options must have the same underlying stock and the same expiration. For shares, a negative value indicates a short position.

Provide data for at least one security:

OPTIONS:				STOCK:	
	Shares	Strike	Price	Shares	0
				Price	0.000
Call #1	0	0	0.00		
Call #2	0	0	0.00		
Call #3	0	0	0.00	RISKLESS BOND:	
Put #1	0	0	0.00		
Put #2	0	0	0.00	$ Initially Invested	0.00
Put #3	0	0	0.00	$ Promised at Maturity	0.00

After entering data, press F1 for results, F2 to graph, or ESC to exit.

To analyze some instruments, enter values for the instrument in question. For the options, specify the number of shares, the strike price, and the price of the option. To show a short position, enter a negative number for shares. If you make a mistake in entering numbers, use the DEL key to erase. As an example, let us assume that you want to analyze the purchase of Call #1 and Put #1, both for one share. Both the call and the put have an exercise price of $40. From Chapter 2, we recognize this position as a long position in a straddle. The call costs $7, and the put trades for $5. The program can either report on the position, or it can graph the expiration outcomes for the position. After entering the data, press F1 for a report or press F2 for a graph of your values or profits. We consider each alternative.

First, assume that you wish a report of the outcomes on this position at expiration. Therefore, press F1 after entering the data as we described. The program presents the Report Menu shown in Figure 6.3. From this menu, we select a report. As an example, assume we select report 6 "Option and Stock Profit Summary." In our example, there is no stock, but the report will show the profits and losses for three categories of assets: all calls, all puts, and the stock. In addition, it shows the total profits and losses for all categories. Figure 6.4 shows the first page of the report. Each report has five pages. Advance the page by pressing ESC. As we expect, we have losses for stock prices around the exercise prices. The position comes into the money stock price above $52 or

---

Figure 6.3

Use This Screen to Choose a Report to Review.

To direct output to a printer, press CTRL-P.
To stop printing, press CTRL-P again.

1	Call Option and Stock Values
2	Call Option and Stock Profits
3	Put Option and Stock Values
4	Put Option and Stock Profits
5	Option and Stock Value Summary
6	Option and Stock Profit Summary
7	General Value Summary
8	General Profit Summary

Press ESC to Exit Report Menu

Your Choice?

Figure 6.4

Option and Stock Profit Summary

STOCK PRICE	CALLS	PUTS	STOCK	TOTAL
15.00	−7.00	20.00	0.00	13.00
15.50	−7.00	19.50	0.00	12.50
16.00	−7.00	19.00	0.00	12.00
16.50	−7.00	18.50	0.00	11.50
17.00	−7.00	18.00	0.00	11.00
17.50	−7.00	17.50	0.00	10.50
18.00	−7.00	17.00	0.00	10.00
18.50	−7.00	16.50	0.00	9.50
19.00	−7.00	16.00	0.00	9.00
19.50	−7.00	15.50	0.00	8.50
20.00	−7.00	15.00	0.00	8.00
20.50	−7.00	14.50	0.00	7.50
21.00	−7.00	14.00	0.00	7.00
21.50	−7.00	13.50	0.00	6.50
22.00	−7.00	13.00	0.00	6.00
22.50	−7.00	12.50	0.00	5.50
23.00	−7.00	12.00	0.00	5.00
23.50	−7.00	11.50	0.00	4.50
24.00	−7.00	11.00	0.00	4.00
24.50	−7.00	10.50	0.00	3.50
25.00	−7.00	10.00	0.00	3.00

Press ESC to Continue Report

Figure 6.5

Menu to Graph Option Values and Profits at Expiration

Press the corresponding letter to select a graph, or press ESC to exit.

	Value Graph	Profit Graph
CALL #1	A	N
CALL #2	B	O
CALL #3	C	P
PUT #1	D	Q
PUT #2	E	R
PUT #3	F	S
ALL CALLS	G	T
ALL PUTS	H	U
ALL OPTIONS	I	V
CALLS AND STOCK	J	W
PUTS AND STOCK	K	X
OPTIONS AND STOCK	L	Y
ALL ASSETS	M	Z

Your Choice?

below $28. On the last page of the report, press ESC to return to the report menu. From the report menu, select a report or press ESC for the data screen.

Now we show how to graph the profits and losses for expiration for the same data we have been considering. From the data screen, press F2 to graph. Figure 6.5 shows the graph menu for Module 1. Choose any graph by typing the corresponding letter. Figure 6.6 shows the graph for our data if we select "V" to graph profits and losses for all options. As the graph shows, a stock price of $40 results in a loss on both the put and the call totaling $12. Consistent with our report for the same data, the graph shows that the straddle comes into the money for stock prices above $52 or below $28.

Module 2
Binomial Call and Put Option Pricing

OPTION! features two modules for the Binomial Option Pricing Model. The first of these is Module 2. Chapter 4 explained the ideas behind the Binomial Model. In Module 2, you may specify the up and down factors that govern the change in the stock price. Figure 6.7 presents the data input screen with data in place and a completed solution. This is the data for the two–period binomial call pricing that we discussed in Chapter 4. The stock price is $100, the up factor is +10 percent, the down factor is –10 percent, and the interest rate is 6 percent. As we found in Chapter 4, this call price is $11.96.

To use this screen, we enter the six data items in the upper portion of the screen. Then press F1 to compute all of the values shown in the bottom portion of the screen. You may specify as many as 100 periods. If you specify three or fewer periods, the program will create the binomial pricing tree for the stock and the put. As the bottom line in Figure 6.7 shows, we can graph by pressing "C" to graph a call option, or "P" to graph a put option. Figure 6.8 shows a graph for the call option of our example. In Figure 6.8, we see that the stock will finish at a price of $121, $99, or $81. The call price will be $21 if the stock price is $121. Otherwise, the call will expire worthless because the exercise price will exceed the terminal stock price. Figure 6.8 displays these different possibilities. After reviewing the binomial tree, press ESC to return to the data entry and solution screen of Figure 6.7.

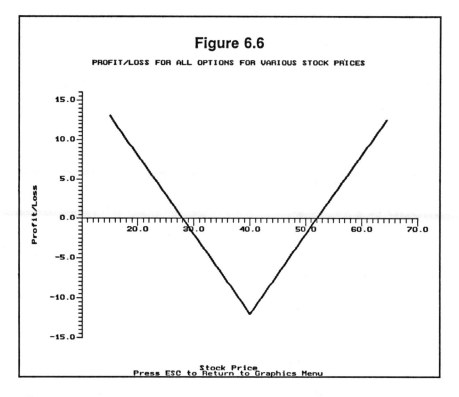

Figure 6.6

PROFIT/LOSS FOR ALL OPTIONS FOR VARIOUS STOCK PRICES

Press ESC to Return to Graphics Menu

Figure 6.7

Binomial Option Pricing

Use this screen to calculate call and put prices using the binomial model.
Enter values for all items in this box. In the binomial model, the price
can either go up or down each period by a fixed percentage. Specify the up
and down percentage movements and the risk-free rate per period. Complete
all items in this box.

Stock Price	100.000	Up Movement in Percent	0.100
Strike Price	100.000	Risk-Free Rate per Period	0.060
Number of Periods	2	Down Movement in Percent	-0.100

The call price is   11.9616
The put price is   0.9612

Maximum Stock Price at Expiration   121.0000
Minimum Stock Price at Expiration   81.0000
Expected Stock Price at Expiration   112.3600

The chance of a stock price increase in each period is   0.8000

Press C or P to graph a binomial tree for a Call or Put; ESC to exit.

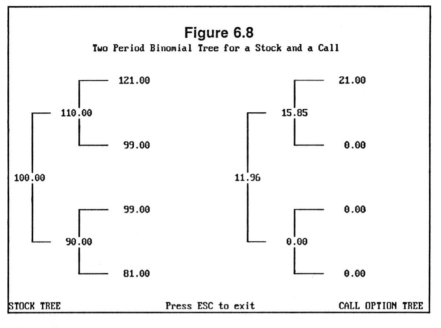

Figure 6.8
Two Period Binomial Tree for a Stock and a Call

STOCK TREE   Press ESC to exit   CALL OPTION TREE

Module 3
Black–Scholes Option Pricing Model

Module 3 provides option valuation by the Black-Scholes Option Pricing Model, which we discussed in Chapter 4. Figure 6.9 presents the data entry and solution screen for Module 3 without data. To use this module, enter values for the five parameters of the Black-Scholes Model in the top portion of the screen. As an option, you may specify a continuous dividend rate in the middle box. After entering the data, press F1 to compute the Black-Scholes prices.

Figure 6.10 shows the Black-Scholes screen with data in place and a completed solution. In our example, the stock price is $100, the exercise price is $100, the risk-free rate is 6 percent, the standard deviation is .10 and 365 days remain until expiration. The bottom portion of the screen shows that the call price for these values is $7.46 and the put price is $1.64. This is the same problem that we computed by hand in Chapter 4. The screen also shows the hedge ratio for the call and put. For the call, the hedge ratio of .7422 matches our calculation in Chapter 4.

With Module 3, you may also graph option price relationships. After entering the data in the top portion of the screen, press F2 for the graphics menu, which is shown in Figure 6.11. You may graph either the Black-Scholes call or put price as a function of the five parameters for the Model. If you entered a dividend rate on the solution screen, the graphs will reflect the dividend.

Figure 6.9

Black-Scholes Option Pricing Model

Use this screen to find put and call prices according to the Black-Scholes Option Pricing Model. The program computes put and call values with or without continuous dividends. Enter data for all items in this box.

Stock Price	0.000
Exercise Price	0.000
Risk-Free Rate per Year (e.g., 0.10)	0.000
Volatility (standard deviation per year, e.g., 0.15)	0.000
Days Until Expiration	0

Enter the estimated dividend rate if there is a dividend. For example, a stock priced at $100 with a $4 annual dividend has a dividend rate = 0.04.

Annual Percentage Dividend   0.000

After entering data, press F1 for results, F2 to graph, or ESC to exit.

Figure 6.10

Black-Scholes Option Pricing Model

Use this screen to find put and call prices according to the Black-Scholes Option Pricing Model. The program computes put and call values with or without continuous dividends. Enter data for all items in this box.

Stock Price	100.000
Exercise Price	100.000
Risk-Free Rate per Year (e.g., 0.10)	0.060
Volatility (standard deviation per year, e.g., 0.15)	0.100
Days Until Expiration	365

Enter the estimated dividend rate if there is a dividend. For example, a stock priced at $100 with a $4 annual dividend has a dividend rate = 0.04.

Annual Percentage Dividend   0.000

Call Price	7.4593	Put Price	1.6358
Call Delta	0.7422	Put Delta	-0.2578

Delta is the sensitivity of the option price to a changing stock price.

After entering data, press F1 for results, F2 to graph, or ESC to exit.

Figure 6.11

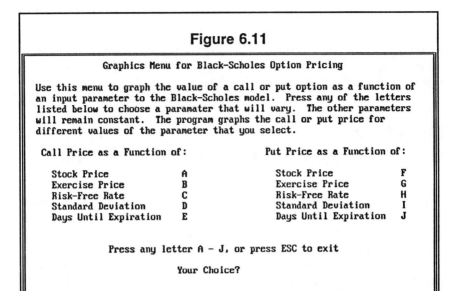

Graphics Menu for Black-Scholes Option Pricing

Use this menu to graph the value of a call or put option as a function of
an input parameter to the Black-Scholes model. Press any of the letters
listed below to choose a paramater that will vary. The other parameters
will remain constant. The program graphs the call or put price for
different values of the parameter that you select.

Call Price as a Function of:		Put Price as a Function of:	
Stock Price	A	Stock Price	F
Exercise Price	B	Exercise Price	G
Risk-Free Rate	C	Risk-Free Rate	H
Standard Deviation	D	Standard Deviation	I
Days Until Expiration	E	Days Until Expiration	J

Press any letter A – J, or press ESC to exit

Your Choice?

Figure 6.12

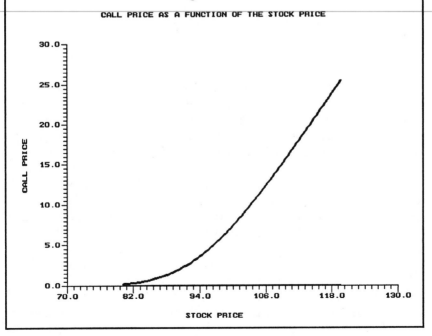

CALL PRICE AS A FUNCTION OF THE STOCK PRICE

For our example call option, Figure 6.12 shows the relationship between the call price and the stock price. This matches Figure 4.8, which graphs the same relationship. After graphing, press ESC to return to the data entry and solution screen. You may study the sensitivity of option prices to the parameters by changing the input data and re-drawing the graph.

Module 4
Binomial Approximation of Black–Scholes

With Module 4, we can approximate Black-Scholes option prices with the Binomial Model. When we discussed the Binomial Model in Chapter 4, we made simplifying assumptions about how stock prices could move. For instance, we specified the number of periods and the up and down movements that might affect the stock price in each period. As we discussed in the section of Chapter 4 on The Binomial Approach to the Black-Scholes Model, we can use more realistic stock price movements and more periods in the Binomial Model to value options more precisely. Module 4 uses a more realistic model of stock price movements and allows us to vary the number of periods to attain better option price estimates with the Binomial Model. Specifically, Module 4 uses the following up and down movements, again matching our discussion in Chapter 4:

$$U = (r - .5\sigma^2)t + \sigma\sqrt{t}$$
$$D = (r - .5\sigma^2)t - \sigma\sqrt{t}$$

With these up and down factors, the Binomial Model will converge to the Black–Scholes Model as the number of periods increases. Holding the time until expiration constant and increasing the number of periods approximates the continuous time framework that underlies the Black-Scholes Model. Figure 6.13 shows the data entry and solution screen for Module 4. To use the module, enter values for the six variables in the top portion of the screen. Figure 6.13 shows values for a stock at $100, an exercise price of $100, three periods until expiration, a 6 percent interest rate, a standard deviation of .1, and 365 days until expiration. This is the same option we used to illustrate Module 3. After entering these six values, press F1, and the program prints the report shown in the bottom of Figure 6.13.

In Figure 6.13, the Black–Scholes call price is $7.46, matching the same value we computed in Chapter 4 and in our discussion of Module 3. With three periods, the Binomial Model gives a price of $7.23. Even with only three periods, the Binomial Model only has an error of 3.08 percent as an estimate of

Figure 6.13

Binomial Approximation to the Black-Scholes Model

As the number of periods increases, the Binomial Model converges to the Black-Scholes Model. By increasing the number of periods, we can make the binomial result come as close as we desire to the Black-Scholes model price. Enter values for all items in this box.

Stock Price	100.000	Annual Risk-Free Rate	0.060
Strike Price	100.000	Annual Standard Deviation	0.100
Number of Periods	3	Days Until Expiration	365

For the Binomial Model:

The binomial call price is	7.2321
The binomial put price is	1.4089
The period length in years	0.3333
The percentage price increase	0.0761
The percentage price decrease	-0.0394

For the Black-Scholes Model:

The Black-Scholes call price is	7.4593
The Black-Scholes put price is	1.6358

After entering data, press F1 for results. Press ESC to exit.

the Black-Scholes price. As the number of periods increases, the error becomes smaller. For example, keeping the values of Figure 6.13, except changing the number of periods to 250, gives a Binomial Model price of $7.4616, compared with the Black-Scholes price of $7.4593. This is an error of only .03 percent. With Module 4, it is possible to explore this convergence.

Module 5
Implied Volatility with Black–Scholes

In its simplest terms, the Black-Scholes Model relates five variables to a sixth. In the normal case, the five variables are the inputs to the Black-Scholes Model and the sixth variable is the option price. As we discussed in Chapter 4, it is possible to change that relationship to secure estimates of stock price volatility. We noted that the standard deviation of the stock price is sometimes difficult to estimate, because the Black-Scholes Model takes the instantaneous standard deviation as an input.

By taking the option price, stock price, exercise price, interest rate and time until expiration as given, we can find the standard deviation. In the Black-Scholes Model, the standard deviation appears in the d_1 and d_2 terms. Because the standard deviation is imbedded in this way, we cannot solve for the standard

Figure 6.14

Implied Volatility

Use this screen to find the volatility implied by a given option price. Best results come from using the option closest to the money. Complete all values in this box and the value for the dividend rate, if any.

Stock Price	100.000
Exercise Price	100.000
Risk-Free Rate per Year (e.g., 0.10)	0.060
Call Price	7.459
Days Until Expiration	365

Enter the estimated dividend rate if there is a dividend. For example, a stock priced at $100 with a $4 annual dividend has a dividend rate = 0.04.

Annual Percentage Dividend   0.000

The implied standard deviation is: 0.099999

After entering data, press F1 for results. Press ESC to exit.

deviation directly. Instead, we need to search for the value of the standard deviation that satisfies the equation.

With Module 5, we can search for the implied standard deviation. Figure 6.14 shows the data entry and solution screen for Module 5. In the figure, data are already in place in the top panel for our example option. The stock price is $100, the exercise price is $100, the risk-free rate is 6 percent, and 365 days remain until expiration. In the top panel, the call price is $7.459. This is the same value that we found in Module 3, as Figure 6.10 shows. In that earlier example, we found the call price by using the other data and a standard deviation of 10 percent for the stock. In Module 5, we assume that we know the call price, and we search for the implied standard deviation. After entering data in the top panel and the optional second panel, press F1. The program searches for the implied standard deviation and reports the answer in the bottom panel. As the figure shows, the program finds a standard deviation of .099999, or .1. This matches our result from Figure 6.10.

Module 6
Cumulative Normal Probabilities

Module 6 is a useful utility for finding cumulative probabilities from the standardized normal distribution. As we saw in Chapter 4, computing Black-Scholes prices requires values for $N(d_1)$ and $N(d_2)$. Here d_1 and d_2 are z-scores from the standardized or unit normal distribution. Taking d_1 as an example, $N(d_1)$ gives the probability of a random drawing from the standardized normal distribution being equal to or smaller than d_1. Instead of using the standardized normal table, which may require interpolation, we can use Module 6 to find very exact values for the cumulative probabilities.

Figure 6.15 shows the data entry and solution screen for Module 6. To use this module, we enter a z-value in the middle panel and press F1. The program reports the corresponding cumulative value in the bottom panel. Figure 6.15 shows the completed screen for a z-value of .65. In Chapter 4, we computed a Black-Scholes call price as an example, where d_1 was .65. This matches the value in Figure 6.15. From the standardized normal table, we found that $N(.65)$ = .7422. This corresponds with the more exact value in Figure 6.15. Intuitively, a value of .7422 means that 74.22 percent of the area under a normal curve lies at or to the left of a z-score of .65. This analysis corresponds to Figure 4.7.

Figure 6.15

Unit Normal Cumulative Probability Calculations

Use this screen to find the cumulative probability of a value from the
unit normal probability distribution. Enter a value in the space provided
and press F1 for results. The program gives the probability of finding a
Z-Value less than or equal to the value you specify. For example, an input
of 1.0 is greater than or equal to 84.13% of random drawings from the unit
normal probability distribution.

Z-Value   0.6500

The cumulative probability is: 0.742154

After entering data, press F1 for results.   Press ESC to exit.

Module 7
Simulate Stock Prices and Option Prices

Module 7 simulates stock price movements over time. For each new stock price, the program computes the value of a call or put. For 250 days, the program graphs the stock price and the corresponding option price. In Chapter 4, equation 4.4, we saw that a standard model of the change in a stock price is:

$$S_t - S_0 = S_0 \mu t + S_0 N(0,1) \sigma \sqrt{t}$$

Module 7 uses this equation to generate 250 daily stock price changes. For each day, the change depends upon two parameters: the expected return and the standard deviation. The stock price change also depends on a random drawing from the unit normal distribution. Thus, for each day, the program draws a random value from the distribution and uses that to compute the stock price change. Based on the new stock price, the program computes the corresponding option value using the Black–Scholes equation. The computation also reflects that the option is getting nearer to its expiration each day.

Figure 6.16 shows the data entry screen for Module 7 with data in place. In the figure, the stock price is $100, the exercise price is $100, and 300 days remain until expiration. Three values are sensitive to the units of time. In this module, the expected stock return, the risk-free rate, and the standard deviation are all expressed in annual units. In the figure, they are 12 percent, 6 percent and .3, respectively.

After entering these values, we can generate graphs for a stock and a call or a stock and a put. To generate a graph for a stock and a call, press F1. Pressing F2 will generate a graph for a stock and a put. Because the program draws a random number for each day, the same input data will give different stock price paths and different option values. The number of days must exceed 250, so the option does not expire before the end of the horizon for which we generate prices. Figure 6.17 shows a graph for the stock and the call based on the data in Figure 6.16. This is just one possible graph the same data can generate.

We can use Module 7 to explore the sensitivity of option values to randomness or to different input values. If we keep the same data and generate repeated price path graphs, we will find radically different results. By the same token, if we change the input parameters, we can also get very different results. For example, if we decrease the standard deviation of the stock substantially, the resulting stock price paths tend to vary much less. Accordingly, the call price will change much more steadily as well.

Figure 6.16

Simulate a Price Path for a Stock and an Option

Use this screen to simulate a stock price path that is consistent with the Black-Scholes Model. Based on the parameters you specify, the program will generate 250 daily price changes. The program graphs the resulting stock and option price paths. Give all time sensitive inputs in annual terms. These are: the expected stock return, standard deviation, and the risk-free rate. You may choose to graph a call or a put.

Starting Stock Price	100.000	Annual Risk-Free Rate	0.060
Strike Price	100.000	Annual Standard Deviation	0.300
Expected Stock Return	0.120	Days Until Expiration	300

Press F1 to graph a call or F2 to graph a put.   ESC to exit.

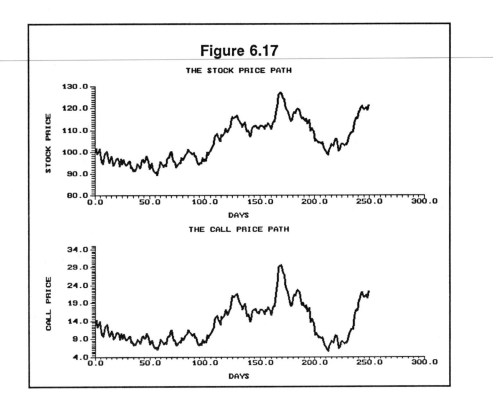

Figure 6.17

THE STOCK PRICE PATH

THE CALL PRICE PATH

Further Explorations

We have discussed the individual modules in **OPTION!** and shown the basic features of each. However, the program is a flexible tool that we can extend to other applications. In this section, we consider just one such application. In Chapter 5, we considered alternative dividend adjustments, including the pseudo-American call valuation model. While **OPTION!** does not have a specific module for the pseudo-American call valuation, we can apply it to this problem with ease.

In Chapter 5, we considered the following data and computed the value of a pseudo American call option.

$$S = \$60$$
$$E = \$60$$
$$t = 180 \ days$$
$$r = .09$$
$$\sigma = .2$$
$$D_1 = \$2, \ to \ be \ paid \ in \ 60 \ days$$
$$D_2 = \$2, \ to \ be \ paid \ in \ 150 \ days$$

In discussing this example, we noted that the first step is to compute the present value of the dividends and subtract that value from the stock price. The present value of both dividends is:

$$D_1 e^{-rt} + D_2 e^{-rt} = \$2 e^{-(.09)(60/365)} + \$2 e^{-(.09)(150/365)} = \$3.90$$

Subtracting this from the stock price gives an adjusted stock price of $56.10. We use this adjusted stock price in all subsequent calculations.

In the pseudo-American call valuation technique, we find the value of a call option for the moment before each dividend and for the actual expiration date. At the moment before a dividend, we subtract the present value of the dividends from the exercise price. After we compute Black-Scholes call values with this technique for all dividend dates and the actual expiration date, we estimate the value of an American call as the largest of the Black-Scholes computed prices.

With two dividends, we need to compute the Black-Scholes price for a horizon matching the actual expiration date of 180 days, for a horizon matching the final dividend date in 150 days, and for a horizon matching the first dividend date in 90 days. On the dividend dates, we need to subtract the present value of the dividends from the exercise price. In 150 days, a $2 dividend is about to be paid, so the present value of the remaining dividends is $2. In 90 days, a $2 dividend is about to be paid and another $2 dividend will be paid 60 days later.

Figure 6.18

```
Black-Scholes Option Pricing Model

Use this screen to find put and call prices according to the Black-Scholes
Option Pricing Model.  The program computes put and call values with or
without continuous dividends.  Enter data for all items in this box.

Stock Price                                             56.100
Exercise Price                                          56.040
Risk-Free Rate per Year (e.g., 0.10)                     0.090
Volatility (standard deviation per year, e.g., 0.15)     0.200
Days Until Expiration                                   90
```

```
Enter the estimated dividend rate if there is a dividend.  For example, a
stock priced at $100 with a $4 annual dividend has a dividend rate = 0.04.

              Annual Percentage Dividend       0.000
```

```
Call Price      2.9011        Put Price        1.6112
Call Delta      0.6118        Put Delta       -0.3882

Delta is the sensitivity of the option price to a changing stock price.
```

```
After entering data, press F1 for results, F2 to graph, or ESC to exit.
```

Together these dividends have a present value of $3.96. Therefore, we need to compute Black-Scholes call prices under three scenarios. In each scenario, the standard deviation, risk-free rate, and adjusted stock price are the same. However, the exercise price and the time until expiration vary. The following table shows the exercise prices, the time until expiration, and the Black-Scholes call price.

	First Dividend	Second Dividend	Actual Expiration
Exercise Price	$56.04	$58.00	$60
Time Until Expiration	90 days	150 days	180 days
Black-Scholes Call Price	$2.90	$2.97	$2.57

Using the pseudo-American valuation technique, we take the highest Black-Scholes price, $2.97, as the estimate of the American call option.

This computation requires pricing three Black-Scholes call options. Instead of computing these by hand, Module 3 of **OPTION!** can speed the calculation. Figure 6.18 shows the screen from Module 3 with data and solution in place of the first dividend date. To find the other two prices, we merely change the exercise price and the days until expiration. Then we press F1 to find the option price. With ingenuity, we can extend **OPTION!** to other computations as well.

Summary

In this chapter, we have explored **OPTION!**, the software that accompanies this text. The seven modules of the program allow a wide variety of computations and graphical displays. We have considered each module in turn and have shown how to use **OPTION!** to solve problems for which there is no specific module.

Module 1 analyzes option payoffs at expiration. It prepares reports of values and profits at expiration. In addition, it graphs the value or profits and losses from different combinations of calls, puts, bonds, and stock. Module 2 computes option values using the Binomial Model. For three or fewer periods, the program can also present the entire tree of payoffs on the stock and an option. Module 3 computes Black–Scholes call and put values. In addition, it computes the call and put deltas. In Module 3, we can also include a continuous dividend adjustment. Module 3 also graphs the value of an option as a function of the five parameters of the Black–Scholes Model. For instance, we can graph the value of a put as a function of a changing time until expiration.

Module 4 employs a standard financial model of stock price movement to simulate Black–Scholes option prices with the Binomial Model. As the number of periods used in the Binomial Model increases, the Binomial Model prices converge to the Black–Scholes Model prices. Module 4 provides a method to investigate this phenomenon.   Module 5 computes the implied standard deviation—the standard deviation that is consistent with the other model inputs and a given option price. Because estimating standard deviations can be difficult, many market professionals use implied standard deviations. With Module 5, it is possible to do this quite easily.

Computing Black–Scholes prices requires the cumulative normal probability of two variables, d_1 and d_2. With Module 6, this computation is easy and very accurate. The alternative to using Module 6 is to use a standardized normal table, such as the one in this book. Module 7 simulates stock price paths. It takes as inputs a starting stock price and an expected return and standard deviation for the stock. Consistent with a well established model of stock price changes, the program allows the stock price to change randomly. For each stock price, the program computes a corresponding call or put price. With Module 7, it is possible to analyze the effect of randomness and changing parameter values on stock and option prices.

Appendix A

Cumulative Distribution Function
for the Standard Normal Random Variable

	.00	.01	.02	.03	.04	.05	.06	.07	.08	.09
0.0	.5000	.5040	.5080	.5120	.5160	.5199	.5239	.5279	.5319	.5359
0.1	.5398	.5438	.5478	.5517	.5557	.5596	.5636	.5675	.5714	.5753
0.2	.5793	.5832	.5871	.5910	.5948	.5987	.6026	.6064	.6103	.6141
0.3	.6179	.6217	.6255	.6293	.6331	.6368	.6406	.6443	.6480	.6517
0.4	.6554	.6591	.6628	.6664	.6700	.6736	.6772	.6808	.6844	.6879
0.5	.6915	.6950	.6985	.7019	.7054	.7088	.7123	.7157	.7190	.7224
0.6	.7257	.7291	.7324	.7357	.7389	.7422	.7454	.7486	.7517	.7549
0.7	.7580	.7611	.7642	.7673	.7704	.7734	.7764	.7794	.7823	.7852
0.8	.7881	.7910	.7939	.7967	.7995	.8023	.8051	.8078	.8106	.8133
0.9	.8159	.8186	.8212	.8238	.8264	.8289	.8315	.8340	.8365	.8389
1.0	.8413	.8438	.8461	.8485	.8508	.8531	.8554	.8577	.8599	.8621
1.1	.8643	.8665	.8686	.8708	.8729	.8749	.8770	.8790	.8810	.8830
1.2	.8849	.8869	.8888	.8907	.8925	.8944	.8962	.8980	.8997	.9015
1.3	.9032	.9049	.9066	.9082	.9099	.9115	.9131	.9147	.9162	.9177
1.4	.9192	.9207	.9222	.9236	.9251	.9265	.9279	.9292	.9306	.9319
1.5	.9332	.9345	.9357	.9370	.9382	.9394	.9406	.9418	.9429	.9441
1.6	.9452	.9463	.9474	.9484	.9495	.9505	.9515	.9525	.9535	.9545
1.7	.9554	.9564	.9573	.9582	.9591	.9599	.9608	.9616	.9625	.9633
1.8	.9641	.9649	.9656	.9664	.9671	.9678	.9686	.9693	.9699	.9706
1.9	.9713	.9719	.9726	.9732	.9738	.9744	.9750	.9756	.9761	.9767
2.0	.9772	.9778	9783	.9788	.9793	.9798	.9803	.9808	.9812	.9817
2.1	.9821	.9826	.9830	.9834	.9838	.9842	.9846	.9850	.9854	.9857
2.2	.9861	.9864	.9868	.9871	.9875	.9878	.9881	.9884	.9887	.9890
2.3	.9893	.9896	.9898	.9901	.9904	.9906	.9909	.9911	.9913	.9916
2.4	.9918	.9920	.9922	.9925	.9927	.9929	.9931	.9932	.9934	.9936
2.5	.9938	.9940	.9941	.9943	.9945	.9946	.9948	.9949	.9951	.9952
2.6	.9953	.9955	.9956	.9957	.9959	.9960	.9961	.9962	.9963	.9964
2.7	.9965	.9966	.9967	.9968	.9969	.9970	.9971	.9972	.9973	.9974
2.8	.9974	.9975	.9976	.9977	.9977	.9978	.9979	.9979	.9980	.9981
2.9	.9981	.9982	.9982	.9983	.9984	.9984	.9985	.9985	.9986	.9986
3.0	.9987	.9987	.9987	.9988	.9988	.9989	.9989	.9989	.9990	.9990
3.1	.9990	.9991	.9991	.9991	.9992	.9992	.9992	.9992	.9993	.9993
3.2	.9993	.9993	.9994	.9994	.9994	.9994	.9994	.9995	.9995	.9995
3.3	.9995	.9995	.9995	.9996	.9996	.9996	.9996	.9996	.9996	.9997
3.4	.9997	.9997	.9997	.9997	.9997	.9997	.9997	.9997	.9997	.9998

Index